Emergency Substitutions

1 cup cake flour = 1 cup minus 2 tablespoons all-purpose flour

1 cup all-purpose flour = 1 cup plus 2 tablespoons cake flour

1 cup self-rising flour = 1 cup all-purpose flour plus ½ teaspoon baking powder and ½ teaspoon salt

1 cup granulated sugar = 1 cup brown sugar or 2 cups confectioners' sugar

½ cup brown sugar = ½ cup granulated sugar plus 2 tablespoons molasses

1 package active dry yeast = 1 cake compressed fresh yeast

1 square unsweetened chocolate = 3 tablespoons unsweetened cocoa powder plus 1 tablespoon vegetable oil or butter

1 cup buttermilk = 1 cup whole milk plus 1 tablespoon white vinegar or lemon juice. Stir and let stand 2 minutes or use 1 cup plain yogurt or sour cream

1 cup plain yogurt = 1 cup sour cream

1 cup whole milk = ½ cup evaporated milk plus ½ cup water. Or use dry milk and follow the package instructions to reconstitute the amount you need.

1 cup raisins = 1 cup currants or other dried fruits such as cranberries, blueberries, and cherries

1 tablespoon cornstarch = 2 tablespoons flour (for thickening purposes)

1 cup corn syrup = 1 cup sugar plus ¼ cup water

1 cup honey = 1¼ cups granulated sugar plus ¼ cup liquid

Pan Size Substitutions

Sometimes you just don't have the right size on hand. If you substitute pan sizes, be sure to closely monitor the baking time of your items. It will most likely change. If you substitute glass for metal pans, be sure to lower the baking temperature by 25 degrees.

Pan	Size	Capacity	Substitutions
Rectangular	12 x 7½	8 cups	None
Rectangular	13 x 9	15 cups	Two 9-inch rounds or three 8-inch rounds
Rectangular	11 x 7	8 cups	None
Square	8 x 8	8 cups	11 x 7, 12 x 7½, 9 x 5 loaf, or two 8-inch rounds
Square	9 x 9	10 cups	None
Round	8-inch	5 cups	10 x 6 or 8½ x 4½ loaf
Round	9-inch	6 cups	None

Baking For Dummies®

Common Food Equivalents

Almonds, 1 pound = 3 cups whole, 4 cups slivered

Apples, 1 pound = 3 medium, 2¾ cups sliced

Apricots, dried, 1 pound = 2¾ cups, 5½ cups cooked

Bananas, fresh, 1 pound = 3 to 4; 1¾ cups mashed, 2 cups sliced

Blueberries, fresh, 1 pint = 2 cups

Blueberries, frozen, 10 ounces = 1½ cups

Butter, 1 pound = 2 cups

Butter, 1 stick = 8 tablespoons, ½ cup

Cherries, fresh, 1 pound = 2½ to 3 cups pitted

Chocolate wafers, 18 wafers = 1 cup crumbs

Chocolate chips, 6 ounces = 1 cup

Cranberries, 1 pound = 3 cups

Cream (heavy, sour, half and half, light), ½ pint = 1 cup

Cream (heavy), ½ pint = 2 cups whipped

Flour, all-purpose, 1 pound = 3 cups sifted

Flour, cake, 1 pound = 4½ to 5 cups sifted

Graham crackers, 15 = 1 cup crumbs

Lemons, 1 medium = 3 tablespoons juice, 2 to 3 teaspoons zest

Maple syrup, 16 fluid ounces = 2 cups

Milk, whole, 1 quart = 4 cups

Oats, rolled, 1 pound = 5 cups

Oil, 1 quart = 5 cups

Peaches (fresh), 1 pound = 4 medium, 2½ cups chopped

Peaches (frozen), 10 ounces = 1⅛ cups slices and juice

Pumpkin (fresh), 1 pound = 1 cup cooked and mashed

Raspberries, 1 pint = scant 1½ cups

Shortening, 1 pound = 2 cups

Strawberries, 1 pint = 2½ cups sliced

Sugar, granulated, 1 pound = 2 cups

Sugar, brown, 1 pound = 2¼ cups packed

Sugar, confectioners', 1 pound = 3½ to 4 cups

Vanilla wafers, 22 wafers = 1 cup crumbs

Walnuts, 1 pound = 3¾ cups halves, 3½ cups chopped

Yeast, ¼-ounce package = 1 scant tablespoon

Measurements

Dash = 2 or 3 drops (liquid) or less than ⅛ teaspoon (dry)

1 tablespoon = 3 teaspoons or ½ ounce

2 tablespoons = 1 ounce

¼ cup = 4 tablespoons or 2 ounces

⅓ cup = 5 tablespoons plus 1 teaspoon

½ cup = 8 tablespoons or 4 ounces

1 cup = 16 tablespoons or 8 ounces

1 pint = 2 cups or 16 ounces or 1 pound

1 quart = 4 cups or 2 pints

1 gallon = 4 quarts

1 pound = 16 ounces

Baking

FOR

DUMMIES®

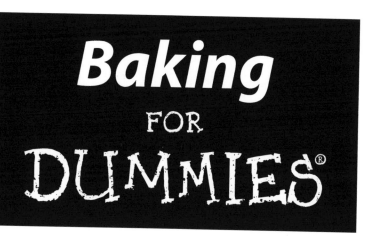

Baking

FOR

DUMMIES®

by Emily Nolan

Wiley Publishing, Inc.

Baking For Dummies®

Published by
Wiley Publishing, Inc.
111 River Street
Hoboken, NJ 07030
www.wiley.com

For general information on our other products and services or to obtain technical support, please contact our Customer Care Department within the U.S. at 800-762-2974, outside the U.S. at 317-572-3993, or fax 317-572-4002.

Wiley also publishes its books in a variety of electronic formats. Some content that appears in print may not be available in electronic books.

Library of Congress Cataloging-in-Publication Data:

Library of Congress Control Number: 2001098043

ISBN: 0-7645-5420-4

10 9 8 7 6 5 4 3 2 1

1B/RR/QR/QS/IN

WILEY

About the Author

Emily Nolan has loved baking for as long as she can remember. Her earliest memories are of digging in her mother's huge tubs of flour as she put together pies and breads. Her mother handed Emily scraps of dough to keep her busy — even at that tender age, Emily had baking in her blood.

Although she majored in English Literature in college, Emily catered to pay the bills, cutting her teeth in the professional food service industry. She learned about food preparation for 10 to 200 people, and was introduced to professional cake decoration, food preparation, and presentation. There she became deft at paying attention to details for food, setting up for parties, and creating menus for prestigious dinners, holiday affairs, and college graduations.

After graduation, Emily was given her first opportunity as a head chef for a month-long program, creating menus and cooking for 150 people, three squares a day. There she applied everything she knew about baking and cooking, providing homemade bread, cakes, and cookies daily. Quality, nutritious food was her goal — and she achieved it.

With that under her belt, Emily traveled to Philadelphia and became the head pastry chef for a restaurant/bakery, Le Bus. She was responsible for fulfilling orders for their three bakeries, plus any special catering orders that came through daily. On top of that, they baked for local four-star restaurants. Emily and her colleagues made everything from scratch, from the croissant dough to the rich, sweet pectin in their apple pies. She was also in charge of developing new desserts for the restaurants.

After spending over a year at Le Bus, she decided to combine her English degree with her love for and knowledge of baking. So, she entered the world of publishing and became a cookbook editor. In her two years as an editor, she learned about cookbook publishing and how to address the needs of the reader and convey information in a clear, concise, usable format. Living in New York City enabled her to keep up with the ever-changing food trends.

After leaving publishing, she returned to the kitchen, where she was the head chef for a month-long program. Again, with a staff of two, she fed over 200 people three time daily. Everything that came from the kitchen was high-quality, homemade fare.

Today Emily does freelance editing, recipe writing, and recipe development. Presently, she is working on Sheila Lukin's new cookbook (to be published in Spring 2002) and is doing recipe development for and contributing food article to magazines such as *Food and Wine*.

Dedication

For my mother, Irene Siembora, and my grandfather, Stephan Siembora — two great souls who taught me the joys of baking.

Author's Acknowledgments

What author doesn't love her editors? I am no exception. A special thanks goes to Jennifer Feldman, publisher of the Dummies cooking titles, for making this book a possibility. I am very grateful to Linda Ingroia, senior acquisitions editor, for giving me the opportunity to write this book and working with me through all the ups and downs along the way. Erin Connell was indispensable with her advice, follow-through, and attention to detail. Project editor Marcia Johnson could not have been more patient and understanding while dealing with technical difficulties and deadlines and ushering me along in the writing process. It gave me great peace of mind knowing that Elizabeth Kuball was the copy editor, and I appreciate the helpful suggestions that technical editor Lauren Chattman offered.

Then, there is the team at home. Thanks to Martha McCoy, my grandmother Agnes, my mom, sister, and all of my aunts for offering their support, recipes, and advice. David Bidwell, I could not have done it without all of your help, support, and tasting suggestions. And, finally, Monkey, who was always ready and willing to rip open bags of flour, boxes of cake mixes, and bags of butterscotch chips in her attempt to prove that even a dog can bake . . . even if her stomach didn't make a good oven.

Publisher's Acknowledgments

We're proud of this book; please send us your comments through our Online Registration Form located at www.dummies.com/register.

Some of the people who helped bring this book to market include the following:

Acquisitions, Editorial, and Media Development

Project Editor: Marcia L. Johnson

Senior Editor: Linda Ingroia

Acquisitions Editor: Erin Connell

Copy Editors: Elizabeth Netedu Kuball, Tina Sims

Technical Editor: Lauren Chattman

Recipe Tester and Nutrition Analyst: Patricia Santelli

Editorial Manager: Pamela Mourouzis

Editorial Assistant: Carol Strickland

Cover Photos: David Bishop

Production

Project Coordinator: Jennifer Bingham

Layout and Graphics: Shelly Norris, Jacque Schneider, Janet Seib

Special Art: Elizabeth Kurtzman, line art

Proofreaders: Laura Albert, John Greenough, Linda Quigley, Marianne Santy, TECHBOOKS Production Services

Indexer: TECHBOOKS Production Services

Special Help: Chrissy Guthrie

General and Administrative

Publishing and Editorial for Consumer Dummies

Business: Kathleen Nebenhaus, Vice President and Publisher; Kevin Thornton, Acquisitions Manager

Cooking/Gardening: Jennifer Feldman, Associate Vice President and Publisher; Anne Ficklen, Executive Editor; Kristi Hart, Managing Editor

Education/Reference: Diane Graves Steele, Vice President and Publisher

Lifestyles: Kathleen Nebenhaus, Vice President and Publisher; Tracy Boggier, Managing Editor

Pets: Kathleen Nebenhaus, Vice President and Publisher; Tracy Boggier, Managing Editor

Travel: Michael Spring, Vice President and Publisher; Brice Gosnell, Publishing Director; Suzanne Jannetta, Editorial Director

Consumer Editorial Services: Kathleen Nebenhaus, Vice President and Publisher; Kristin A. Cocks, Editorial Director; Cindy Kitchel, Editorial Director

Consumer Production: Debbie Stailey, Production Director

Contents at a Glance

Cartoons at a Glance

By Rich Tennant

page 7

"Oh for gosh sake — you've got to figure out what you're doing wrong when you make upside-down cake, or you're gonna kill yourself."

page 273

"I know it tastes a little odd. Let's just say you should store your bundt cake in a cool dry place, other than your husband's cigar humidor."

page 293

"QUIT MOPING—YOU WON FIRST PLACE IN THE MEATLOAF CATEGORY, AND THAT'S GOOD. I'M THE ONLY ONE WHO KNOWS IT WAS A CARROT CAKE YOU ENTERED."

page 93

"...because I'm more comfortable using my own tools. Now-how much longer do you want me to sand the cake batter?"

page 61

Cartoon Information:
Fax: 978-546-7747
E-Mail: richtennant@the5thwave.com
World Wide Web: www.the5thwave.com

Recipes at a Glance

Cookies

Cakes

Frostings

Pies and Tarts

Crisps, Cobblers, and Other Delights

Quick Breads, Muffins, and Biscuits

Yeast Breads

Savory Baked Goods

Baking with Mixes and Premade Doughs

Low-Fat Baking

Table of Contents

Introduction

A t some point in your life — maybe now, since you've picked up this book — the mystery of baking has attracted you. The desire to create becomes stronger than the desire to pick up a pack of cookies at the store, and you think, "Hey, I'm a smart person. I can do this!" And you can!

Knowing how baking works and which role each ingredient plays enables you to understand how to *bake* instead of how to just follow a recipe (there is a difference). When you understand how to bake and master the various techniques to make you successful, you'll gain confidence in the kitchen and become a proficient baker. You'll also find yourself confidently experimenting with some recipes, too! So, roll up your sleeves, clean off the countertop and get ready to start baking.

About This Book

The purpose of this book is to fill you in on how to become a proficient and independent baker. You may feel like you know nothing now, but as you dive into this book, you'll become competent in the kitchen and realize baking skills are something you can easily master. This book will acquaint you with familiar, as well as unfamiliar, ingredients, and also tell you a few things you may not know, such as the secret to flaky pastry crusts and how to zest a lemon. From organizing your kitchen to be an efficient workspace to storing your baked good properly, this book gives you the tools you need to become a successful baker and plenty of tantalizing recipes to practice with.

This book introduces you to the *hows* and *whys* of baking. From mixing a batter to putting the finishing touches on your baked goods, you'll discover all kinds of information in this book. This book also explains various techniques for all kinds of baking situations — and with good technique, the sky is the limit. Practice makes perfect, so the more familiar you become with baking and handling your ingredients, the more proficient you will become as a baker.

Conventions Used in This Book

The recipes in this book are very straightforward and easy to understand. But here are a few notes on the ingredients, which apply to all the recipes:

- ✔ All oven temperatures are given in Fahrenheit.

- ✔ Unless specified in the ingredient list, you can use any degree of fat in milk (whole thru skim).

- ✔ All eggs are large.

- ✔ All flour is all-purpose flour, unless specified otherwise in the ingredients list.

- ✔ All sugar is granulated sugar, unless specified otherwise in the ingredients list.

- ✔ If a recipe calls for butter and not margarine, don't use margarine. A few recipes just won't taste good if margarine is substituted.

- ✔ All dry ingredients are measured using nestled dry measuring cups (not the glass ones with the graded amounts on the side), and all ingredients are measured level, unless specified.

- ✔ *Lemon zest* or *orange zest* refers to the outer colored peel, not any of the white pith.

- ✔ Generally, canned, fresh, or frozen fruit can be substituted, unless the recipe specifies one or the other.

And keep in mind:

- ✔ If you don't know about an ingredient or technique in a recipe, be sure to check in Part I or II for an explanation.

- ✔ Make sure you have all the equipment you need. Double-check that the pans you have are the right size before you get started.

- ✔ You can double most recipes in this book, unless the recipe states otherwise.

Foolish Assumptions

Baking For Dummies is a tool for both beginning and experienced bakers. No matter which group you fall in, this book will open you up to new ideas, techniques, and recipes. I make the assumption that you already know your way around a kitchen, but you probably favor the top of your stove more often than the oven. You may rely too often on the grocery store or local bakery for your baked goods.

You don't need any prior baking knowledge to use this book. If you love to bake, or you love the idea of baking, you'll find what you need here. You won't get lost either, because every technique and ingredient is explained.

The recipes are basic but delicious and interesting. All of them can be embellished a little with additional ingredients, frostings, whipped cream, or powdered sugar. They use easy-to-find ingredients and simple instructions for extraordinary results. No matter what skill level you start with, this book assumes you want to become a better baker. Not only will you discover your untapped talent, you'll master a lifetime of skills, tips, and shortcuts to keep you baking for years to come.

How This Book Is Organized

This single-subject cookbook is organized into five parts that guide you through every aspect of baking. It's full of thoughtful advice, interesting information, as well as obvious and not-so-obvious baking tips. The goal of this book is to get you baking as soon as possible. Successful baking starts with the basics, and that is where the book begins as well. When you get the lowdown on ingredients, utensils, technique, and kitchen preparation, then the recipes begin. They're organized so you can go to your section of choice — cakes, cookies, breads, and so on.

Part 1: Baking Essentials

Before you get up to your elbows in batter, get to know some of the fundamentals of baking. This part covers the very basics in baking, letting you know what to keep in the pantry and what gear you'll need when you step into the kitchen to create. You'll also discover the role of basic ingredients — how they affect the baking process. So the more familiar you become with what they do, the less intimidating baking as a whole will be for you.

Part 11: Basic Training

You know you have an oven, but do you know how it works? This section prepares you for the process of baking. You'll find information for getting your oven in top working order. It also gives you advice on how to read recipes, what to watch for, and how not to get yourself in over your head if you're a baker just starting out. I offer up tips on how to measure all kinds of things, from flour to fats. And I provide information on basic techniques you'll need to perform when you want to try out some of the intermediate to challenging recipes. This part unlocks many of the mysteries of the kitchen.

Part III: Ready, Set, Bake!

In this part, you get to try your hand at baking — and the best part about it is you can eat the results! As you practice with the recipes in this section, you'll become more and more familiar with ingredients and baking techniques.

Part IV: Other Important Stuff

This section is chock full of suggestions and ideas for baking. I give you lots of suggestions for sprucing up cakes and cookies, plus tips for special presentations and how to do some easy cake decorating when you want to make your cakes extra special. I also let you know how to store baked goods properly to ensure they'll remain fresh as long as possible.

Part V: The Part of Tens

What happens if your cake is lopsided or your cookies are burned on the bottom? This section gives you ten tips for conquering the most common baking conundrums. You'll also find ten fantastic baking sources that offer everything from great baking supplies to show-stopping recipes.

Appendixes

Appendix A at the end of this book is a Glossary of Baking Terms. Don't go into the kitchen without it. Appendix B makes metric conversions a piece of cake.

Icons Used in This Book

Look for these icons peppered throughout the book to help you find helpful bits of information:

This icon staves off potential mistakes or mishaps in the kitchen. Heed the warning to avoid a kitchen calamity.

I use this icon when you need to keep a "baking basic" in mind so nothing bad happens.

This icon is used to identify information that may be just a little more than you actually need to know for successful baking, but that is interesting nonetheless. If you're in a hurry and just want to get the information you absolutely need, you can skip the paragraphs marked by this icon and come back to them later when you have more time.

Who doesn't like to save a bit of time here and there? Follow these tips to get your baked good in the oven and on the table faster!

Here you'll find little gems of information that you may not have known about the recipe or technique you're using. This icon points to information that will make things just a little bit easier to do.

Where to Go from Here

Now that you know what the book has to offer, pick your favorite spot and begin. Perhaps you want to brush up on some technique know-how in Chapter 5 or dive right into your first batch of cookies in Chapter 7. Because you don't have to read this book cover to cover to make the most of it, you can start anywhere.

Above all, enjoy yourself. Baking should be fun and an activity you share with your loved ones. Whether the inspiration for baking is remembering a birthday, making a sweet treat for the family, bringing dessert for a dinner party, or welcoming a new neighbor or co-worker, you can certainly taste a difference when something is baked with love. You're saying that the people you're baking for are important enough that you took the time to do something special. Happy baking!

Part I
Baking Essentials

In this part . . .

Once you have a well-laid foundation for baking, it's easy to build upon it. The chapters in this part provide such a foundation. Here you find out about common ingredients and how they react with one another to create delicious baked goods. I also provide an in-depth look at the gear you'll need and hints on saving money and choosing wisely when you need to purchase some small electric appliances that can make baking easier.

Chapter 1

Bake, For Goodness' Sake!

So you've decided you want to find out how to bake? Congratulations! Perhaps you have tinkered in the kitchen but feel uncertain about what you're doing, or maybe your attempts at creating something in the oven have not been very successful. Or perhaps you just have some general questions about baking. Reading this book is a good start for getting answers to the fundamental questions that arise when you bake. Soon you'll be well on your way to becoming a better baker!

Baking is rewarding in many ways. First and most basic, it allows you to feed yourself and provides you with the ability to choose what you eat. You can give up the ammonium alginate, disodium guanylate, and guar gum you find in cake mixes. Your breads will no longer be preserved with sodium propionate. And your pies will be heptylparaben-free. Welcome to the world of butter, sugar, flour, and vanilla.

There's something deeply satisfying about taking those basic ingredients and turning them into something that everyone loves, such as cakes and cookies. Freshly baked treats say "You are special to me" to the people you share them with. And recipients feel special because you took the time to create something for them. Welcome a new neighbor with fresh bread, surprise your office workers with a crumbcake for their coffee break, or treat your children to homemade cookies.

Baking is a way to enjoy the simple pleasures of life. An afternoon spent in the kitchen baking bread or making cookies to pack in lunches for the rest of the week is a nice gift to give yourself or your family. Mixing up a batch of cookies with your children, roommates, or loved ones is a great activity that doesn't cost a lot of money and that will give you lasting memories.

Baking really is a lot of fun when you feel comfortable in the kitchen and at ease with what you're making. Unfortunately, baking can also be a source of great anxiety and frustration when you're not sure what you're doing or feel like the ingredients are staging a rebellion against you. But it's time to calm the troops. You've chosen the right book to get started!

Knowing How to Get Started

If baking is so great, then why does it sometimes seem like it's so hard? Did you ever get a chance to practice the basics? How many bad experiences have you had in the kitchen with burned cookies or dry cakes? Now is the time to forget all that you don't know (and perhaps your past kitchen disasters) and look toward a new horizon. You're about to equip yourself with the knowledge of how to bake.

Baking differs dramatically from other forms of cooking. It involves a kind of magic. From mixing up batters to working bread doughs firmly but gently to watching your dough rise, baking brings a spectacular feeling. Other forms of cooking are more about sustenance — feeding hunger. But baking is something special. It's both an art and a science. And the science really does count — instructions and ingredients work together to create delicious results. Wondrous aromas will waft from your kitchen, filling your home with flavors today and sweet memories tomorrow.

Sometimes it's hard to know where to start when you're trying something new. This book is a good start. It not only helps familiarize you with *what* you're baking but also explains *how* to bake. Knowing how to bake involves more than knowing how to read a recipe and following the instructions; it's also about understanding the following:

- The variety of ingredients available
- The roles of the various ingredients in a recipe
- What happens when you combine certain ingredients
- Various baking techniques

When you equip yourself with this knowledge, you'll discover how easy and fun baking can be!

Getting organized

As you set out to bake, the most important thing is to get organized. Kitchen counters are often dumping grounds for dirty dishes, yesterday's mail, car keys, or stray kitchen items that haven't been properly put away. Take the

5 minutes it takes (if that much!) to clean off the space you need. Visit Chapter 6 for more tips and ideas for organizing your baking space.

Before you crack your first egg, be sure that you have all ingredients on deck. Nothing is more frustrating than thinking you have a full box of raisins on hand and then finding that you have only half the amount you need when you go to pour them out. Read more about stocking up on staple ingredients in Chapter 2.

And one more thing: Do you know where both your beaters are for your electric mixer? Are you sure you have both the top and the sides for the springform pan you want to use? How about all the parts for your food processor? One thing I've learned over the years is that you can never be too prepared when you start to bake. Sometimes I tear my kitchen apart looking for my square pan, only to remember that I lent it to my neighbors. Or, I will search high and low for parts to my mixer, only to find them on the drainboard or put away in a different drawer. Have the tools you need in front of you before you start baking. Check out Chapter 3 for more details.

Finally, make friends with your oven. If you haven't paid much attention to it lately, read some helpful advice in Chapter 4 to make sure that your oven is in proper working order. No matter how good the recipes are, if your oven is off, there is little hope for baking success.

Familiarize yourself with baking techniques

If your eyes glaze over after reading a recipe, make a quick stop at Chapter 5 to get to know the common, and not so common, baking terms and techniques. There, you discover how to zest, fold, cut in, and whip. You should be aware that sometimes cooking terms dictate the kitchen tool you use. For example, you whip or whisk eggs with a wire whisk, you cut in butter with a pastry blender, and you fold with a rubber spatula. If a recipe uses equipment you don't have, you have time to consider alternatives or choose another recipe. So understanding the techniques not only helps you know what to do but also lets you know whether you need a specific tool to do it properly.

Practice

If you ask any professional bakers or cooks whom you respect how they acquired all their baking talent, I'm sure that you'll discover they spent a lot of time practicing their craft. The more you practice baking, the more you'll get a feel for it and the more successful you'll be.

Eventually, you'll know by the look and feel of certain foods what is going on with your dough or batter. You'll find yourself adding a pinch of this or that or kneading the dough a little more or less just because you know how it *should* feel or behave. Practice is the key to successful baking, and Part III of this book is full of recipes to practice with. You'll discover what a good cake batter should look like, how bread dough should feel, and what to do if your recipes aren't turning out the way you want.

Practicing baking is lots of fun, too, because the results are usually delicious and people are always happy to participate in your experimenting. I was quite popular with family and friends as I was developing and testing the recipes for this book, so I know that you, too, will be just as popular as you try these recipes.

Enjoying What You Bake

Who doesn't get excited when a co-worker or family member bakes up a treat? Everyone is happy when homemade desserts are brought in to be shared. The reason you bake dozens of cookies or multiple loaves of bread is to share the results. There never was a baking book titled *Baking for One or Two* because baked goods are meant to be shared.

Cakes will last for days, and cookies can stick around for a week or so if stored properly. So be sure to read Chapter 17 to pick up some great tricks and hints on how to keep every last bite of pie tasting as good as the first ones.

If you want to really wow your fellow friends, turn to Chapter 18 for some easy and neat ideas to spruce up your finished product. You can find some tips on how to package your baked goods or add some extra special touches that elevate the ordinary to the extraordinary.

Chapter 2

Stocking Up

• •

• •

A well-stocked pantry really makes a difference when it comes to baking for several reasons:

✔ It's a huge time-saver because it eliminates a trip to the grocery store.

✔ It enables you to create delicious treats whenever the mood strikes.

✔ If you happen to run out of one ingredient, a well-stocked pantry will ensure that you have a substitute or an extra ingredient on hand.

You don't need a lot of room to have a good pantry, but you need to be organized and store your ingredients well to maximize not only space but also the ingredients' shelf life. This chapter presents a list of staples you should have on hand when you begin baking. Of course, you don't have to purchase everything all at once, but you may be surprised at how quickly you'll build your pantry and how accommodating it will be to have a well-stocked kitchen for future baking.

When shopping for your pantry, be a smart shopper. Look for items on sale at your local grocery store. If space is not an issue, buy two or three popular items when they go on sale (my theory is you can never have enough baking soda or sugar). Also, take a look in discount stores and those ever-popular dollar stores. Recently, I found nonstick cooking spray at the dollar store and stocked up, because one can costs double or triple that amount in my local grocery store. This also goes for spices; I almost always purchase spices "loose" at a local store that sells them prebagged. I never spend more than 75 cents for what most people pay $3 to $4 in a supermarket. You may be surprised at how inexpensively you can stock your pantry when you shop around.

TIP

Storing bulk foods

If your supermarket or natural-foods store has a bulk section, purchasing ingredients there is an economical choice. However, never store items in the plastic bags for more than a week. Instead, save your jars and containers! Washed, clean jars or containers from spaghetti sauce, salsa, yogurt, peanut butter, and applesauce make great containers to hold items you purchase in bulk. Baby food jars, in particular, recycle into great spice jars. Don't forget to mark your jars with masking tape and permanent marker. (Don't use nonpermanent marker — it can rub off, and you'll be left wondering what you put in those jars!) You may someday need a reminder of what's in them and when you bought it!

If you hope to bake a lot or the holidays are coming, it is good to purchase flour, sugar, chocolate, and nuts in bulk at warehouse clubs. Of course, do this only if you will go through the ingredients quickly. If you're a part-time baker, I find that the "bulk section" of my food store is good if I need smaller amounts of ingredients. I can purchase just what I need, and there is no waste.

Your dry pantry can be in the cabinets, on shelves, in a cupboard or in a designated pantry or closet. Make sure to keep the floor clean. Remove everything and wipe down the shelves at least twice a year (spring and fall are good times for this type of cleaning). And, of course, if you spill anything, clean it up right away to avoid any sort of animal or insect infestation.

Flour

Flour is the primary ingredient for most cakes, cookies, pastries, and breads. Although it is one of the most basic baking ingredients, it also can be the most confusing, because of the wide variety available on grocery store shelves. Some flours are perfect for bread baking but disastrous for piecrusts or tender pastries. What makes a flour good for one recipe and bad for another? The amount of protein it contains. The more protein a flour has, the more gluten it will produce when it's kneaded. And the more gluten you have, the less tender your baked good will be.

TECHNICAL STUFF

Gluten is the protein that forms weblike structures present in wheat and other flours. When the flour is moistened and the bread is kneaded, or doughs and batters are mixed together, gluten forms and adds an elastic and cohesive nature to the food. This elasticity allows the dough to expand and trap the carbon dioxide, produced by the leavening, which makes the dough rise and stretch. Gluten makes it all possible!

Several different kinds of flour are available for baking; all-purpose, cake, bread, self-rising, and whole wheat flour are just a few. Become acquainted with three basic types of flour: all-purpose flour, cake flour, and bread flour.

✔ **All-purpose flour** is a blend of hard and soft wheat flours. The presence of more and tougher gluten in the hard wheat results in a rather elastic product. This produces the texture you want for cakes and cookies.

 Bleached and unbleached all-purpose flours can be used interchangeably, but unbleached flour has a higher nutritional value. Southern flours, such as White Lily, are made with a softer wheat, which means that they have cake flour–like qualities. Southern flour is great for tender biscuits and piecrusts.

✔ **Cake flour** is made with soft wheat, producing less gluten when mixed, so your cake will be more delicate, with a slightly crumbly texture. When purchasing cake flour, don't buy self-rising cake flour unless the recipe specifically calls for it. If you do buy it by mistake, omit the baking powder or baking soda and salt from the recipe.

✔ **Bread flour** has a higher gluten-forming protein content, making the dough nice and elastic. This makes it ideal for bread-making.

Don't store any of your flours in the paper sacks you buy them in. Instead, transfer them into airtight canisters and store them in a cool, dry place to make sure your flour won't absorb any odors or off-flavors. Label the containers to ensure that you can tell the difference between the different varieties (they tend to look the same out of their bags). Flour can last up to six months if stored properly in the pantry and indefinitely if stored in the freezer. If you bought the flour from a natural food store, place it in the freezer for a few days to make sure nothing will hatch.

If you use flour slowly, you can store your flour in the freezer. Double-bag the flour in sealable freezer bags and be sure to label it. Flour stored in the freezer can last for several years.

TIP

Substituting for cake flour or all-purpose flour

If your recipe calls for cake flour and you have only all-purpose flour on hand, you can substitute 1 cup *minus* 2 tablespoons all-purpose flour for 1 cup of cake flour. If you need all-purpose flour and have only cake flour on hand, substitute 1 cup *plus* 2 tablespoons of cake flour for 1 cup of all-purpose flour. The texture will be different, but if you have no other choice, it's okay. If you have instant flour on hand, such as Wondra, combine 2 tablespoons in the cup measure, then add enough all-purpose flour to make 1 cup (which would be about ¾ cup plus 2 tablespoons). That will also give you a cake flour–like flour.

Sugar

Sugar, another basic in baking, gives tenderness and sweetness to doughs and batters. Sugar also causes browning because it *caramelizes* (turns brown) when heated. Sugar also is a food source for yeast, making it rise.

In baking, you need to have three different types of sugar on hand: granulated sugar, confectioners' sugar, and brown sugar (light or dark).

- ✔ **Granulated sugar** is standard white sugar, either from sugar cane or sugar beets, and is the most popular and readily available sweetener in baking. Superfine sugar is a form of granulated sugar that dissolves easily in liquid. You can make your own superfine sugar: Place 1 cup of granulated sugar in the blender, cover, and process for 1 minute. Let it sit for about 1 minute longer to let the "smoke" settle. This produces 1 cup of superfine sugar. Sometimes superfine sugar is used in frostings and certain cakes. It dissolves quickly, so it doesn't need much cooking time.

- ✔ **Confectioners' (powdered) sugar** has been refined to a powder and contains a small amount of cornstarch to prevent lumping. Confectioners' sugar dissolves instantly in liquid and has a smoothness that makes it a popular choice for frostings, icings, and whipped toppings. It's also perfect for dusting cake tops and brownies. If your confectioners' sugar becomes lumpy, you can sift it.

- ✔ **Brown sugar,** both light and dark, is a mixture of granulated sugar and molasses. Brown sugar has a deeper flavor than granulated sugar. The color of brown sugar depends on the amount of molasses mixed in; dark brown sugar has more. Light brown sugar is the most common type used in baking, but the more assertively flavored dark brown sugar is also used. Recipes specify which brown sugar to use when it makes a difference; otherwise, you can use whichever you have on hand.

When measuring brown sugar for recipes, be sure to pack it into the measuring cup for accurate measuring.

When exposed to air for an extended amount of time, brown sugar has a tendency to harden. If this happens to your sugar, there's a quick fix: Place the hardened brown sugar in a heatproof bowl, and place the bowl in a baking pan containing about an inch of water. Tightly cover the entire baking pan with aluminum foil and place it in a 200-degree oven for 20 minutes or until softened. Use the softened brown sugar immediately, because it will re-harden when it cools. You can also use your microwave to soften brown sugar. Place the hardened sugar in a microwavable dish. Add a wedge of apple. Cover and microwave on high for 30-45 seconds. Let stand for about 30 seconds, then use normally.

Store all your sugars in airtight containers in a cool, dry place.

Salt

Salt is invaluable in the kitchen. It not only adds its own flavor but also helps bring out the flavor of the other ingredients. When used in baking, following the precise amount called for in the recipe is important.

Three types of salt are available for baking:

- ✔ **Table salt:** This is by far the most popular variety.
- ✔ **Kosher salt:** This salt has less of a salty taste than table salt and can be coarser.
- ✔ **Sea salt:** This salt has a fresher taste and is usually used in salt grinders.

All these salts can be used measure for measure in baking.

Most table salt has an anticaking agent added to help prevent it from clumping. However, on humid days (especially during the summertime) salt still tends to stick or clump. To prevent this, add about a teaspoon of rice to your salt shaker. The rice will absorb the moisture and keep your salt free-flowing. You never want to add the rice to anything you bake, though. If you need to get the rice out of your salt, run the salt through a fine-mesh strainer.

Eggs

Eggs thicken custards and sauces, help cakes to rise and be tender, and enrich and add sheen to baked doughs. Eggs come in two different colors — white and brown — but there's no nutritional difference between them. Eggshell color and color of the yolk (light yellow to deep orange) are the results of the breed and diet of the chicken and say nothing about the nutritional value or quality of the eggs.

Always buy large, fresh eggs. All the recipes in this book were tested with Grade A large eggs. Egg sizes are determined by their weight and volume, so substituting one egg size for another can affect the outcome. For example, two large eggs equal approximately ½ cup. It takes three medium eggs to equal the same ½ cup. Feel free to use free-range or organic eggs in any of the recipes in this book, as long as they're the right size.

How do you know your eggs are fresh? An easy way to tell is to place the egg in a bowl of tap water. If the egg sinks to the bottom, it is fresh. If the egg stands up and bobs on the bottom, it is not so fresh. If it floats, it is likely to be rotten. What makes the eggs float? Eggs naturally have a small pocket of air. As they age, this pocket increases, which causes the eggs to float in water. Check the expiration date on the box to ensure that your eggs are the freshest available.

Taking care with eggs

Care must be taken when handling eggs because they can carry *salmonella*, a bacteria that can cause dangerous food poisoning. Although salmonella is rare, prevention is the best cure. Of course, pregnant women, young children, the elderly, and those with a compromised immune system should not eat anything that contains raw or undercooked eggs. Here are some tips that can help:

✔ **Always buy the freshest eggs possible.** Buy only the number of eggs you will use within two weeks' time to ensure the freshness of your supply. If you don't use eggs that often, try to buy them by the half-dozen.

✔ **Be sure to wash your hands with hot, soapy water before and after handling raw eggs.** If you use a bowl to hold raw eggs, wash and dry the bowl before reusing it for another purpose.

✔ **Don't store eggs in the egg holder on the door of the refrigerator.** It might be convenient, but it's also the warmest part of the refrigerator. Salmonella does not grow in temperatures of less than 40 degrees. And it's killed at temperatures above 160 degrees.

✔ **Never use an egg with a cracked shell.** If you detect an off-odor after you have cracked an egg, discard it immediately.

✔ **If a recipe calls for eggs at room temperature, don't allow the eggs to sit at room temperature for more than 20 minutes.** Never use eggs left at room temperature for more than two hours.

Do not store your eggs in the refrigerator door. This is the warmest part of the refrigerator, and you want your eggs to be cold. Keep the eggs in the carton and store them in the refrigerator. That way, you'll always know the expiration date on the carton, and you'll know which eggs to use first. Keep them away from strong odors as well.

Leaveners: A Baker's Best Pick-Me-Up

Leaveners cause a dough or batter to rise by producing carbon dioxide, which rises throughout the batter and gives it a light, porous texture. There are two types of leaveners: chemical and yeast. Chemical leaveners include baking soda, baking powder, and cream of tartar. Yeast is just that, yeast — which, if you want to get technical, is a fungal leavener.

Now for a quick bit of Chemistry 101: When an acid and an alkaline are combined in the presence of a liquid, carbon dioxide is formed. All three elements are needed to produce the rise. When they're combined, the reaction is immediate, and, thanks to the heat of the oven, the gases in the batter expand, acting as another rising agent. Of course, too much rise is not desirable, because then the cake or bread or whatever you're baking will fall.

Baking soda

Otherwise known as *sodium bicarbonate,* baking soda is an alkali that must be mixed with something acidic (such as lemon juice, buttermilk, chocolate, or molasses) to react. Because baking soda reacts immediately, you should place the batter in the oven as soon as you've finished putting it together. If you taste baking soda, you will feel it tingle on your tongue.

When mixed with an acidic ingredient such as sour milk, buttermilk, yogurt, or citrus, baking soda acts as a leavening agent for cookies, cakes, and muffins. But baking soda has many other uses in and around the kitchen (listed here), so keeping a couple boxes on hand is always a good idea.

- ✔ **Baking soda is great for removing coffee stains from metal pots or ceramic mugs.** Just sprinkle a tablespoon or two inside the pot, rub with a dishcloth, and watch the stain disappear.
- ✔ **Baking soda is essential for destroying odors and keeping your refrigerator and freezer fresh.** Arm & Hammer now makes a special design just for the refrigerator and freezer.
- ✔ **Baking soda puts out grease fires.** Keep a box of baking soda near the stove in case of an emergency.
- ✔ **Baking soda is a great addition to a hot bath.** I like to have a box in the bathroom to add to my bath after a day of baking in the kitchen — it softens my skin and keeps me fresh-smelling!

Note: Baking soda and baking powder should *not* be substituted for one another.

Baking powder

Baking powder usually comes in a small, round, sturdy container with an airtight lid. Baking powder is essential for cakes, cookies, muffins, and quick breads and acts as the leavening agent. Choose double-acting baking powder, which is the most readily available.

Baking powder contains both an acid and an alkali (which is almost always baking soda), so just the addition of liquid is necessary to create a rise. Double-acting baking powder is true to its name — it reacts twice: once when the liquid is mixed in and then again when the batter is placed in the oven. Today, almost all baking powder sold is double-acting.

Although baking powder contains baking soda, don't substitute one for the other. Too much baking powder will make your baked goods taste acidic and may cause the product to collapse.

Baking powder can be stored in its own container, but if your baking powder has been sitting around for several months, be sure to test it for potency. Dissolve 1 teaspoon in ¼ cup of hot water. If it does not foam within a few seconds, it is time to get a new container.

In a pinch, you can make your own baking powder. Combine ¼ teaspoon baking soda and ½ teaspoon cream of tartar to equal 1 teaspoon baking powder. Or you can use 1 teaspoon baking soda plus 2 teaspoons cream of tartar for each cup of flour called for in the recipe. If you do make your own baking powder, make just what you need for the recipe; it can't be stored.

Cream of tartar

After the manufacturing of wine, the acid left in the wine barrels is made into cream of tartar. Not widely used in baking, cream of tartar is generally added to egg whites when whipping to help stabilize them. It is also often used in candy-making.

Cream of tartar is sold with all the other spices in the supermarket. It's used in baking when you are whipping egg whites to help "stabilize" them, which means they keep their shape. It's also good to have on hand, because you can mix it with baking soda if you run out of baking powder (see the preceding section).

Yeast

Yeast is the leavening agent for breads and rolls. Mostly used in bread making, yeast gets its rising powder from the combination of the right amount of warmth, food for it to eat (sugar), and liquid, which causes the yeast to release carbon dioxide.

In general, there are two types of yeast: active dry yeast and fresh compressed yeast.

- **Active dry yeast,** which I use for all the recipes in this book, is available in most supermarkets in premeasured packets, containing ¼ ounce (or about 1 tablespoon). You can also buy active dry yeast in jars that contain larger amounts.

  Active dry yeast should be dissolved in lukewarm water, no hotter than 110 degrees, which is actually just slightly warmer than lukewarm. Test the water on the inside of your wrist or run the tap over a candy thermometer until you reach this temperature. If you're unsure, it's better to err on the side of cooler water than hotter because all yeast will die if exposed to temperatures over 120 degrees.

✔ **Fresh compressed yeast** is moist yeast, available in 0.6-ounce squares. A square of fresh yeast can be substituted for one package of active dry yeast.

You can also find bread machine yeast, which I don't recommend for any of the recipes in this book. It's a special strain of fine-granulated, dehydrated yeast, specially designed to dissolve during the kneading and mixing processes of bread machines. Another type of yeast is rapid-rise or quick-acting yeast, which is just another strain of dehydrated yeast. Although this type of yeast can be substituted for active dry yeast measure for measure, I don't often use it. I haven't found it to significantly reduce rising time for my breads and am somewhat wary of its sustained rising power. If you do choose to use this variety of yeast, be sure not to *proof* it (to dissolve it in water and sugar before mixing it into the flour mixture to make sure that it's working). It may expire before your dough finishes rising.

Before starting any recipe, be sure to check the expiration date on your package of yeast. Don't bother trying to use yeast that has passed that date. I like to store active dry yeast in the refrigerator to ensure its freshness, although you don't have to. You must store compressed cake yeast in the refrigerator or freezer, because it's highly perishable. You can also proof your yeast to make sure that it's still alive.

Fats: The Good Guys with a Bad Rap

Fat is just a generic way of referring to butter, margarine, lard, oil, and shortening. How rich a cake, pastry, cookie, or other baked item tastes depends largely on the type of fat used in it and how the fat was incorporated. Although fat has gotten a bad reputation, it really does play an important role in baking, adding tenderness and flavor to baked goods. It also retains moisture and helps the leaveners in batters.

Several different types of fats are used in baking. Although butter, stick margarines, and shortenings are pretty interchangeable, using the ingredient the recipe calls for is always best.

Butter

Of all the fats, butter has the best flavor for baking. Most professional bakers would not think of baking with anything else. It is made from the richness of cream and gives a wonderful melt-in-your-mouth taste to baked goods.

Butter varies in taste from brand to brand, so finding the brand you like is important. Because butter can be expensive compared to your other choices (margarine, oil, shortening, and so on), your best choice is usually the brand that's on sale.

At the market, butter comes in sticks or whipped in tubs. For baking, choose the stick form — whipped butter gives a much different texture to baked goods because it has air whipped into it. You also have to choose between salted and unsalted. For the recipes in this book, it doesn't really matter which one you use, although you may want to choose unsalted butter for less salt content in your baked goods. Most professional cooks are "butter purists" and use only unsalted butter for baking. They vow that salty butter will alter the taste of their recipes, so they like to control that by choosing only unsalted. Personally, I have not yet found a recipe where the salted or unsalted butter has made or broken a recipe, but I'm sure that many would passionately disagree. I respect their choices, but I believe that the choice is yours. No need to get too fussy here.

Keep butter wrapped in the refrigerator, away from strong odors (the butter compartment of your refrigerator is always a good choice). You can also freeze butter (which is a great reason to load up when there's a sale). Just remember that butter is a sponge for odors, which can dramatically change its flavor. So wrap your butter in aluminum foil or seal it well in plastic wrap or plastic bags before freezing and rotate your stock (first in, first out). Think about storing your butter near an open box of baking soda, too.

Butter will keep frozen for up to one year, and in the refrigerator for several weeks. If you're in doubt about freshness, just give it a taste. It should taste like nothing but butter. When butter goes bad, it becomes rancid, which is indicated by a bad odor and taste. If it has picked up refrigerator odor, you will also be able to easily detect that.

One stick of butter or margarine weighs 4 ounces and equals 8 tablespoons or ½ cup.

There is nothing like butter, which imparts it own fresh, creamy flavor to baking. But stick margarine can be substituted in recipes where butter is called for, unless otherwise stated.

Margarine, butter blends, and vegetable spreads

Butter is 100 percent saturated fat, which is a drawback for many. A wide variety of oils and solid fats are used in making margarine, which gives you an unsaturated butter substitute with no less than 80 percent fat. Butter blends are a combination of about 60 percent margarine and 40 percent butter and can be used interchangeably with butter or margarine.

Margarine and butter blends come in sticks and in tubs. Use the sticks for baking; the margarine in the tub is too soft.

For the most part, stick margarine can be used in place of butter. Because of the oils that are added, margarine has a higher melting point than butter (110 degrees compared to 96 degrees). This also means it remains softer even when refrigerated. Textures and flavors vary, so you may have to try several brands before you find one you prefer.

Don't use reduced-calorie or low-fat butter or margarine for baking. Margarine products called *vegetable oil spreads,* which are lower in fat and cholesterol than butter or margarine, are available in sticks, tubs, or as liquid spreads. Because the fat is decreased and water is increased in these products, I don't recommend them for baking — you won't like the results! If you must use them for health reasons, don't use any product with less then 65 percent fat for baking, and choose only the sticks. These products affect the texture and quality of any baked item. Never use a liquid spread for the recipes in this book.

Shortening

Shortening is 100 percent fat and is great for creaming and whipping because it doesn't break down or melt (like butter or margarine can) from the friction created by creaming fats. Many bakers swear by vegetable shortening for the flakiest piecrusts. Solid vegetable shortening is great for incorporating air into the batter, which gives added volume to cookies and cakes and makes them softer and spongier.

Unfortunately, shortening does not impart much flavor to baked goods (although its lack of flavor makes it ideal for greasing cookie sheets and pans). Although there are butter-flavored shortenings, they still fall short of the real thing. Shortening is a good choice when the flavor of the fat is not that important. For example, you may want to use shortening for a spice or chocolate cake, and it makes a great choice for crunchy chocolate chip cookies. It's a bad choice for sugar cookies, however, because butter is an important flavoring ingredient in that recipe. Substitute shortening for butter, measure for measure. You also can use half butter and half shortening in some baking recipes.

Solid vegetable shortening comes in cans and, unopened, can be stored indefinitely. Once opened, it will last for several years if it's stored in an airtight container.

Lard

Lard is rendered pork fat, which is 100 percent animal fat and means that, like butter, it contains cholesterol. Lard makes for a great flaky piecrust, and the pork fat gives good flavor, especially good for savory recipes, and is inexpensive. You usually can find lard in the supermarket where the shortening is kept. You also can get lard from a butcher. Piecrusts aside, lard is not recommended for cakes, cookies, or other baked goods because of the strong flavor of the pork fat. When serving, you may want to inform your guests that there is lard in the crust, in case there are any vegetarians in the crowd.

Oil

Oils impart a tenderness and moistness to baked items. Mild-flavored vegetable oils such as corn, canola, or peanut are often called for in quick-bread, muffin, and some cake recipes. Oil also can be used to grease baking sheets or pans.

Vegetable oils are a good choice in baking because they are low in saturated fats and contain no cholesterol. When oil is called for in a recipe, be sure to choose one with a very mild flavor, such as safflower, canola, vegetable, peanut, or corn. I learned this the hard way. When I was a beginning baker, I once decided to make fresh blueberry muffins for guests visiting from Russia. The only oil I could find in the kitchen was extra-virgin olive oil, so I used it. Although the muffins looked fine, the assertive flavor the olive oil gave to the muffins made them pretty unpleasant-tasting (although the jolt was better than coffee!). Our guests were extremely gracious and even sampled one or two, but in the end we used the muffins to feed the birds. However, you can use "light" or "pure" olive oil for baking because it does not have the same flavor qualities that extra-virgin olive oil has.

You don't have to refrigerate vegetable oils (unless it's extra-virgin olive oil, which is not used for baking). They will keep for a year or longer in an airtight container. You'll know that it's gone rancid if it tastes stale or smells oddly pungent. You can, however, refrigerate oils for even longer storage.

When baking, use oil only when a recipe calls for it. Because oil mixes up differently than solid fats, the outcome of using it when it isn't called for may be undesirable.

Nonstick cooking spray

I love nonstick cooking spray for one-shot super-easy greasing action. It's especially great for greasing Bundt pans, because the molded design makes it particularly difficult to grease. You can also find a product called Baker's Joy, which "greases and flours" your baking pans for you.

Liquids

Liquids are added to a batter to help dissolve the salt and sugar and to create steam, which helps a cake rise and adds to its texture. Liquids also moisten the leavener, which helps to activate it. Although liquids include everything from water to fruit juice, the liquids I define here are dairy liquids, because these are the ones you'll come in contact with most often:

✔ **Fresh milk:** When a recipe calls for milk, it refers to cow's milk. Several varieties of fresh milk are available in the market: whole, low-fat, and skim. Although all the recipes in this book were tested with whole milk, unless otherwise specified, you can substitute the milk of your choice.

Fresh milk without the fridge? Keep a constant supply of milk on hand in your pantry. Parmalat makes a boxed milk that can be stored in the pantry for months without refrigeration. Open it, use what you need, and then store it in the refrigerator. Its flavor is slightly sweeter than traditional milk, but that's undetectable when it's used in baking. You can find this milk in your grocery store's baking section.

✔ **Buttermilk:** This milk contains no butter but was once a by-product of butter-making. Most commercial buttermilk is fermented from milk mixed with lactic acid (like yogurt and sour cream). Buttermilk adds a tangy flavor to doughs and batters, and it is lower in fat than whole milk.

If a recipe calls for buttermilk and you don't have any on hand, you can substitute 1 cup of regular milk plus 1 tablespoon vinegar or lemon juice for 1 cup of buttermilk. Let it sit for a few minutes before using. You can also substitute plain yogurt, measure for measure.

If you purchase buttermilk and you don't use the whole container, freeze it! Pour the buttermilk in 1-cup yogurt containers, and then you'll always have a small amount ready when you need it.

✔ **Cream:** Cream is produced when the butterfat of milk is separated out of the liquid. The different types vary depending on the amount of butterfat in them.

• **Heavy (whipping) cream** is the richest of all the creams, containing between 36 and 40 percent butterfat. It's used to make whipped cream and for some cooked frostings. Ultra-pasteurized heavy cream has been sterilized and will keep for several weeks in the refrigerator. Regular heavy cream will keep for up to one week.

• **Light cream** is only about 20 percent butterfat. It is much richer than milk and can be substituted for milk in many recipes. It's good for making sauces or baking when you don't want all the richness of heavy cream. It's also tasty in coffee. Light cream will not whip up, though.

- **Half-and-half** is a mixture of light cream and milk and contains between 10 and 12 percent butterfat. If you ever run out of milk, half-and-half makes a great substitute.

✔ **Evaporated milk:** Available in small cans, evaporated milk is whole milk with half the water removed. The mixture is slightly thicker than whole milk. Skimmed evaporated milk is widely available and can be used interchangeably with regular evaporated milk.

Keeping a can of evaporated milk on hand is always a good idea. If you ever run out of fresh milk while baking, just mix equal parts evaporated milk and water to make up the amount of milk you need.

✔ **Sweetened condensed milk:** Also available in small cans, this is similar to evaporated milk with sweetener added. It's often used for cream pies and candy making.

Cocoa and Chocolate: A Chocoholic's Dream

Chocolate comes from cocoa beans that have been fermented, roasted, and crushed into nibs. These nibs are then reheated and ground into a paste called *chocolate liquor,* which contains at least 53 percent cocoa butter. All chocolate and cocoa start out this way but are made into many different products.

Chocolate

Solid chocolate used for baking and eating comes in many varieties. Their differences lie not only in their varying proportions of chocolate liquor, sugar, and cocoa butter, but also the addition of vanilla and sugar.

Usually, baking chocolate comes in individually wrapped 1-ounce squares (usually in 8-ounce boxes). Many varieties of chocolate are available:

✔ **Unsweetened chocolate** is pure chocolate liquor, containing at least 50 percent cocoa butter and no added sugar.

✔ **Bittersweet, semisweet, dark, and sweet chocolate** vary from one another by the amount of sugar added to the chocolate liquor.

✔ **Milk chocolate** has dried milk powder, cocoa butter, and sugar added.

✔ **White chocolate** is not really chocolate because it doesn't contain chocolate liquor, but most brands of white chocolate have cocoa butter in them. Make sure that the brand you choose contains cocoa butter. Without it, the flavor is inferior. White chocolate is also called *vanilla chips* or *vanilla baking bar.*

When a recipe calls for a specific type of chocolate, such as unsweetened chocolate, don't substitute any other type, such as milk chocolate. You run the risk of a bad baking outcome.

Store chocolate in a cool, dark place (do not refrigerate). It should remain at a constant temperature, between 65 degrees and 78 degrees, and stored well wrapped in aluminum foil or plastic wrap. If stored at a high temperature or exposed to air for a long period of time, the chocolate will *bloom,* meaning that it will have a whitish haze or may become crumbly. What has happened is the cocoa butter has separated from the solids, and your chocolate gets a grayish exterior color. Not to worry, though — the quality of the chocolate is not affected. Stored properly, chocolate has an extremely long shelf life — up to one year.

When melting chocolate, never do so over direct heat. It is very delicate and burns easily. See Chapter 5 for the correct chocolate-melting procedure.

Cocoa

Unsweetened cocoa comes from pure chocolate liquor that has been separated into cocoa butter and solid cocoa cakes. These cakes are ground into cocoa powder, which is used often in baking cakes, cookies and commonly used to make brownies. Unsweetened cocoa is much different than cocoa for hot chocolate drinks, which have milk powder and sugar added. They cannot be substituted for one another, although you can add sugar and milk to cocoa to make hot chocolate.

You may notice that you now have a choice between Dutch process cocoa powder and regular cocoa powder. Simply put, the Dutch process treats the cocoa beans with an alkaline solution, and it has a different pH (about 7 or 8) than regular cocoa (about 5.5) before grinding the nibs. The result is a darker color and milder flavor than regular cocoa powder. This "Dutch process" finds favor with many pastry chefs.

Cocoa powder comes in a tin with a fitted lid. Cocoa powder is great if you bake a lot with unsweetened chocolate because it makes a good substitute and you don't have to melt it. Many people also feel that cocoa powder gives a more intense flavor than unsweetened chocolate.

Add-Ins and Flavorings

Many times, you don't want just "plain," so you stir in a little fun. Nuts, coconut, raisins, and other ingredients make fine additions or toppings for many recipes. Extracts and syrups also add flavor to baked goods. These ingredients may come in small packages, but they're essential for good flavor.

Nuts

Nuts add a wonderful flavor to baked goods, and they can also double as decorations. Here's a list of the nuts most commonly used in baking (shown in Figure 2-1):

- **Almonds:** Almonds are oval-shaped with a light brown exterior. They are available in or out of the shell, *blanched* (skinned) or *unblanched* (raw), halved, sliced, slivered, toasted, smoked, buttered, or salted. Whew!

Blanching your own almonds is easy. Just place the almonds in boiling water for 30 seconds to 1 minute. Drain and run under cool water to cool, and then rub them in a clean kitchen towel to loosen the skins. Or you can pop them straight out of their skin by just squeezing them a little.

- **Hazelnuts:** Also called *filberts,* hazelnuts seem to be the nut of the decade. You can find just about anything flavored with this nut, from coffees to gourmet desserts. Their round shape makes them perfect for garnishing, too. Hazelnuts have a light-brown skin and can be used whole, ground, chopped, or as a paste to flavor fillings for desserts.

To skin hazelnuts, spread them out on a baking sheet and bake at 350 degrees for 10 minutes, or until the skins begin to crack. Rub the nuts in a clean kitchen towel to remove the skins.

- **Pecans:** Pecans are an American original, made famous in such dishes as pecan pie and pecan cookies and grown primarily in the southern part of the United States. They're in season from September to November and are largely available shelled, in pieces. Whole halves are the most expensive and used largely for decorating.

- **Pine nuts:** Also called *piñon,* these buttery-tasting nuts have grown in popularity in recent years because of their starring role in pesto, but they're delicious in cookies, piecrusts, and breads. Shaped like a tiny ivory teardrop, these little nuts have a high oil content, so they should be stored in the freezer and used within six months of purchase. Although the pine nut is grown worldwide, and many varieties are available, don't purchase the Chinese pine nut, which has a strong, piney flavor.

- **Walnuts:** The most common variety of walnut is the English walnut, which has a wonderful mild flavor and is usually found in cookies, pies, and brownies. Walnuts are available in halves or in pieces (which is usually the least expensive way to buy them). Less well known is the black walnut, which has a very assertive, almost bitter flavor. All the recipes in this book that call for walnuts use the English walnut.

Be sure to get the freshest nuts possible. Store all your nuts in airtight containers in a cool, dry place if you will use them in less than a month. Otherwise, pop them into your freezer, away from strong odors, where they can keep for up to one year. Because most nuts have a high oil content, they can go rancid quickly if they're not frozen. You can still chop and grind frozen nuts without any defrost time, so there really isn't any reason not to freeze them.

Raisins and other dried fruits

Raisins are essential ingredients in many breads, cookies, and quick breads or muffins. I love to have them around to throw into something that may need a touch of sweetness.

You also can use dried currents, blueberries, cherries, and cranberries in place of or in addition to raisins. They are a wonderful flavor burst and can be used measure for measure as a substitute.

For moist, chewy raisins, soak them in hot water for a half hour or so. Just place them in a small bowl and add hot water to cover (you can flavor the water with coffee, rum, brandy, or bourbon if you like). When they become plump, drain the raisins and use as directed in the recipe.

Oats

Rolled oats are essential for oatmeal cookies and an important ingredient if you are making any sort of streusel or crumbly pie or cake topping. I also like to use them for making oatmeal bread.

Old-fashioned and quick oats generally come in a large cardboard container with a tight-fitting lid, which is fine to keep them in for storage. You can also find oats in the bulk section of many supermarkets. Do not store the oats in the plastic bag; instead, transfer the oats to an airtight container. If you do not use your oats often (for example, only a couple times a year), store them in the freezer. Also, never use instant oats for baking (which are different from quick oats). Instant oats absorb the water immediately and "cook," which then turns your baked good into cement.

Peanut butter

Peanut butter is great for peanut butter cookies and peanut butter pie, among other things. Peanut butter will store for many months in the pantry. If you purchase an all-natural brand, you can store that in the refrigerator so that it won't separate. Do not be alarmed if the oil separates from the ground peanuts. That's normal for unprocessed (natural) peanut butter to do.

You can also find lots of other nut butters — cashew, almond, and soy. Although you can interchange them with peanut butter for baking, the flavor of your baked good will be very different.

Coconut

Coconut is great for decorating cakes and cookies and is the essential ingredient for coconut cream pies and meringue cookies. Your recipe should specify whether you should use sweetened or unsweetened coconut. (If a recipe calls for unsweetened and you can't find it at your grocery store, look for it in a whole-foods or natural grocery store.) Store it in an airtight container or a sealable bag. Unopened coconut will keep for six months. Opened, it will keep for several weeks. You can refrigerate or freeze coconut if you don't use it very often.

Liquors

Liquors (bourbon, rum, brandy, and so on) add a nice flavor to many cakes, pies, and cookies. The alcohol evaporates during cooking, so unless a cake is soaked in the liquor or is uncooked, there is not much of a chance to overindulge. Always choose a moderate-quality alcohol when baking — the quality will be passed on to your finished product.

Maple syrup and extract

Maple syrup is the boiled sap from the maple tree. I always use pure maple syrup, but it's quite expensive (unless you live in Maine or Vermont, where it's much cheaper — if you travel or live there, look for it in grocery stores for the most reasonable price).

Keep your maple syrup in the refrigerator. Trust me when I say this — I once lost a whole gallon of pure maple syrup to mold because I did not refrigerate it. It may turn darker in the refrigerator, but it will not affect the flavor. Also, believe it or not, it takes quite a bit of syrup to impart maple flavor to baked goods or even frosting, so pick up some maple extract and try that before using your precious syrup, which I like to drizzle over cakes, cookies, and breads.

Molasses

Molasses is a strong-flavored syrup and comes from what is left over after granulated sugar has been extracted from sugar cane. It comes in light or dark varieties and is used to make gingerbread and to flavor cakes and muffins. Molasses will keep for a long time and should be stored in tightly closed jars in a cool place.

Spices and extracts

Spices and extracts lend a wonderful flavor accent to all baked goods. They should never overwhelm a dish and should be as fresh-tasting as possible.

Spices

Spices come from the seeds, bark, roots, and nuts of different plants and add flavoring to baked goods. The most common spices used in baking are

- ✔ Allspice
- ✔ Cardamom
- ✔ Cinnamon
- ✔ Cloves
- ✔ Ginger

✔ Mixed spice (also called *apple pie spice*)

✔ Nutmeg

Recipes usually call for ground spices. When spices are ground, the oil that gives them their fresh flavor evaporates over time. For best results, buy small quantities of ground spices to ensure a high turnover in your own cupboard. Store them in tightly closed containers (glass is best) and keep them in a cool, dry place (not near the stove) to minimize the loss of the oil. Still, you should consider replacing spices you've had for more than one year, after which the flavor will have dissipated.

Buying spices "loose" is much less expensive than buying them in jars at grocery stores or supermarkets. Find out if your local natural-foods store or baking supply shop carries loose spices so that you can scoop just the right amount (usually ¼ ounce is plenty). Just don't forget to label the jars you store them in.

Extracts

Extracts often are the essential oils of many foods or plants. They are extracted as a concentrated oil, such as orange, lemon, or almond, and then mixed into an alcohol base. The most common extract used in baking is vanilla.

At the market, you have a choice of pure or imitation extracts. For the best flavor, always choose pure extract if you're baking it in a simple recipe that contains few ingredients. Although pure extract can cost almost twice as much as imitation, it's a smart investment because the flavor it gives your baked goods is so much better than that of imitation.

Because alcohol evaporates, be sure to keep the lids of extract bottles on tight and store your extracts in a cool, dry place. If you do, they will keep indefinitely.

Fresh Fruits

Cakes, pies, and tarts made with fresh fruit make a wonderful ending to any meal. The better the fruit you choose, the better the end result will be. Always buy fruit in season, at the peak of ripeness. The following guidelines can help you select the best of each season's crop:

✔ **Apples:** Choose apples that have a fresh, bright look and smooth, tight, unbruised skin. They should be firm and crisp. The best apples for baking are the more tart or sturdy varieties, such as Granny Smith, Winesap, McIntosh, and Golden Delicious. Keep in mind that Red Delicious apples may look pretty and are great for snacking, but they aren't a good choice for baking.

TIP

Frozen fruit

In the summertime, I love to go to pick-your-own farms and stock up on all kinds of fresh fruit. Then I freeze my harvest for the winter months, when a fresh blueberry pie lifts my spirits. You can also keep frozen berries and fruits on hand (you can pick them up at the supermarket if you like) for pies, muffins, pancakes, and other desserts.

REMEMBER

Always store apples in the refrigerator. At room temperature, they ripen up to ten times faster and turn mealy. Yuck!

✔ **Bananas:** Bananas should be lightly firm and golden yellow with speckles of black spots; you don't want green stems or tips. If your bananas have green tips, let them ripen at room temperature for a few days.

✔ **Berries:** All berries, especially raspberries, are highly perishable and should be refrigerated and used within a day or two of purchase. Don't wash berries until you're ready to use them. Inspect packages of berries carefully; you should see no sign of mold. Fresh berries should give off a pleasant, fresh aroma. If they don't have much of a smell, they won't have much flavor either.

✔ **Cherries:** Unfortunately, cherries have an extremely short season — July and August — so grab them while you can. Look for firm, plump, glossy cherries with a dark maroon color. Avoid soft or brown cherries; they're overripe. Wash cherries only when you're ready to use them (within a few days of purchase).

✔ **Citrus fruits:** This category includes lemons, limes, grapefruits, and oranges. Choose fruits that are firm and feel heavy for their size. (The heaviness comes from the fruit being juicy.) Avoid lemons and oranges that have tinges of green skin. Always wash the fruit if you plan on using it for *zest* (the colored skin, not the white pith underneath).

Keep lemons on hand for freshly grated zest and for their juice. These bright, cheery fruits will keep for several weeks in the vegetable crisper.

✔ **Cranberries:** You can usually find cranberries only in the autumn, and they're often sold in plastic packaging. Look for bright, plump, glossy cranberries. Shriveled or soft berries are a sign of age — and certainly steer clear of any brown or moldy packages. Rinse fresh cranberries before using them. Cranberries freeze very well, so consider stocking up on them for a year-round supply. Just don't defrost them before baking.

✔ **Mangoes:** Mangoes are becoming more and more popular, and finding them is no longer such a chore. Purchase your mango while it is still slightly firm but gives a bit when pressed. Look for smooth skin with red and yellow coloring. A little touch of green is okay, but avoid mangoes that are all green.

✔ **Nectarines and peaches:** Choose fruits with an orange-yellow or creamy-yellow skin, a nice red blush, and a fragrant smell. Any green on the skin means that the fruit was picked unripe and will never sweeten. If the fruits have nice color but are slightly hard, set them out at room temperature for a few days to ripen. Refrigerate peaches and nectarines when they're ripe.

✔ **Pears:** A good pear has a nice pearlike fragrance. Because pears bruise so easily, choose your fruits slightly firm. They will ripen at room temperature in a few days. Avoid very green or bruised fruit.

✔ **Pineapple:** Choosing a good pineapple can be tricky, because the fruits will not continue to ripen, or sweeten, after they're picked. Some pineapples are labeled *field ripened,* and these should be your first choice. Otherwise, look for fresh-smelling, deep-green leaves. Pineapples should be firm but give slightly when squeezed. Pulling a leaf from the center of the pineapple is not a good indicator of the fruit's freshness or sweetness (a popular misconception). Avoid pineapples that are soft or smell like they're beginning to ferment.

Extras That Are Nice to Have on Hand

Although the following ingredients are not must-haves, you will come across them every once in a while when you're baking. A well-stocked pantry will keep many of these ingredients at your fingertips so that you'll be ready to bake on a moment's notice.

✔ **Cornmeal:** I am a lover of cornbreads and spoonbread, and cornmeal is great for keeping pizza crusts from sticking to the baking sheet, so I always keep some cornmeal on hand. Cornmeal can be white or yellow — where you live will probably dictate the availability and choice or preference. White cornmeal is a bit lighter and more delicate but doesn't give you as chewy or strong a flavor as yellow cornmeal does. Store cornmeal like you would flour: in an airtight container in a cool, dark place.

✔ **Cornstarch:** Sometimes cornstarch is used in baking to thicken the juices in pies. It's also used to thicken gravies and sauces. Cornstarch keeps forever — just make sure to store it in an airtight container in a cool, dry place.

✔ **Decorative frostings:** Tubes of different colors of decorative gels or frostings make adding spur-of-the-moment decorations to cakes and cookies easy. They keep forever and are always ready to turn the ordinary into something extraordinary.

✔ **Dried beans (for pie weights):** Dried beans may seem like a strange thing to keep in the kitchen for baking, but they act as inexpensive pie weights when you're baking a piecrust without a filling.

✔ **Food coloring:** Food coloring is great to keep on hand to tint coconut or frostings and to make colored hard-boiled eggs. Be careful when using it, though — it can stain!

✔ **Frozen dough:** Piecrust, well wrapped, will keep for up to a year in the freezer. Just defrost the dough before rolling it out. You also can keep puff pastry and bread doughs on hand in the freezer.

✔ **Instant tapioca:** Tapioca comes in several forms: pellets, flour, and granules. I love to use instant tapioca (which is made up of small pellets and is found where puddings and flavored gelatin are sold) when I bake fruit pies. It acts much like cornstarch does, thickening fruit juices, but I think it give the pies a better overall flavor.

✔ **Yogurt:** Plain yogurt is often used in quick breads and muffins. Its tangy flavor and richness add a nice component to baked goods. You can substitute yogurt for sour cream in many recipes as well. Unless a particular type is specified, you can use nonfat, lowfat, or whole-milk yogurt in any recipe.

Chapter 3

Going Over the Gear

*B*aking is a good activity because there is relatively little startup cost. If you have a bowl, a mixing spoon, and some baking sheets, you don't need much more to make cookies or even bread. I'm a huge lover of kitchen gadgets, but I live in a tiny apartment, so I have to streamline what I buy in the interest of having walking-around room. Because I love to bake, I've put together a list of the basics you need in order to use this book.

If you're starting from scratch, I recommend looking for bakeware and appliances on sale. Department stores usually have a good sale every few weeks in their housewares section, so keep an eye out for quality products at reasonable prices. Outlet malls are also a good place to find discounted stuff for the kitchen. If you aren't fully committed to the idea of baking, you can always find heavy-duty aluminum foil baking pans in just about every shape and size at the grocery store. You can usually use the pans only once, so they're not an economical choice, but they're perfect if you don't bake often or are bringing a baked good to a friend's house — you don't have to worry about getting the pan back.

Cost is not always the best indicator of value. Look for sturdy pots and pans; despite the price tag, if something feels flimsy, it is. Your bakeware should feel sturdy and heavy. They'll be going in and out of a hot oven throughout their lifetime, so you want to choose equipment that won't warp and will withstand the wear and tear of baking. Before using any new bakeware, be sure to wash it thoroughly in hot, soapy water.

Baking Pans

You won't get very far in baking if you don't have some baking pans. Although you don't need many, it's a good idea to familiarize yourself with the variety and sizes of pans available. From springform pans to muffin tins, discover all you need to know about the pans that make baking possible.

Generously grease insides of pans with solid vegetable shortening. Use a pastry brush to spread the shortening evenly, making sure that all the inside surfaces are well covered.

Baking (cookie) sheets

To keep yourself sane, I recommend owning at least two cookie sheets so that you can always have a batch of cookies ready to go into the oven. I recommend four baking sheets for an avid baker. Choose heavy, shiny aluminum baking sheets. Avoid dark baking sheets — they tend to burn cookies faster.

Cookie sheets either are flat (with no sides) or have a lip running around all four sides (see Figure 3-1). I prefer a baking sheet with a lip because I can use it for many things, such as placing it under juicy pies as they bake so that it catches the juice and the juice doesn't drip into the oven.

Figure 3-1:
Baking sheets can be flat or have a lip running around all four sides.

Thin baking sheets will warp in the oven, so make sure that yours are sturdy.

If you find that your baking sheets with nonstick coating are browning your cookies too fast, reduce the oven temperature by 25 degrees. You also can buy insulated baking sheets — they're a little pricey, but they keep your cookie bottoms from getting too brown. You may find that you need to increase your baking time by a few minutes if you use insulated sheets.

You can create your own insulated baking sheets instead of spending extra money to buy them. If your cookies are burning on the bottom but raw on top, stack two baking sheets together (one on top of the other) and continue baking as usual. This should prevent further burning.

Baking (muffin) tins

Muffin tins are little cups, usually 6 or 12 cups per pan, pressed out of one sheet of metal. They're used for making muffins, cupcakes, or rolls or for baking small cakes. Like other baking tins, the best muffin tins

- ✔ Are sturdy.
- ✔ Are made of heavy aluminum.
- ✔ May have a nonstick coating.

Specialty muffin tins are also available in mini-muffin size, as well as muffin-top pans (from which you get only the crunchy tops of the muffins and not the cakey bottoms).

Bundt and tube pans

Bundt and tube pans allow a hurried cook to make a beautiful, tall cake without the worry of layers. The secret is the funnel, which cooks the cake from the inside out. Bundt pans almost always have some sort of cut-crystal design molded into the pan and have tall sides with a hollow tube in the center. Check out Figure 3-2 to see what a Bundt pan looks like.

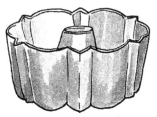

Figure 3-2: Bundt pans let you make fancy cakes, sculpted cakes.

BUNDT PAN

A tube pan (shown in Figure 3-3), or angel food cake pan, has a funnel in the center, too, but the sides of this pan are smooth, which allows the batter to climb up the walls of the pan as it bakes. Tube pans often have *feet,* which are little metal nubs that stick out above the rim of the pan, allowing the pan to be flipped over while it cools without smashing the cake inside. If your tube pan doesn't have feet, chances are the tube center is higher than the sides of the pan, which will give you the same clearance that feet would. Angel food cakes need to cook this way so that they don't collapse in the pan.

Figure 3-3:
The funnel in the middle of this tube pan helps your cake bake evenly.

If you don't know how many cups of batter your Bundt or tube pan holds, fill the pan to capacity with measured water to find out what its volume is. The same goes for any baking pan you need to use.

Cake pans

Cake pans come in several sizes. The most common are 8-inch round and 9-inch round. When you're buying a cake pan, make sure to get one that's at least 1½ inches deep. You'll need two 9-inch-round baking pans for making a layer cake. I recommend heavy aluminum pans, with or without a nonstick coating, and with straight sides. Be sure your pans are sturdy; you don't want them to warp and produce an uneven cake.

These pans will mold the batter you put into them, so you want them to be straight and flat.

Loaf pans

Loaf pans come in two standard sizes: 9 x 5 x 3 inches and 8½ x 4½ x 2½ inches. Either size is fine for the recipes in this book. You can find loaf pans made of glass, shiny metal, and nonstick aluminum. Glass pans and dark, non-stick pans have a tendency to brown your breads a bit faster than shiny metal, so you may have to lower the oven temperature by 25 degrees.

Always have two loaf pans for bread-baking, because most recipes make two loaves of bread, and you'll need both pans to put the bread in to rise; you can't really bake one loaf of yeast bread at a time. I also don't recommend baking quick breads one at a time. The leavening will become active when the wet ingredients are mixed together, and if the batter sits around for too long, the leavening may become inactive.

Pie plates (pans)

The most common sizes for pie plates are 8 inches and 9 inches. Pie plates can be a bit tricky because the size refers to the diameter, not the depth, of the plate, so they vary in the amounts they hold, even if they're the same diameter. Pie plates come in a variety of materials:

- ✔ **Glass:** A glass pie plate is often the best choice for pies that bake for 30 to 50 minutes. The glass radiates and conducts heat at the same time, so it cooks the crust quickly. If you have only glass pie plates and you need to cook a pie for more than an hour, lower the oven temperature by 25 degrees so that the crust won't burn in the pan.

- ✔ **Aluminum:** A thick aluminum pie plate gives you a more evenly baked crust than a thin plate does. Dull metal or dark pans also absorb heat faster and cook faster than shiny pans. Be sure to adjust the cooking time and temperature accordingly.

  A shiny pie plate reflects heat, so your pie will end up with a soggy bottom crust if you bake your pie for less than an hour.

- ✔ **Ceramic:** Ceramic pie plates are less popular, but they are available. They behave like thick aluminum pie plates, baking crusts evenly and slowly. They're a good choice for quiches and double-crust pies that require a longer cooking time.

Springform pans

Springform pans are clever contraptions. They allow the cake to bake, but then you can remove the sides of the pan (there is a clasp on the side) without having to invert it, and you're left with a lovely cake ready to be cut and served (see Figure 3-4). They're the perfect pans to make cheesecakes in. The most common sizes of springform pans are 8 inches, 9 inches, and 10 inches. Finding sets of springform pans sold in these three sizes is common.

When shopping for a springform pan, make sure that the bottom fits in tightly and the clasp is strong. Carrying a cake to the oven and having your clasp give out on you, bottoming out the whole pan and leaving you wearing the cake, is not a pleasant experience. Even worse is when this happens when you're carrying the finished cake to the cooling rack!

Figure 3-4:
The sides spring off of a springform pan so you don't have to disturb your cake.

To make sure that your springform doesn't spring a leak, place it on a baking sheet when you place it in the oven. The baking sheet will help catch any drips and allow you to transport your cake without any risk of the bottom falling from the cake pan.

Basic Pots

You don't need that many pots and pans for baking. However, you may have to melt chocolate for a cake or cook a filling for a potpie or even a pudding for a pie. This section presents a very short list of essential pots you need to have in the kitchen. For all pots, I recommend heavy, stainless steel cookware (with or without a nonstick coating).

What? No double boiler?

If you're in a pinch and need to make a double boiler, take two saucepans of different sizes or a saucepan and a stainless steel or tempered glass bowl to fit on top. Fill the larger saucepan with about 2 inches of water and rest the smaller saucepan on top of the water (it doesn't matter whether the second saucepan touches the water, because the bottom of a regular saucepan is sturdier than the bottom of a double boiler) or insert the bowl in the saucepan. Use as you would a regular double boiler.

A word of warning: Because the two pans will not be fitted, you need to make sure that none of the simmering water gets into the top saucepan. Also, be very careful when removing the top bowl if you're using a bowl. It will be hot!

Or you can use a stainless steel bowl large enough to sit on top of the pan of simmering water. What's nice about this setup is that there's no danger of the water mixing in with your melting chocolate. Just remember that the bowl will be very hot to touch, so use an oven mitt.

Saucepans

You should have at least a 1-quart saucepan and a 2-quart saucepan on hand for stovetop procedures such as scalding milk and melting chocolate. Heavy-bottomed saucepans are better conductors of heat, and you're less likely to burn or scald the bottom than if you use thinner metals. I prefer stainless steel saucepans because they're *nonreactive* (they don't react with acidic ingredients, which can cause discoloration) and durable. They also don't pick up food odors or stain easily.

Double boiler

If you melt chocolate, you need a double boiler. A double boiler consists of two nesting saucepans or a saucepan with a fitted bowl inside. To use a double boiler, heat water in the lower pot until it steams with the upper pot in place. This warms the bottom of the upper pot or bowl. Make sure that the bottom of the bowl doesn't touch the simmering water. Then the chocolate can melt with no risk of burning. This method of indirect heating also is used for making some creams and sauces.

Never use the top saucepan of a double boiler over direct heat, because the metal used to make the upper pan is not as sturdy as the bottom saucepan.

Dutch oven

Its name is said to have come from its Dutch ancestry, dating back to the 1700s. These large pots or kettles are good for going from the stovetop to the oven, which is great if you're making potpie or stew and dumplings. Make sure that your Dutch oven has a tight-fitting lid and is flameproof (oven safe). This includes the handles and lid knobs.

Electric Tools

Although most baked goods don't require electric gadgets, these convenience tools certainly speed up the baking process. Electric mixers enable you to speedily beat sugar and butter, whip egg whites, and mix together batters. Food processors and blenders can chop and puree in no time.

Blender

A blender is great for a number of tasks, such as

- Pureeing fruits
- Making cheesecake
- Crushing crackers or cookies for a crumb crust
- Grinding or chopping nuts

There's no better tool than a blender when you need superfine (quick-dissolving) sugar and have only granulated sugar on hand. Just dump the amount you need into the blender and whiz it for a minute or so, and — voilà! — superfine sugar. (I once tried this in my food processor and the results were not the same.)

Food processor

A food processor (shown in Figure 3-5) is a wonderful kitchen tool because it's strong, simple to use, and pretty quiet — but it's also quite expensive. I absolutely love my food processor and use it all the time. You can use a food processor to

- Make pastry dough with the dough blade.
- Chop nuts or citrus zest with the metal blade.
- Puree fruit with the metal blade.
- Juice lemons or limes with the juicer attachment.
- Shred carrots with the shredder attachment.
- Slice apples with the slicing attachment.

Food processors can do these tasks and more — all in a fraction of the time required to do it by hand.

If you're considering purchasing a food processor, don't skimp on quality. Make sure that you purchase a reputable brand with a good, durable motor. The money you spend on it upfront will save you money and time in the long run.

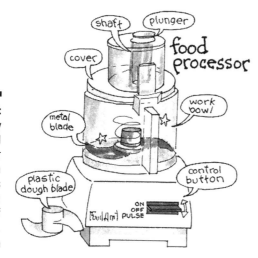

Figure 3-5:
A quality
food
processor
comes with
numerous
blades for a
variety of
tasks.

Handheld mixer

A handheld mixer is relatively inexpensive and great to have on hand. You can use a handheld mixer for

✔ Whipping up cake batters and light cookie doughs.

✔ Whipping cream and egg whites.

Handheld mixers have three speeds: slow, medium, and fast. They are portable and easy to clean (the beaters just pop off when you're finished), which can save you a great deal of time and frustration.

Although the motor in a handheld mixer is not as strong as the one in a standing mixer, you can find sturdier, more expensive models that come with attachments for creaming thick cake batters and dough hooks for bread doughs. The advantage of a handheld mixer is that it's portable, which means that you can use it wherever you need it (as long as you can plug it in).

Stand (table) mixer

A good stand mixer (shown in Figure 3-6) has been called the most efficient tool known to man. It can handle just about any workload you dish out, because the motor is about six times stronger than that of any handheld mixer. It also has a wider range of speeds than a handheld mixer.

A stand mixer generally comes with its own bowl attachment, which is usually generous in size, and three standard attachments, including

- ✔ **A paddle,** which blends batters and creams ingredients together.
- ✔ **A wire whisk,** which incorporates air into batter and whips egg whites.
- ✔ **A dough hook,** which kneads dough.

You also can purchase special attachments for some models, including a pasta maker, a grinder, a shredder, a slicer, and a juicer.

Stand mixers are not quite as convenient and do not disassemble as neatly as handheld mixers, so you will more than likely store yours on the countertop or in an easy-to-access place.

A wide range of stand mixers are available in a wide assortment of prices. My best advice is to determine how much baking you'll be doing. If you bake about once a month, I recommend investing in a quality mixer, such as a KitchenAid. It's expensive but well worth the money. My mother has had hers for well over 25 years and has never had problems with it — and I plan on having mine for that long or even longer!

Other Essentials

You need bowls, racks, and cutting boards for preparing doughs and batters. Then, when your finished creations come out of the oven, you need cooling racks to help them cool quickly. This section describes the essentials for a good baking kitchen.

Mixing bowls

You don't have to go out and purchase new bowls — you can use any bowl you have on hand to make the recipes in this book. However, if you plan to buy bowls, this section offers some tips for selecting the best ones.

For mixing cake batters and cookies, I like a wide stainless steel mixing bowl. These come in a variety of sizes, but look for bowls with flat bottoms and wide, sloping sides. They make mixing easier and are less likely to tip over if you leave a whisk or spoon in them than a narrower bottomed bowl. Stainless steel is also durable, unbreakable, and nonreactive (it won't react with acidic ingredients, turning the bowl different colors).

When I make bread, I like to let the dough rise in a heavy ceramic bowl. The ceramic bowl keeps my dough well insulated and at a more consistent temperature.

When choosing a mixing bowl, make sure that you will have enough room to fit all the ingredients and still have space to mix them up. Also take into account what ingredients will be going into it. This is especially important when you're whipping egg whites or cream, because egg whites can grow up to six times their original volume, and cream will at least double.

Cooling racks

Cooling racks are wire racks that allow air to circulate around baked goods while they cool, preventing them from having a soggy or moist bottom. A wide variety of shapes and sizes are available; just make sure that your rack has feet on it so that it won't lay flat against the countertop, thereby defeating the purpose of circulation. Also, look for the rack's wires to be close together. This will prevent delicate cakes from sinking too much and smaller cookies from slipping through the spaces between the wires.

Cookie and biscuit cutters

Cookie cutters come in all shapes and sizes. They're generally made of plastic or metal. When choosing your cutters, look for somewhat simple shapes that won't cut your cookies into a variety of thicknesses. For example, a cookie cutter that cuts out giraffes may be tricky because the small head might burn before the body is done cooking. Avoid cutters that are too detailed.

Biscuit cutters generally are nothing more than 1- or 2-inch-round cutters. If you don't have a biscuit cutter, you can use a clean soup can with both top and bottom removed instead.

Cutting boards

Cutting boards offer smooth, even surfaces for tasks such as chopping, cutting, peeling, and rolling out doughs. You can choose from a few different materials:

- ✔ **Wood:** A wooden cutting board is your best choice for preserving the sharp edges of knives, because they don't blunt as quickly as they do on plastic, metal, or marble. Don't place your wooden cutting board in the dishwasher or let it soak in water for any length of time. The heat from the dishwasher will warp your board, and the water will soften the board's bonded sections. Keep one side of your cutting board knick-free and smooth so that it's suitable for rolling out cookie or pastry dough.

- ✔ **Polyurethane:** Polyurethane boards will not warp and are soft enough for knives to be used without dulling. They also can be sterilized in the dishwasher.

- ✔ **Thin plastic:** My new favorite cutting boards are very thin, flexible chopping surfaces. They are bendable, are so easy to use, and take up hardly any space, plus they seem easier to clean and don't retain odors. I promise that if you purchase one, you'll use it time and time again.

Knives

A good sharp knife can be your best friend in the kitchen. Just be sure to hold it carefully! (See Figure 3-7.) Good, professional knives are quite expensive and not really necessary for the home baker. Still, you should have four basic knives in your kitchen:

- ✔ **A large cleaver:** This knife is perfect for chopping, and its side is ideal for crushing things.

- ✔ **A serrated knife:** This knife is great for slicing breads and delicate cakes.

- ✔ **A medium-sized knife (chef's knife):** This knife is best for slicing cakes, cutting pastry, and for less heavy work than the cleaver.

- ✔ **A paring knife:** This knife is ideal for cutting small foods, peeling fruits, hulling strawberries, and performing many other detail tasks.

Although a knife's sharp edge can be dangerous, dull knives are even more dangerous. You need to apply more pressure to cut with a dull knife, therefore increasing your chances of slipping and injuring yourself. Always tuck your fingertips under when cutting with a knife so that if your knife does slip, it will cut your knuckle, not your fingertip (see Figure 3-8).

the handle grip
works best for
small hands

the blade grip
works best for
LARGE hands

Figure 3-7:
The proper
grip ensures
safe cutting.

Figure 3-8:
Curling your
fingertips
under
enables you
to work
quickly
without
risking your
fingertips.

SAFE FINGER PLACEMENT
WHEN SLICING

Measuring cups

Measuring cups are essential for every kitchen. You won't find many recipes that don't require measurements of some kind. Measuring cups come in two basic types:

- **Graded:** Graded cups (see Figure 3-9) range in sizes from ¼ cup to 1 cup and can range from 4 to 6 cups in a set. Use graded cups to measure dry ingredients and solid fats, such as shortening.

- **Glass:** Glass cups (see Figure 3-10) are available in a wide range of sizes, the most common being 1 cup, 2 cups, and 4 cups. Use these cups for measuring liquids. Make sure that you read your measurement at eye level, with the cup on a flat surface.

Figure 3-9:
Every baker
needs
a set of
measuring
cups.

dry measure cups

Figure 3-10:
Use a glass
measuring
cup to
measure
and pour
liquids.

liquid measure cup

When measuring thick, sticky liquids such as honey, molasses, and corn syrup, spray the inside of the measuring glass with nonstick cooking spray or grease it a little with oil. The liquid will then be much easier to remove.

Measuring spoons

Graded measuring spoons usually come in sets of four or six, ranging from ¼ teaspoon to 1 tablespoon. Sometimes sets have ⅛ teaspoon and 1½ tablespoon, too. You use these measuring spoons for both dry and liquid measures.

Potholders and oven mitts

Potholders and oven mitts enable you to hold hot baking sheets and pans without burning yourself. I like to have both an oven mitt and potholders (generally square pads) on hand for different tasks. I use the mitt if I'm reaching into the oven and run the risk of burning my whole hand. I choose the square pads when I need to hold the sides of a dish, such as a soufflé.

I highly recommend that you forgo the decorative potholders that are so commonly found in stores' housewares sections. If you have them, use them for display. Few of these decorative potholders provide adequate protection from heat. Make a special trip to your kitchen supply store and purchase insulated potholders. They're slightly more expensive than regular potholders, but I trust them in every situation — whereas the decorative holders wear in strange spots and inevitably end up burning your hands.

Always have two sets of potholders. No matter what kind of potholder you have, if it gets wet, stop using it until it dries. It can no longer protect your hands.

Rolling pin

You use a rolling pin to roll out pastry dough. Many types are available, but I recommend a relatively heavy pin with handles, such as the one shown in Figure 3-11. The weight of the pin helps distribute the dough evenly, so don't push down on the pin when using it.

Figure 3-11:
Heavy
wooden
rolling pins
are best
for rolling
out pastry
dough.

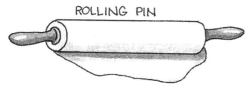

ROLLING PIN

There are such things as *cool pins,* made of plastic or marble. Some you can even fill with water and freeze. These rolling pins ensure that your dough stays cool while you're working with it. I don't recommend buying a cool pin unless you've worked with one and prefer it to the traditional wooden pin. The marble variety is too heavy for my liking. The plastic is too light. And the frozen pins are a waste of money in my opinion. Not only are they awkward to work with, but the frozen center sweats as the water comes to room temperature, so it can make your dough sticky. So stick with a sure thing: wood.

To minimize sticking, always dust your rolling pin with flour before using it and wipe it clean when you're finished. Never put your rolling pin in the dishwasher.

Spoons

You should have two types of spoons in your kitchen: metal and wooden. You want at least two metal spoons, one solid for stirring and one slotted for lifting foods from liquids. Wooden spoons are great for stirring custards and sauces made in nonstick pans and for stirring batters and doughs. Nothing beats a sturdy wooden spoon. They are inexpensive, so you may want to get two or three.

Great Gadgets

This section provides a list of helpful tools for the kitchen. Although you don't need to go out and purchase each and every one of these items, it's good to know that they're out there to help make your life in the kitchen that much easier.

Apple corer

Apple corers (see Figure 3-12) come in two basic types. One is a wooden handle attached to an elongated curved metal cylinder with a cutting edge. This tool is indispensable when you want to core an apple or pear without slicing through it, making it perfect when you want baked apples or pears. You just press down vertically into the apple at the stem with a slight twisting motion until you reach the bottom. Another version cores the apple and slices it into segments. This tool has sets of metal spokes that meet in the circle in the center. Press directly over the apple and it slices and cores the apple easily.

Box grater

Graters are usually made of metal (although plastic is available) and usually have four sides, offering a choice from fine to coarse grating, as well as a slicing blade that I like to use for cheese and carrots. If you don't own a box grater, choose a sturdy one with four sides and comfortable handle. You also can find a flat grater, which usually offers a choice of only two holes, but I find them cumbersome to use and unsteady. In their favor, flat graters take up less space and are easier to clean than box graters.

Clean your box grater from the inside out. Scrub the inside with a stiff brush, under running water, to push food from the back through to the front. Then hang the grater to air-dry.

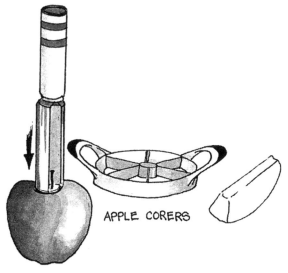

APPLE CORERS

Cake tester

Thin plastic or metal needlelike instruments, sometimes with a round handle, are sold as cake testers. You insert the tester into the center of the cake to determine whether it's done. If dough clings to it, the cake is not yet finished. If the tester comes out clean, the cake is finished. But I find that a wooden toothpick or even a thin, small knife works just as well.

Citrus juicer (reamer)

A citrus juicer is a hand tool that enables you to juice a lemon without getting too much pulp or seeds. Some are handheld; some you place over a bowl and strain out the seeds and pulp so that only the juice falls into the bowl; and others collect everything at their base. Citrus juicers come in many different shapes and sizes, so choose one that works well for you.

TIP

If you don't have a citrus juicer and you need to get more juice out of a lemon than squeezing will allow, try this: Squeeze the lemon — roll it on the counter while mashing down with the palm of your hand — before cutting. Then insert a teaspoon and gently squeeze again while twisting the spoon around the inside of the lemon. This will help release additional juice.

Flour sifter

A flour sifter (see Figure 3-13) removes any lumps or debris from your dry ingredients by sifting them through a fine mesh. Although most of the flour you find today is presifted, it has a tendency to settle during storage, so sifting flour or just stirring it up with a spoon before measuring it is a good idea so that the flour isn't so densely packed. This is especially important with cake flour. Sifting also is a good way to blend all dry ingredients evenly and aerate dry ingredients.

Figure 3-13:
Use a flour sifter when you want smooth, evenly textured flour.

If you don't have a sifter and you need sifted flour for a recipe, you can use a wire mesh strainer instead (see Figure 3-14 for instructions).

How to Sift Flour If You Don't Have a Sifter

Figure 3-14:
In a pinch, you can always use a strainer to sift flour.

1. Pour flour into a strainer

2. Use your hand to lightly tap the strainer

– OR –
tap the strainer on the inside of the bowl

Funnel

Funnels come in handy in the kitchen in many ways. They're ideal for hanging an angel food cake pan over or for filling salt shakers. They're also helpful if you need to return liquids to containers without spilling. You may not reach for a funnel every time you bake, but when you need one, you'll be glad you have it.

Kitchen scissors

Keeping a pair of scissors in the kitchen for food-related jobs is a good idea. Kitchen scissors are perfect for trimming pastry dough, cutting paper to line a pan, opening plastic bags, cutting fresh herbs, and snipping strings. The heavier and stronger the scissors you have, the better they will help you in the kitchen — heavy-duty scissors can easily cut through doughs or frozen items in one try. Also, the weight of sturdy scissors makes the cut more precise.

When cutting up fruits, especially sticky ones like dates, figs, apricots, and so on, lightly oil or butter the scissors first.

Nutmeg grater

A nutmeg grater is a fun, but not necessarily essential, item for the kitchen. Spices are so much more flavorful when they're freshly ground. Nutmeg is no exception. A nutmeg grater is a small tool used to turn the whole egg-shaped nutmeg seed into a ground spice. The slightly curved surface has a fine rasp, and you rub the seed across the surface to grate it. A little door slides open in the back of the grater, which stores the nutmeg seeds for you.

Oven thermometer

If you were to run out immediately and purchase just one item for the kitchen, I would recommend an oven thermometer. A good oven thermometer is inexpensive and can save you from ruining your baked goods. Because you rely on your oven for baking, you need to be sure that the heat is accurate. Many home-oven thermostats are not always true, so the best way to monitor your oven's temperature is with a thermometer. Look for one with a hook for hanging. I hang my thermometer on the oven's center rack and can easily double-check the temperature. Installing an auxiliary oven thermostat is the best thing you can do for your oven and the success of your baking. Flip to Chapter 4 for more on oven thermometers.

Pastry bags and tips

I like a sturdy nylon cloth pastry bag for decorating cakes. If you're going to purchase one, I suggest getting one slightly larger than you think you need (it's always better to have more room than you need). Pastry tips are hard little metal cones that are either dropped into the pastry bag (coming out the small end) or screwed onto the coupler on the outside of the bag (making switching tips quite easy). The tip you use determines the pattern you pipe onto the cake. For more on using a pastry bag, see Chapter 9.

For small, quick piping jobs, use a small zipper-top plastic bag rather than digging out the pastry bag. Fill it with icing, remove the excess air, seal the top, and snip off a tiny bit of one corner. You're now ready to pipe away!

Pastry blender

A pastry blender is a handheld tool with a set of steel cutters (see Figure 3-15). The most common use for a pastry blender is to cut fats into flour quickly so that the fats won't melt and your dough remains tender. To use a pastry blender, mix the ingredients while cutting into the fats with the blender using a rocking, up-and-down bouncing motion. If you don't have a pastry blender, you can use two knives or two forks to cut in the fat.

Figure 3-15:
Using a
pastry
blender to
cut fat into
flour makes
the job
quick and
easy.

Pastry brush

A pastry brush (see Figure 3-16) is a small tool that makes life in the kitchen a lot easier — there's no substitute for a brush. You use it to spread melted butter, glaze pastries, and brush breads with egg wash. If you enjoy working with phyllo dough or pastry, you may want to purchase a pastry brush. Look for one with very soft bristles. Rough or stiff brushes will tear your pastry, so avoid them if you can. Wash your brush with hot, soapy water after each use and hang to dry. Do not store with the weight on the bristles or you will cause them to curve and not brush effectively anymore.

Pie weights

When you prebake an empty pie shell, sometimes you'll need to weigh down the crust with pie weights to prevent it from bubbling up. Pie weights are available at any kitchen supply store and are usually ceramic or metal round pellets. To use them, pour them onto an unbaked, foil-lined piecrust and then place the crust in the oven, as shown in Figure 3-17. About 5 to 10 minutes before the crust has finished baking, remove the weights by lifting out the foil and return the crust to the oven to finish browning.

Figure 3-16:
A pastry
brush.

Figure 3-17:
Using pie
weights
when
baking an
empty
piecrust.

TO USE PIE WEIGHTS, POUR THEM INTO AN UNBAKED, FOIL-LINED PIECRUST. PLACE IN THE OVEN.

ABOUT 5 TO 10 MINUTES BEFORE THE CRUST HAS FINISHED BAKING, REMOVE THE WEIGHTS BY LIFTING OUT THE FOIL AND RETURN THE CRUST TO THE OVEN TO FINISH BROWNING.

If you don't have pie weights, you can use dried beans instead. Follow the same directions as for the pie weights. Keep the beans in a special jar — you can reuse them many times. Unfortunately, after you've used beans in place of pie weights, the beans can no longer be cooked — they will have dried out too much.

Sieve (strainer)

A sieve is great for sifting flour, dusting cakes with confectioners' sugar, or straining liquids from solids. A sieve generally has a bowl-shaped bottom made of fine mesh and a long handle. You also can mash soft fruits through the mesh to make a puree, which is especially good for removing all the seeds from a raspberry puree.

Spatulas

Two kinds of spatulas are important in baking: rubber and metal. A rubber spatula (shown in Figure 3-18) is great for scraping down the sides of bowls during mixing, getting all the batter into pans, and folding together ingredients. Choose a spatula with a flexible, but stiff, blade. The stiffness in the blade gives you more scraping control. Don't expose your rubber spatula to heat, because most will melt or crack.

Figure 3-18: Rubber spatulas are great for scraping every bit of batter from a mixing bowl.

A metal spatula (see Figure 3-19) has blunt edges and a rounded tip and is the perfect tool for spreading frostings and fillings. These are available in a wide range of sizes, but for finished cakes, you may want to have a 10-inch blade so that you can sweep across the entire top of the cake for a smooth finish. Make sure that the blade fits snugly in the handle and that the handle is comfortable to hold.

Figure 3-19:
Metal
spatulas are
especially
useful for
spreading
frostings.

Timer

A timer is an inexpensive item that can save you money in the long run by reminding you when to take your baked creations out of the oven, therefore preventing wasted batches.

Always set your timer for the minimum amount of time given in a recipe, and check for doneness. You can always leave your goodies in the oven for a few more minutes — just don't forget to reset the timer!

Tongs

Think of tongs as an extension of your hands. Tongs are great for retrieving foods from hot water, flipping cooking foods, and lifting hot lids.

Trivets

A trivet can be made of wood, cork, or ceramic. It's usually round or square and is placed underneath the bottom of a hot pot or pan to prevent it from burning the surface it's placed on. Trivets also protect glass and ceramic baking dishes from the sudden shock of cold surfaces, which can cause them to break.

Vegetable peeler

There's nothing like a comfortable vegetable peeler for removing the skins of fruits and vegetables. A vegetable peeler also makes great chocolate curls. Look for a stainless steel blade so that it won't react with acids.

Wire whisk

Not a week goes by when I don't use my wire whisk. It has many purposes: It mixes, blends, and aerates batters and ingredients. It's essential if you want to make puddings, smooth lumpy liquids, or blend liquids into solids. If you don't have a whisk, I recommend that you get one. Purchase a stainless steel whisk that's comfortable to hold and use. Avoid a narrow handle because your hand might get tired holding it. And look for one that's well manufactured so that food doesn't get stuck in it.

Part II
Basic Training

The 5th Wave   By Rich Tennant

"...because I'm more comfortable using my own tools. Now—how much longer do you want me to sand the cake batter?"

In this part . . .

Sure, you're familiar with terms such as *beat, blend, mix,* and *whip,* but when the recipe calls for the dough to *come together* or for you to *blanch* the almonds, *hull* the strawberries, or *zest* the lemons, you may start feeling faint and begin searching for the number to the nearest bakery. Well, put down the phone and get ready to pick up some new lingo so you can talk shop with the best of them. This part also helps you discover the role of basic ingredients so that baking in general becomes less intimidating to you.

You know you have an oven, but do you know how it works? This section preps you for the process of baking. You can find information for getting your oven in top working order and what to look for when baking and how to combat troublesome ovens. It also gives you advice on how to read recipes, what to be on the watch for, and how not to get yourself in over your head if you're a novice baker. I also provide tips on how to measure all kinds of things, from flour to fats. You also get information on basic techniques you'll need to perform when you want to try the intermediate to challenging recipes. Find out about whipping egg whites and melting chocolate. This section unlocks many of the mysteries of the kitchen.

Chapter 4

Understanding Your Oven

● ●

In This Chapter

▶ Knowing the different types of ovens

▶ Knowing how to position your racks

▶ Figuring out how to avoid hot spots in your oven

▶ Making sure that your oven is the right temperature

● ●

Most people take their oven for granted — it has always been there and it always will be in the kitchen. Some people don't think twice about their oven. They just put food in and it cooks. Others find that they're constantly battling the demons that live inside. If you have a love-hate relationship with your oven, read on to discover how to uncover the quirks of your oven and overcome common oven issues. Even if you don't have a worrisome oven, in this chapter I tell you how to make sure that your oven remains in tiptop working order.

Knowing the Difference Among the Three Types of Ovens

You can imagine how important a properly working oven is. Three different types of ovens are on the market: gas, electric, and convection ovens. Gas and electric are the most common varieties found in homes, and convection ovens are generally found in professional or top-of-the-line kitchens.

Before conventional ovens were in homes (the first gas stove was introduced into American homes in the 1850s), the majority of cooking was done over open fires, and the baking was done in beehive-like ovens usually above or behind an open fire. Temperature was gauged by touch — how long your hand could remain in the oven. Judging when an oven was hot enough was one of a baker's most difficult challenges. Bakers today have it easy — they even have choices. The next time you have to purchase an oven, consider the information in the following sections.

Gas ovens

Gas ovens generally have a constantly running pilot light, and the heat comes from a perforated bar that runs down the center or in a T shape in the bottom of the oven. This bar is usually covered by a false bottom of the oven. An advantage of this false bottom is that you can set pans of water on the bottom of the oven floor if you want to make your oven "moist" for baking bread. Another advantage to a gas oven is that it tends to be warm because of the pilot light (although many modern ovens have eliminated this constant burning pilot and replaced it with a "self-starting" pilot). If you have the older type, inside the oven is the perfect place to let bread dough rise because it's warm and draft free.

What's going on in there?

Everyone knows what an oven is, but have you ever given much thought to how your oven works? Food cooks in an oven because it's surrounded by hot, dry air. How quickly or evenly the food cooks depends on the temperature of the oven. The way food is baked in the oven is due to *conduction*, or transfer, of energy (heat, in the case of baking) from the air to the batter or dough.

The foods you bake are made up of many elements: proteins, starches, sugars, water, and fats. Heat has an effect on all these elements, each producing a specific and necessary reaction. Slowly, the heat from the air inside the oven is transferred to and penetrates the food from the outside inward (that's why the outside of a cake may look cooked, even though it's still wet and gooey inside). The metal pan helps to retain the heat from the oven and acts as an insulator for the heat. Heat affects the batter in several ways:

✔ The proteins (eggs and gluten) begin to lose moisture, shrink, and coagulate.

✔ The liquid in the starches begins to become gelatinous and firms up (for example, the flour begins to absorb the liquids and becomes firm and dry).

✔ The sugars begin to caramelize, which is why baked goods turn golden brown. The type of sugar used affects how brown the food becomes.

✔ Water also evaporates, which can happen rapidly as the internal temperature of the food increases.

✔ Fats begin to melt.

✔ The air that has been incorporated into the batter — either because of beating it or because of the gases produced by the chemical leaveners — begins to expand, which gives cakes and cookies rise.

So, basically, the food enters the oven; the surface begins to lose the moisture and firms up; and the food browns, which completes the cooking process. Pretty neat, huh?

What happens if your oven temperature is off?

If the temperature of your oven is too cool, the surface of a cake will dry out too quickly, leaving the middle still uncooked. When it does cook through, the cake will be too dry because it will have evaporated too much of the moisture.

If the temperature of your oven is too hot, all the chemical reactions happen too quickly. A cake can rise unevenly, or too quickly, and the outside of the cake will be cooked and browned while the inside is still raw batter.

Electric ovens

Electric ovens have large, exposed coils placed in the top and bottom of the oven, so they heat from both areas (unless you broil, in which case only the top element does the heating). Because electric ovens heat from the top and bottom and gas ovens heat only from the bottom, many people claim that electric ovens supply more even heat, which results in more even cooking. Also, gas ovens will surge on and off with the heat to maintain the temperature, and electric ovens do not. I like electric ovens because you can broil items in the same space that you bake them. This is great if you want to brown the top of a cake or custard and you don't have to worry if the pan will set into the broiler section of the gas oven area.

Convection ovens

Convection ovens use an internal fan to circulate the hot air, so every part of the oven is the same temperature and it can cook lots of food at one time. These ovens are almost always free-standing and have many racks. In general, convection ovens cook food faster than conventional ovens, so if you're using one, you may have to reduce the heat called for in a standard recipe by 25 to 50 degrees or reduce the baking time by 25 percent.

Turn on an oven 15 to 20 minutes before you plan to use it to allow time for it to heat to baking temperature.

Rack Chat

Although it may sound odd to you, the position of the racks within your oven affects the way your foods cook. The center of your oven is where the temperature is most moderate, giving your baked goods what I consider the best placement for even cooking. Depending on the placement of the heating elements inside your oven, you're likely to have hot spots. In general, the lower third of your oven is hotter than the middle (because generally the source of heat is located in the bottom of the oven), and the top third of your oven is also hotter (because heat rises) than the middle but not as hot as the floor.

If your oven heats from the top *and* bottom, you may find your oven to be equally hot at the top and bottom and moderate in the middle. This is why it's important to bake items in the center of the oven. It's where the temperature is most consistent. You can bake in the top and bottom thirds, but you will have to rotate the items from top to bottom and turn the pans 180 degrees to ensure even baking.

Hot spots in the oven result in uneven cooking. You can't really do anything about that, but if you notice that you need some extra protection, try placing all your pans on baking sheets before you put them in the oven. The baking sheet will actually help insulate the pans and help bake things more evenly. If it seems that your oven cooks your food unevenly, give the food a half-turn halfway through the baking time, so what was in the back is now in the front and what was on the left is now on the right.

If you need to adjust the racks in your oven, do so while the oven is cool. Racks usually don't just slide in and out easily, because most are designed to pull out and still support the weight of the baked good on it without tipping forward. So there is usually some sort of up-and-over motion you have to finesse when removing the racks from each level. You certainly don't want to be trying to manipulate tricky racks when they're hot.

I recommend using only one rack, the center rack, when you bake. However, if you want to use two racks, position the racks as close to the center of the oven as possible (usually that means one rack will be in the center and one rack will be positioned directly below). Don't place the pans one on top of the other, but position them off-center so that air can circulate around both pans (see Figure 4-1). Halfway through baking, rotate the top and bottom pans and turn them back to front so that they will bake most evenly. You many notice with two pans in the oven at once that you'll need to increase the baking time. Of course, if you have a convection oven, you won't need to rotate the pans or worry about rack placement since every inch of the oven is the exact same temperature.

Figure 4-1:
Staggering
pans for
even baking.

Preheating

You'll notice that almost all recipes say to preheat the oven. You may think that this step is frivolous, but it's actually very important.

A preheated oven allows the ingredients to react properly, ensuring a good finished product. If you place anything to bake in a cold oven, the ingredients will react much differently with each other and the results are most undesirable. Preheated ovens contribute a lot to your finished product:

- ✔ They give breads their final growth spurt.
- ✔ They give soufflés a good push up.
- ✔ They give cakes a good rise.
- ✔ They keep cookies from spreading all over the pan.

Properly preheating an oven takes about 15 to 20 minutes, so turn your oven on when you begin your recipe, and it will have reached the proper temperature by the time you're ready to put your items in the oven.

Gauging and Adjusting the Heat

If you've been baking and the results are not what you expected, it may not be the recipes, but the temperature of your oven. Don't trust the oven dial with which you set the temperature. Even ovens that may have been tried and true for many years may suddenly become uncalibrated and, without warning, increase their temperature by 25 to 50 degrees!

An unsuspecting baker wouldn't know that her oven has become uncali-brated — unless she has placed an additional auxiliary thermometer in her oven. You can find oven thermometers in any kitchen-supply store or hard-ware store; they should cost only a few dollars. The time and frustration an oven thermometer will save and the piece of mind it gives even a casual baker are worth every dime. Place your oven thermometer in a central loca-tion in your oven. You can hang it off the center of your oven if you like (don't place it on the floor of the oven — it gives you an inaccurate reading). If you're convinced you have a tricky oven, you may want to invest in two ther-mometers — one for the front of the oven and one for the back — to make sure that the temperature is even throughout your oven.

No peeking: Every time you open the oven door, you lower the oven's temper-ature. If you keep the door open, you can lower it by 25 to 50 degrees, so constantly checking on your items can be detrimental. Always check after the minimum baking time given. If you need to peek, turn on your oven light and look from the outside. It's the best way to keep your oven the right temperature.

Chapter 5

Basic Techniques

· ·

In This Chapter

▶ Getting your measurements just right

▶ Keeping your goodies from sticking to your pans

▶ Separating eggs

▶ Whipping egg whites and heavy cream into shape

▶ Peeling, zesting, and sectioning fruits

▶ Working with chocolate

▶ Scalding milk — it's not cruel, really!

▶ Bringing out the flavor of nuts by toasting them

· ·

*W*hen you read a recipe and it calls for scalding milk or tempering chocolate without providing further explanation, it can cause your head to spin. This chapter walks you through some basic techniques that are good to familiarize yourself with.

Measuring Ingredients

You probably know someone who bakes a lot, and it seems like she just tosses this in and that in and presto, out come cookies or a pie or something delicious. It seems like magic, so you may wonder how important it is to be accurate in measuring. The answer is: *very important.* Proper measuring is critical to baking. Baking is a science, and when you mix together ingredients, you're creating chemistry, albeit edible chemistry, so being precise is important. There is balance with flour, leaveners, fats, and liquids.

Extra salt or baking soda can ruin otherwise perfect cookies. Too much flour makes muffins taste dry and flavorless. No beginning cook should be nonchalant about measuring. The success of your recipe depends on it.

Packing it in

Sometimes ingredients, such as brown sugar, shredded cheeses, coconut, or herbs, are called for as lightly or firmly packed. Why pack? Generally, these ingredients are bulkier and can form big air pockets if you use the traditional spoon-and-level method of measuring. If you apply light or slightly firm pressure to the ingredients, you eliminate some of the air pockets and get a more accurate measurement. Never push the ingredients in so much that you actually crush them or pack them in so tightly that you have difficulty getting them out the of cup measure. If you do so, you will overmeasure, adding too much of the ingredient. A good visual cue that you have lightly packed something is that after you pour it out of the measuring cup, it will lose the shape of the cup it was in. If it's firmly packed, it will slightly retain the shape of the measuring cup after it's dumped out into the bowl, but it will be easy to stir apart.

As you begin to feel more comfortable with baking, you may feel inclined to experiment a bit, maybe add some chocolate chips to peanut butter cookies, or throw some nuts or dried cranberries into oatmeal cookies, or substitute pecans for walnuts. That's all well and fine, but give it time. You're never too good or experienced to measure.

Measuring with teaspoons and tablespoons

Teaspoons and tablespoons are pretty simple, and you can use the same measuring tools for both liquids and dry ingredients. For liquids, fill the spoon until it's full. For dry ingredients, pour or scoop into the spoon until it's full, leveling off the spoon with the straight side of a spatula or knife.

Never measure over the bowl of ingredients you're using for the recipe. If you overpour or level extra into the bowl, your measurements will not be accurate.

Measuring dry ingredients

To measure flour, sugar, breadcrumbs, and other dry ingredients (with the exception of brown sugar in many cases), spoon the ingredients lightly into the measuring cup. Then level off the cup with the straight side of a butter knife — do not use the cutting side (see Figure 5-1). Leveling it off gives you one level cup. If the recipe calls for a heaping cup, do not level off the cup. Instead, leave a small mounded top of ingredients.

To measure chopped nuts, shredded cheese, fresh herbs, and coconut, spoon the ingredients into the measuring cup and pack down lightly.

Accurate
Measuring

Figure 5-1:
Measuring
dry
ingredients.

Measuring fats and other solids

To measure shortening, spoon the ingredients into a cup and pack down firmly with a spoon or rubber spatula to eliminate any air holes. Lucky for us, we don't often have to measure fats because butter and margarine come in conveniently measured sticks. One stick equals 8 tablespoons. Two sticks equal 1 cup. You still have to measure solid shortening, but now they make shortening sticks, so even that task has been greatly simplified.

If you're measuring fats, an easy way to keep the cup clean (and save yourself time by not having to wash it) is to place a piece of plastic wrap in the measuring cup first. Then, once the shortening is measured, pull the ends of the plastic out of the cup. The measuring cup stays clean and you have perfectly measured shortening.

Measuring liquids

Always use a glass measuring cup for measuring liquids For an accurate reading, always rest the cup on a level surface and read at eye level (see Figure 5-2).

Figure 5-2:
Measuring
liquids at
eye level.

Sometimes the container in which you purchase an ingredient might be labeled in ounces when your recipe calls for cup or spoon measurements (or vice versa). Check out Table 5-1 for some common equivalencies.

Table 5-1	Measurement Equivalents
If a Recipe Calls or This Amount	**You Also Can Measure It This Way**
Dash	2 or 3 drops (liquid) or less than ⅛ teaspoon (dry)
1 tablespoon	3 teaspoons or ½ ounce
2 tablespoons	1 ounce
¼ cup	4 tablespoons or 2 ounces
⅓ cup	5 tablespoons plus 1 teaspoon
½ cup	8 tablespoons or 4 ounces
1 cup	16 tablespoons or 8 ounces
1 pint	2 cups or 16 ounces or 1 pound
1 quart	4 cups or 2 pints
1 gallon	4 quarts
1 pound	16 ounces

Preparing Pans

For many basic recipes, you need to grease the pan. Always prepare your pan before you start mixing up the batter. The only exception to this is if you use nonstick spray. Then just quickly spray the pan just before you pour the batter into it. That way, the coating won't slide down the sides of the pan while you mix up the batter. You also can dust the greased pan with flour for an added barrier of protection. When you grease a pan, you're essentially creating a thin barrier that keeps the cake from sticking to the pan.

When you grease a pan, it's best to use solid shortening. Many people use the residue of butter or margarine wrappers, which is okay, but if you have shortening, use it. Shortening does not contain water, which can cause the batter to stick to the pan, and it also can withstand higher temperatures without burning. Flour you use to dust with also adheres better to shortening than to butter or margarine.

Place about ½ tablespoon of shortening in the pan that is to be greased and spread it into a thin layer with your fingers or a piece of waxed paper. Professional bakers use a medium-stiff pastry brush to apply grease, but I think fingers work just as well, and you already have them at the ready. If your recipe tells you to dust with flour, place about 1 tablespoon of flour in the bottom of your pan. Rotate and tap the flour around in the pan until it clings to the bottom and sides of the pan (this is also a good way to see that you have completely coated the pan with grease, because the flour won't cling if you missed a spot).

If you're making a chocolate cake, dust your pans with sifted cocoa. Then you won't have the telltale marks of flour on your cake when you turn them out of the pans.

Nonstick cooking spray is a baker's best friend, particularly if you're making muffins (greasing a muffin tin can be cumbersome) or greasing a decorative Bundt pan that has lots of nooks to get into. Nonstick sprays contain emulsified oil beads that literally rest on the pan's surface creating a barrier between the batter and the pan. A nonstick flour/oil spray on the market called Baker's Joy does two jobs with the press of a button.

If a recipe calls for greased pans, always do it even if the pans you're using have a nonstick coating. It's up to you which method of greasing you use. Nonstick spray is quick and easy, but I enjoy the ritual of greasing and flouring pans by hand. Plus, it's the perfect task to give the little ones when they want to help out in the kitchen.

Occasionally, a pan has to be lined with parchment, waxed paper, or other liner to prevent a cake from sticking to the pan. Sometimes liners are used if the batter is very sticky and greasing the pan won't be sufficient. Other times, you won't want to grease the pan, but you want to ensure that the baked item won't stick. Many professionals prefer to line their pans because it's the surest of ways to prevent baked goods from sticking to the pans. If you need to line a pan, the recipe will tell you. To hold the liner in place, place a dab of shortening on the pan, and then place the liner on top. Figure 5-3 shows you how to line a variety of pans.

PREPARING PANS

FOR A ROUND PAN:
PLACE THE PAN ON A SHEET OF
PARCHMENT OR WAXED PAPER.
TRACE THE SHAPE OF THE PAN
ONTO THE PAPER....

...CUT OUT THE CIRCLE AND PLACE IT
IN THE PAN. YOU CAN GREASE AND
FLOUR THE PAPER AND THE SIDES
OF THE PAN TOO!

FOR A LOAF PAN:
TAKE 2 LONG PIECES OF PARCHMENT.
OR WAXED PAPER. CUT ONE TO FIT THE
LENGTH OF THE PAN AND A SECOND TO
FIT THE WIDTH. GREASE THE PAN, THEN
FIT BOTH PIECES INTO THE PAN!
(THEY WILL OVERLAP AND THERE
WILL BE SOME OVERHANG)

Figure 5-3:
Making
liners for
baking pans.

✔ **To cut a liner to fit a round pan:** Place the pan on a sheet of parchment or waxed paper and trace the shape of the pan onto the paper. Cut out the circle and place it in the pan. You can grease and flour the paper and the sides of the pan, too, to ensure that it will not stick to the cake once it is baked and it will be easy to remove.

To prevent paper liners from slipping out of place, grease the pan with shortening or butter and then insert the paper. The liner will stick in place.

✔ **To cut a liner to fit a loaf pan:** Take two long pieces of parchment or waxed paper. Cut one to fit the length of the pan and the second to fit the width of the pan. Allow extra for overhang. Grease the pan, then fit both pieces of paper.

✔ **To line a jelly roll pan:** Trace the pan onto a piece of waxed paper or parchment. Secure the paper onto the jelly roll pan by greasing it first, and then flatten the liner onto the pan to fit.

✔ **To line a tube pan:** Trace the pan on a piece of waxed or parchment paper. If possible, stick the pencil inside the tube and draw around its base. If you can't reach, hold the pan upside down and press the paper onto the base to mark the outer and inner edges of the pan. Cut out the paper and ring. Don't line the sides of a tube pan if it's a sponge cake or an angel food cake. Those batters need to climb the walls of the pan.

The simplest and most common liners are those that you use when you prepare cupcakes or muffins. You can purchase muffin cup liners at the grocery store to fit the cup and pour the batter directly into the paper cup.

Working with Eggs

Eggs are important ingredients in baking. They add leavening, texture, color and richness. Plus, they also add an element of nutrition. Eggs help with binding and hold batters together, and the protein in eggs help the structure of the dough hold its shape.

Separating an egg

Baked goods often call for egg whites or egg yolks without their counterpart. You can buy egg whites without the yolks, but separating the eggs yourself is nearly as fast and is much cheaper.

Eggs separate best when they're cold. Not having any egg yolk in the whites is important, but it's okay if the whites get mixed into the yolks. If you will be separating many eggs, minimize your risk of leaking egg yolk into the whites by doing one at a time over a small bowl and then adding the clean white into a large bowl. Transfer the egg white after each separation to prevent any accidental egg yolk breakage from contaminating the whole batch of whites.

When working with raw eggs, keep in mind that eggs can carry a bacteria that may be present in the porous shells of the eggs, which can cause salmonella poisoning. Although this is rare, it is helpful to know that nearly every box of eggs sold in the United States has a toll-free number on it, as well as an expiration date for the eggs. You can call the supplier to see if any cases of salmonella have been reported. (Not many have.)

That said, you can choose how you want to separate your eggs. Look at Figure 5-4 to see these methods in action.

✔ The most common practice is to crack the egg cleanly in half over a bowl and pass the yolk from one shell to the other, allowing the white to gradually fall into the bowl below. This method can be a bit messy, and you run the risk of the yolk getting punctured. It's important that you not let any yolk contaminate the whites, because egg yolk will prevent the whites from whipping to their full volume. Also, some whites will be lost to the shell.

Note that most food safety experts would not recommend this practice due to the risk of introducing salmonella into the egg product even though the risk is quite small and people have been doing this safely for decades. If you do use this technique, make sure your egg shells, particularly eggs from a farm stand, do not have any foreign matter sticking to the shells.

✔ My favorite method is to crack and break the egg into your cupped hand held over a bowl. Gently relax your fingers, which allows the white to spill through and drop into the bowl below. After all the white has separated, you're left with a perfect, round yolk. Wash your hands thoroughly before and after using this method.

✔ You can also separate an egg by using an egg separator. Place the egg separator over a small bowl or glass. Crack the egg open, and let it fall into the center of the separator. The whites will slip through the slots of the separator and into the bowl, and the yolk will stay in the separator, which can be transferred easily into another bowl.

3 WAYS TO SEPARATE AN EGG ⊖

(1.) CRACK THE EGG IN HALF, OVER A BOWL...

..AND PASS THE YOLK FROM 1 SHELL TO THE OTHER, ALLOWING THE WHITE TO GRADUALLY FALL INTO THE BOWL BELOW.

(2) CRACK THE EGG AND BREAK THE EGG INTO YOUR CUPPED HAND HELD OVER A BOWL. GENTLY, RELAX FINGERS, ALLOWING THE WHITE TO SPILL THROUGH INTO THE BOWL BELOW.

(3.) USE AN EGG SEPARATOR! PLACE IT OVER A SMALL BOWL OR GLASS. CRACK THE EGG OPEN AND LET IT FALL INTO THE CENTER.

THE WHITE WILL SLIP THROUGH THE SLOTS AND THE YOLK WILL STAY IN THE SEPARATOR.

Figure 5-4: A few ways to separate an egg.

Whipping egg whites

The purpose of whipping egg whites is to incorporate as much air as possible into the whites, which gives good lift to your cakes or meringues. If you have good arm strength, the best tools are a copper bowl and a whisk with a large balloon. The most common method of whipping egg whites is with a mixer with a whisk attachment. A pinch of salt helps break up the gelatinous texture of egg whites; a pinch of cream of tartar helps to stabilize them. If you use a copper bowl, you don't need the cream of tartar or salt, because the copper of the bowl helps stabilize the egg whites naturally.

Egg whites increase their volume best if they come to room temperature first. Remember that egg whites can expand up to six times their natural volume, so make sure the bowl you choose can accommodate them. Also, be sure the bowl and whisk you use are perfectly dry and clean; any amount of moisture, egg yolk, or other debris will prevent the egg white from whipping up properly.

Beating whites to *soft peaks* means the whites flop gently over when the beater is removed; *stiff peaks* hold their shape when the whisk is lifted (see Figure 5-5).

Pasteurized egg whites are being sold in the refrigerated sections of many grocery stores. *Do not* use these egg whites if the recipe you're using requires you to beat them. The pasteurization process breaks down the egg whites' ability to whip up and hold their shape. If you try to do this, you'll end up with a frothy top and liquid on the bottom of your bowl.

Figure 5-5:
Soft and stiff
peaks.

Be careful not to overbeat the egg whites, or else they will become dry. If you're nervous about overbeating egg whites, you can always stop using the electric mixer when the whites reach soft peaks and finish beating them by hand with a wire whisk. Also, be sure not to beat the egg whites until you're ready to use them. If you let them stand around, they'll deflate.

Whipping Heavy Cream

Many types of cream are on the market. The best cream for whipping is called heavy whipping cream (which is different from plain whipping cream, which has less fat — only 30 percent — and will whip up, but won't hold its shape well). Heavy whipping cream contains 36 to 40 percent butterfat and will whip up and hold its form without much effort. Remember, it doubles in volume, so if a recipe calls for 2 cups of whipped cream, you just need to whip up 1 cup of heavy whipping cream.

Use a whisk or handheld or electric mixer. Pour the cream into a chilled metal bowl and whip until it thickens and just forms soft peaks (do not overbeat). Add 2 tablespoons of granulated sugar or 4 tablespoons of confectioners' sugar and 1 teaspoon of vanilla when the cream begins to thicken but before it forms soft peaks.

To prevent whipped cream from deflating, store it in the fridge with a paper towel covering the container. Tupperware containers work great for this if you put the paper towel under the lid before closing. You'll be amazed at how long you can keep whipped cream this way.

Be very careful not to over-whip heavy cream, or else it will turn into butter. This will happen suddenly, especially with electric mixers, so be careful. To avoid overbeating your cream, if you use an electric mixer, stop beating the cream when it begins to thicken, and finish whipping it by hand with a wire whisk.

Working with Fruits

Fresh fruits are a wonderful filling for pies, cakes and many baked desserts. Refer to the tips in this section the next time you're working with a recipe that calls for fruit.

Peeling and pitting fruits

Keep these tips in mind to get the best fruit for your recipes:

- **Apricots or nectarines:** You do not need to peel apricots or nectarines. Just slice them in half and pop out the pits.

- **Apples and pears:** Peel off the skin with a standard vegetable peeler, cut the fruit into quarters, then remove the core and stem bits from the center.

  If you need the fruit to stay whole, remove the stem and core using an apple corer, which has a handle attached to an elongated curved piece of metal with a cylindrical bottom and a cutting edge. (See Chapter 3.) Just press down vertically with a slight twisting motion until you reach the bottom.

✔ **Cherries:** While cherry pitting can be tedious, it is actually quite easy. Simply make a slit, north to south, around the circumference or the cherry and pull it apart, and then pop out the pit with the tip of a paring knife or your finger. This method will result in the cherries being both pitted and halved, which is the way most recipes require them. A cherry pitter tool is unnecessary unless you're preparing large quantities for canning or jam.

✔ **Peaches:** If your peach is perfectly ripe, sometimes the skin will slip right off, without even so much as a knife, but that's not always the case. This method will makes peeling peaches a snap, leaving the beautiful flesh unmarked.

Have ready a medium-sized bowl of ice water. Set a 2-quart pan on the stove to boil. While you wait for the water to boil, lightly cut a small X on the bottom of each peach. Try not to cut into the flesh, but just the skin. When the water is boiling, gently drop the peach into the water. Wait about 30 seconds (you will see the cut skin start to loosen and flutter a bit in the water). Remove the peach from the water and plunge it into the ice water for 1 minute. The skin should slip right off. If not, return the peach to the hot water for 30 more seconds. This method also works for plums and tomatoes.

Zesting and sectioning citrus fruits

The *zest* of citrus is the colored part of the skin, which contains essential oils. The *pith* is the white membrane between the skin and the fruit, which is bitter. You want to get the zest and not the pith when zesting citrus fruits. The most common citrus fruits used for zesting are lemons and oranges.

There are two ways to zest a citrus fruit:

✔ You can use a *citrus zester,* a kitchen tool that removes the zest of the fruit and leaves the pith behind. Hold the fruit in one hand and the zester in the other, and run the citrus zester along the length of the fruit. The peel should come off in thin little strips. You can either dice the strips or use them whole (the recipe will call for one or the other). You can see what this looks like in Figure 5-6.

✔ You can also use the coarse, sharp-edged holes of a grater (not the large holes used to grate cheese). Rub the fruit against the sharp edges, rotating the fruit after a few rubs, until the peel grates off and the desired amount is grated (see Figure 5-7). Be careful of your knuckles and fingers when using a grater, because the holes are very sharp.

Figure 5-6:
A citrus
zester.

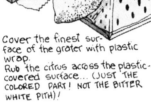

Figure 5-7:
Using a
grater to
zest citrus
fruits.

Cover the finest sur-
face of the grater with plastic
wrap.
Rub the citrus across the plastic-
covered surface... (JUST THE
COLORED PART! NOT THE BITTER
WHITE PITH)!

When you think you've grated enough,
lift off the plastic and scrape up
the zest with a flat edge.
Use a measuring spoon to see
if you've grated enough.

Using a vegetable peeler to remove the zest can be tricky business and is not recommended. I speak from experience. Unless you have a very dull peeler, the chances you will remove zest and pith together are very high. Then you will have wasted the zest you did remove. Remember, the white pith is bitter and should be avoided.

You probably won't run into too many recipes that call for sectioned fruit, but this is a handy technique to know, and sectioned fruit always makes a nice garnish.

Citrus fruits, particularly oranges and grapefruits, have a tough skin that can be difficult to chew. When you section a citrus fruit, you remove the fruit from the tough membrane, making it easier to eat.

Start by cutting off the top and bottom of the fruit. Cut to the fruit and don't leave any white pith on the fruit. Lay the fruit on its cut end. Being careful not to cut too deeply, cut away the peel and the white pith, following the shape of the fruit. Hold the fruit in one hand. It will be juicy, so you may want to do this over a bowl. You will see the membranes that hold the fruit together. Make a cut parallel and right next to the membrane, cutting toward the center to release the fruit. When you get to the center, turn the knife and cut away, next to the other membrane, following the shape and size of the section of fruit and continue cutting until the section of fruit is free. Repeat until all the sections are free. Figure 5-8 shows you how to do this.

Sectioning an Orange to Eliminate Membranes

Figure 5-8: Sectioning an orange isn't as difficult as you may think.

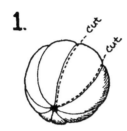 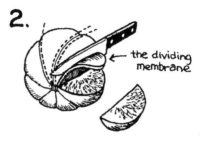

Melting Chocolate

There is nothing so versatile or universally welcomed as melted chocolate. You can stir it into recipes, drizzle it over finished baked goods, dip cookie bottoms into it, or stir it into frosting for a flavor burst. Melting chocolate is easy, but you do need to pay attention when you are doing it.

Never melt chocolate directly over heat. It burns very easily and must be melted over low heat. Because quality varies from brand to brand, follow the manufacturer's instructions for best results. If none are given, here are some guidelines:

1. **Cut the chocolate into pieces smaller than a 1-ounce square.**

2. **Place the chocolate pieces in the top part of a double boiler, and set it over simmering, not boiling, water.**

3. **As the chocolate melts, stir it often; remove it from the heat when almost all of it has melted.**

4. **Continue stirring until all the pieces have melted and the chocolate is smooth.**

The microwave is also a great tool for melting chocolate. Chocolate melts very easily, so set your temperature to medium-low and follow the manufacturer's directions for time (usually 1 to 2 minutes). Check the chocolate after 1 minute. It will not melt the same way it does over a double boiler, so you'll have to stir it and keep a close eye on it, because it will burn easily. White chocolate needs particularly close attention and very low heat.

To quickly and easily melt chocolate, place in a metal bowl and put in the oven, with the temperature turned on the lowest possible setting. Close the door. After about 5 minutes, turn the oven off. In about 10 minutes, the chocolate should be melted.

Scalding Milk

Scalding has fallen out of favor among many cooks because now that milk is pasteurized, it is an unnecessary step to retard the souring of milk. However, it's also a good idea to scald milk that you use for bread baking to enhance the sugars, which will promote better texture in your breads. To scald, you heat the milk to just below its boiling point. Follow these steps:

1. **Measure the milk into a saucepan and place it over medium heat.**

2. **Heat the milk, stirring occasionally.**

3. **As soon as the surface of the milk begins to bubble, remove the pan from the heat.**

   If the milk does boil, it might form a thick film on top. Remove the film before using the milk underneath.

Here's a trick that I learned at the bakery: Rub some butter along the inside edge of the pan. Even if the milk does foam up when it's heated, it will stop foaming when it reaches the butter.

Toasting Nuts

Toasting nuts helps to bring out their wonderful flavor and removes some of their raw taste. To toast nuts, place them in a shallow baking dish and bake in a 350-degree oven, stirring often, until they're golden brown and smell toasted, about 5 to 10 minutes, depending on the nut (pine nuts take the least amount of time; almonds and hazelnuts take a bit longer). Don't overbake them or their flavor will become bitter.

You can also toast nuts in a dry skillet over medium heat. Stir the nuts frequently until they become golden brown and smell toasted, about 5 to 10 minutes, depending on the nut.

If I have a small amount of nuts to toast, I use my toaster oven. I spread the nuts on the small tray and set the toaster to the lowest setting. After the nuts finish toasting, I let them sit for a few minutes and then check to see if they're golden brown. If they aren't, I just push down the toast button again. The second time around, I closely monitor them to make sure that they don't brown too much.

If you've burned your nuts, discard them — they'll ruin the flavor of your baked item.

Chapter 6

Getting Ready to Bake

*B*aking, like cooking, is just a series of different techniques. Be familiar with the ingredients and know their different variables. Knowing how ingredients react together is a great way to understand baking and to prevent disaster.

The best way to become comfortable with baking is to practice and practice some more. At first, don't overchallenge yourself when you select recipes. Choose ones that call for familiar ingredients and involve familiar techniques. Once you've mastered those, move on to more challenging recipes — maybe try a recipe for which you have to pick up an unfamiliar ingredient or try one new technique. If you continue progressing in a slow and steady manner, you'll soon become a proficient baker, and you may wonder why you ever bought a cake from a grocery store.

Preparing Your Kitchen

One of the best first things to do when you're getting ready to bake is to look around your kitchen, because that's where all your baking will take place. If you don't spend a lot of time there, take stock of the equipment you have.

Inspect your oven

Take a peek in the oven — the tool without which you could not bake at all. Does it need to be cleaned?

So how do you know if your oven needs to be cleaned? You generally can tell that your oven needs to be cleaned if lots of spilled food has burned onto the oven's surface and smokes or gives off a burned odor when you bake. You should clean your oven about twice a year if you use it regularly, yearly if you use it occasionally. If you can't remember the last time you cleaned your oven or if it smells stale when you open the oven door, it's time to clean.

When was the last time you used your oven for baking? I know a woman who lived in her apartment for six years and never once used the oven. If you're unfamiliar with your oven or you tried baking before and it didn't work out, I strongly suggest that you purchase an oven thermometer to put in your oven — the problem may not have been what you made but how it baked. Ovens tend to acquire minds of their own. Just recently (thanks to my oven thermometer), I discovered that my own oven interprets just about all temperatures as 350 degrees Fahrenheit, even when I set the dial at 300 degrees. I never would have discovered this problem without the thermometer, and now I know that I have to set the oven temperature lower. For more about ovens, see Chapter 4.

Organize your space

Look around your kitchen. Do you have a lot of counter space or just a little? Do you have a lot of cabinet space? I have very little counter and cabinet space in my kitchen, so I have organized things to hang on the walls just about everywhere I can. A utensil or pot or pan is within reach just about anywhere I stand in the kitchen, which simplifies my baking time immensely. Think about what you use and, as you read through this book, keep in mind what you may need to make your kitchen efficient.

Counter space is the hottest real estate in the kitchen. If you have a lot of things cluttering up your counter (spice racks, napkin holders, paper towel holders, appliances, and so on), it may be time to reorganize. Take a good look around your kitchen and decide what you can put away and what you want to leave out. If you make coffee only on the weekends, for example, tuck your coffeemaker in a cabinet so that you have more counter space during the week. If you always seem to be searching for utensils in drawers, think about organizing your most frequently used utensils in a can or small crock on the counter.

Never store your knives with other utensils. If you reach for a spoon, you could easily cut yourself on a knife's sharp blade.

Take a look in your cabinets. Do you have a lot of opened, half-used bags of flour? Half-used boxes of brown sugar that are now rock hard? Store-bought cookies that you forgot about? Clean out your cabinets at least twice a year, once in the spring and once in the fall, to get rid of forgotten treasures — now trash — and to prevent insect infestation.

Three-tiered hanging baskets are a huge space-saver in the kitchen. You can use them in literally hundreds of ways (and not one of them has to be food related), such as storing plastic container lids, spice jars, scraps of paper, loose pens and pencils, recipes, and so on.

Take the time now to organize things so that later you won't be looking for all the parts of the food processor or the bottom plate to your springform pan. Feeling comfortable in your kitchen is a huge part of feeling comfortable with baking.

Working with Recipes

If you know how to read, you can read a recipe. However, you need to keep a few things in mind as you select and work with recipes to make sure that you won't experience any surprises along the way.

Consider your skill level

If you want to improve your baking skills, the best thing to do is practice. Start out with an easy recipe — one that doesn't require a lot of ingredients or involve numerous steps. Practice beating butter and cream together. Get used to mixing, measuring, scooping, and timing. (For basic techniques, see Chapter 5.) Once you master basic techniques, try recipes with longer lists of ingredients. Then move on to intermediate recipes, which may involve slightly more difficult techniques, such as whipping egg whites. When you feel comfortable with what you're doing, move on to even more challenging recipes. Before you know it, you'll be baking like a pro.

Understand the instructions

What's crystal clear to recipe writers may not be so easy for you to understand, especially if you aren't an experienced baker. If you run across any unfamiliar words as you read a recipe, be sure to look them up. Use the Glossary of Baking Terms at the back of this book or use a dictionary.

Recipe writers follow certain rules that sometimes confound beginning bakers. For example, if a recipe calls for "1 cup walnuts, chopped," you may wonder whether that means to chop the walnuts and then measure them or to measure out 1 cup of walnuts and then chop them. The answer is simple. When you're supposed to do something to an ingredient *after* you measure it, the action is listed *after* the ingredient; if you're supposed to do something to the ingredient *before* you measure it, the action is listed *before* the ingredient.

Therefore, "1 cup walnuts, chopped" means that you should measure the whole walnuts and then chop them. If you were supposed to chop the nuts before measuring them, the recipe would have called for "1 cup chopped walnuts."

Read the recipe all the way through before you start

When you find a recipe you want to try, read all the way through it carefully before you start baking. You want to preview a recipe . . .

- ✔ To make sure that you're familiar with all the terminology used in the instructions.
- ✔ To know how much prep work you will have to do before you begin.
- ✔ To get a sense of how much time it will take you to make it.
- ✔ To familiarize yourself with all the necessary ingredients and methods the recipe requires.

Look up what you don't know *before* you start baking. Leafing through a book is harder when you're up to your elbows in batter!

Keep in mind that many times it's easier for recipe writers to shorten the main recipe by including some steps in the ingredient list. For example, a recipe may call for "3 apples, peeled, cored, and diced," so you have some work to do to the apples before you get started. I've been caught in the middle of a recipe without nuts chopped, pasta cooked, or vegetables peeled and chopped because I didn't read the recipe fully — I just read it quickly to make sure that I had the necessary ingredients. Similarly, if you read through once, you'll know whether the ingredients need to be chilled or marinated, which may determine whether you can do the recipe now or later. If you develop one good habit of baking, make it this one. You'll thank me later.

Keeping your recipes out of harm's way

The kitchen can be a dangerous place for papers, recipes, and even books. A cookbook can get into a lot of trouble on a kitchen countertop. Place the cookbook you're using in a convenient place, but not in direct contact with ingredients, especially liquids. Read the recipe several times before you start, place the book a few steps away from the action, and go back and forth to read the recipe. You can tape recipe note cards onto cabinets, at eye level, so that they're always in view but not in harm's way.

Check how many people it serves

As you're deciding what to make, be sure to take the number of servings into account. It's easy enough to figure out whether 4 dozen cookies are enough for your needs, but you may not be sure about how many people a given pie or cake will serve. Table 6-1 gives you some guidelines.

Table 6-1	How Many People Your Goodies Will Serve
Baked Good	*Yield*
8-inch layer cake	8 to 10 people or more
8-inch cheesecake	10 to 12 people
9-inch layer cake	10 to 12 people
9-inch cheesecake	12 to 14 people
9-inch pie	8 to 12 people

To slice your cakes and pies so that you get an accurate yield, see Chapter 18.

Generally, the richer the dessert, the smaller the slices you want to cut. Of course, you must take your guests into consideration when choosing a dessert. If you know that someone has a particularly sweet tooth, she may want seconds. Better to have too much than too little.

If you're attending a potluck or expecting a crowd for dessert, think about making something with a high yield, like a sheet cake or cupcakes. Almost all cake recipes can be made into sheet cakes or cupcakes, which feed between 16 and 24 people.

Take inventory

After you've read through your chosen recipe, it's time to assemble all your ingredients and equipment. You don't want to remember halfway through a recipe that you polished off the brown sugar last week and forgot to pick up more at the market. You can avoid last-minute dashes to the market by doing a quick inventory check before you start baking to ensure that you have an adequate supply of all the necessary ingredients.

If you bake infrequently, your flour supply may be lower than you remember. I'm always thinking that I have more eggs and butter in the refrigerator than I really do. It takes only a second to check, and doing so will save you a lot of time in the long run. Start composing a shopping list if you need one.

Premeasuring: Make it easy on yourself!

Chances are that, at some point in your life, you have happened on a cooking show and have seen the cook dumping in bowls of this and that into bowls or pans. Although you don't see what these pro cooks do beforehand, know that they premeasure everything into these bowls, making it possible to throw together several dishes in a short time. If you premeasure everything (or, in cooking terms, prep everything), you will make baking the easiest thing in the world to do. Once you have your ingredients at your fingertips, ready to be mixed together, you may wonder why you ever felt intimidated by baking. Of course, you may dirty an additional bowl or two, but the payback in pleasure and ease of baking is worth the extra few seconds it takes to wash the bowl.

If you know that you'll be pressed for time, you can even prep in advance and store your ingredients in the refrigerator overnight. You will just have to take them out so that everything can come to room temperature before you use it.

During this stage, you may discover that you're out of materials. If you're baking muffins, for example, make sure that you have liners for the tins. Also, you may be low on shortening to grease the baking sheets, or you may need more nonstick spray. These things may not be listed among the recipe's ingredients, but they're just as essential as any of the ingredients you add. Assembling the tools and going over ingredients are two surefire ways to ensure that you'll have a successful baking experience. (But you can find useful substitutions on the Cheat Sheet at the front of this book if you get stuck without a necessary ingredient.)

After you've assembled all the ingredients and equipment, it's time to start baking.

Use the right tools for the job

When you read through a recipe, you also need to read about the equipment that's called for. If you have to beat together butter and sugar, you'll more than likely want to have at least a hand mixer available. If you're making rolled cookies, you'll need a rolling pin. The right tools make baking much easier and save you quite a bit of time.

Before starting a recipe, be sure that you have the pan size that the recipe calls for. If you use a larger or smaller pan than is called for, your finished product will be different, and you run the risk of it burning or never cooking through. Certain pans can be fudged a little, though. Loaf pans, for example, come in 8½ x 4½ and 9 x 5 sizes, and, in most cases, either can be used with the same result. If the recipe calls for a covered casserole, you can create a cover with aluminum foil.

Of course, much of baking can be done with just a few simple tools, so if you want to bake, you don't have to go out and stock your kitchen with a variety of expensive pans and tools. The following is a list of what I consider the essential tools for baking. (Flip back to Chapter 3 for more detailed descriptions and for a more comprehensive list of baking tools and gadgets.)

- Measuring cups/spoons
- Wooden spoon
- Rubber spatula/plastic spatula
- Whisk
- Mixing bowls (at least two sizes)
- Knives (at least a cleaver and a paring knife)
- Pots/skillet (at least a 1-quart, a 2-quart, a stockpot, and a 10-inch skillet)
- Baking sheets
- Cake/pie pans
- Cooling racks (two racks are a good start)

If you look around your kitchen, I'm sure you'll find a lot of these items already there. I baked for several years without any electrical appliances; you don't have to spend a lot of money when you're just starting out. Hand mixers, stand mixers, and food processors certainly make quick work of preparing and mixing ingredients and are the workhorses in the kitchen, so if you really start to enjoy baking, invest in one or more of those appliances. They really do make baking a breeze.

However, if you are a simple kind of person or can't fit too many more appliances in your kitchen, try out these recipes from this book. They use a minimum of tools and don't require special machinery to get the job done:

- Crisp Sugar Cookies (Chapter 7)
- Crispy Chocolate Chip Cookies (Chapter 7)
- Granola Bars (Chapter 7)
- Martha's Chocolate Cake (Chapter 8)
- Blueberry Muffins (Chapter 12)

Timing It Right

The recipes in this book include preparation times as well as baking times. However, not everyone bakes at the same pace, so be sure to give yourself ample time to prepare your baked goods. You'll find it much more relaxing when you don't have to play beat-the-clock.

Certain times are *not* included, such as the 15 to 20 minutes it will take for a cake to cool enough to handle. If you want to frost the cake, you will need to allow even more time for the cake to cool so that you can frost it. What if you run out of an ingredient and have to run to the store? Allow for such mishaps. Even if you don't need additional time, you'll be better off having planned for it. I have cooked under relaxed conditions and flustered conditions alike, and when I'm under the gun in regard to time, the recipes inevitably reflect my rushed approach.

Baking at High Elevations

People who live at elevations above 3,500 feet face some interesting cooking challenges. Because baking is a science, the higher altitude (thanks to the change in air pressure and humidity) causes different reactions in baking. You may notice that once-dependable recipes baked at sea level become a bit out of whack up in the mountains.

Air pressure is lower up there, so water boils at a lower temperature and liquids evaporate much faster. Gases also expand more rapidly, so you may find that your cakes rise so much that they actually collapse on themselves. This means that your tried-and-true recipes may start behaving poorly when the altitude increases.

You have to adjust recipes to compensate for differences in altitude. Unfortunately, you're left to trial and error for the most part. If you're new to high-altitude cooking, you can contact your local U.S. Department of Agriculture Extension Service, listed in the phone book under county government, for help with any questions. Or contact Colorado State University's Food Science and Human Nutrition Department or log on to www.colostate.edu/Depts/FSHN/.

Here are some things to keep in mind if you're baking at a higher altitude:

✔ If you're boiling foods, they will take longer to cook because the temperature at which water boils is between 203 and 207 degrees, not the usual sea level 212 degrees.

✔ You need to cream butter and sugar less and beat eggs less so that less air is incorporated into your finished products and they won't rise as much.

✔ Most baked goods made with baking powder or baking soda will be better off if you make the following adjustments: Increase the liquid by 1 to 4 tablespoons, decrease the leavening by ¼ (so if the recipe calls for 1 teaspoon, you should use ¾ teaspoon), decrease the sugar by 1 to 3 tablespoons per cup, and/or use a larger pan size (for example, if the recipe calls for an 8-inch square pan, use a 9-inch square). For butter-rich cakes, decrease the butter by 1 to 4 tablespoons.

✔ You may want to increase the oven temperature by 25 degrees and shorten the baking time to compensate for the loss of moisture.

✔ If egg whites are your primary leavener, beat them only to soft peaks so that less air is incorporated into them.

✔ Quick breads, cookies, biscuits, and muffins require the fewest adjustments. Experiment with increasing the liquid by ¼ to ½ cup and decreasing the leaveners and sugar by ¼ if necessary.

✔ Yeast breads rise more rapidly at higher altitudes, so shorten the rising time and be watchful of your breads because they may overrise. Also, they may dry out faster, so use the minimum amount of flour called for in the recipe, decrease the amount of flour by ¼ to ½ cup, or increase the liquid by ¼ to ½ cup.

✔ Cooked frostings become concentrated more quickly because of the faster evaporation of the water. Watch very closely and reduce the recipe temperature by 2 degrees for every 1,000 feet you are above sea level.

Cleaning Up as You Go

When I was younger and would bake at home, I was always amazed at the large mess I would end up with. I seemed to dirty every single bowl, spoon, countertop, and article of clothing that came near me. When I entered college, I catered to earn a living. A huge sign in the kitchen read: *Clean as you go.* Why hadn't I thought of that? I began that practice and wow, what a difference it made! Not only did I use fewer utensils, but my mess wasn't nearly as large.

Now, I have one of the world's smallest kitchens, and I always seem to be getting in my own way. So, when I bake, I have no other choice than to clean as I go. Doing so not only makes my life easier (I'm not saddled with a huge pile of dishes at the end) but also frees up space on my counters.

Here are some tips for cleaning as you go to make your baking easier and your cleanup time at the end shorter:

✔ **Recycle bowls and utensils as you bake.** If you use a spatula to scrape down the sides of the bowl while you're mixing, use it again to scrape the batter into pans. If a bowl had sugar in it and you need to beat eggs, either give the bowl a quick rinse or just use it as is. You might be amazed at how few utensils you really need, and you'll save time in washing the dishes.

✔ **Make use of your downtime.** If you have to mix dough for 5 minutes, wash the bowls that held the ingredients for the dough while your electric mixer does the work. If the dough needs to chill, wipe down the appliances you used and put them away if you won't be using them anymore. I always find it convenient to have a container of hot, soapy, clean water ready in the sink to wipe down counters, rinse off utensils, or soak things.

✔ **Wash your hands often** — not only for sanitary purposes at the start of baking, but also because your hands will become dirty or sticky while you bake. If you don't wash them often (a quick rinse in soapy water usually does the trick), you'll find batters and dough stuck to your refrigerator handle, on your appliances, and all over your clothes or whatever else you touch, which means more cleaning for you later.

✔ **Keep cutting boards clean.** The flavor of one food can be transferred to another if the foods share the same space. For example, if you chop onions or garlic, be sure to wash and dry (and even flip over) the cutting board before you set out to slice your strawberries; otherwise, your berries might taste like onions.

✔ **Wipe down your countertops often.** They're the most likely things to have ingredients spilled on them and be messy. A quick wipe every so often will help keep whatever you put on them clean, too.

✔ **Always check to see whether your garbage needs to be emptied before you begin baking.** You may be amazed at the amount of trash you can produce, and you don't want to pile the garbage so high that you run the risk of spilling it onto the floor or having to stop what you're doing to take out the trash.

✔ **Put away ingredients and equipment as soon as you finish using them.** Doing so frees up quite a bit of counter space, giving you room to work with dough or spread out pans for batter, for example.

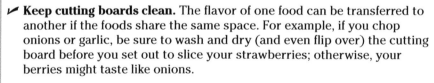

Part III
Ready, Set, Bake!

The 5th Wave   By Rich Tennant

"QUIT MOPING—YOU WON FIRST PLACE IN THE MEATLOAF CATEGORY, AND THAT'S GOOD. I'M THE ONLY ONE WHO KNOWS IT WAS A CARROT CAKE YOU ENTERED."

In this part . . .

Now comes the fun part of the book — making mouth-watering baked goods to serve your family or give away to friends and family. These ten chapters include a variety of baked products. You can find such diverse items as Dense Chocolate Brownies, Pumpkin Cheesecake, Cran-Apple and Pear Pie, Fluffy Dinner Rolls, and Chicken Potpie. There's even a chapter of low-fat recipes that taste so good you'll never miss those extra calories. Each recipe includes easy-to-find preparation and baking times and yields. I also assign a level to each recipe: easy, inter-mediate, or challenging, so as you get more and more practice, you can advance to the next level of recipes. Easy recipes require nothing more than measuring ingre-dients and mixing them up. Intermediate recipes may have a trickier step or additional technique. Challenging recipes have specific techniques that, if done incorrectly, may affect the baked product. But, not to worry, because I'm here to guide you every step of the way.

Chapter 7

Understanding Cookies

*F*inding someone who didn't like cookies in some form or another would be a difficult task. Cookies come in any shape or size, and they're portable treats that are appropriate for just about every event. They can be dressed up or eaten plain, drowned in milk or quietly accompanied by a cup of tea. Most cookies are pretty easy to make and not at all intimidating when you're just starting out. Cookies don't need much equipment, they have a relatively high yield (as long as you don't snack on too much of the dough for quality control), and you probably have most of the ingredients on hand — you may even have all the ingredients ready to go in your kitchen right now.

Just as there is a cookie for everyone, there is an opinion about cookie making, too. Some people like thin, crunchy cookies; some like softer cookies; some like a crispy drier cookie; and some prefer them to be soft and gooey. You know who you are, so just take the time to find the perfect cookie for you.

Despite the simplicity of making cookies, you do need to be aware of a few basics so you get the most from your cookie-baking experience. Some things can go wrong — maybe your cookies spread too much, maybe they spread too little, or maybe they're too crunchy. Because you're baking such small amounts of batter, it's easy to see when the dough is not quite right — maybe it spreads too much or too little or it isn't behaving the way you want it to. In this chapter, I explain the fundamentals of what makes your cookies crumble — in addition to providing lots of recipes to get you started.

Making Cookies like a Pro

Cookies are crowd pleasers on many levels. Also, if you're a beginner baker, cookie recipes are a surefire way to experience success — just keep the information in the following sections in mind as you bake.

Measuring accurately

Always measure your ingredients carefully when making cookies. Too much or too little of just one ingredient will affect the outcome of your cookie. Because cookies are miniature baked goods, you'll see right away if something is off. Remember, test your dough first and always bake a test cookie.

Understanding the effect of fats

You can interchange stick butter or margarine or shortening when you make cookies. Use vegetable oil only when it's specifically called for in the recipe. Cookies baked with butter or margarine will flatten out more than cookies baked with shortening, but the ones with butter or margarine have a richer taste. Sometimes I call for half butter and half shortening when I want a round cookie with good flavor.

Knowing the proper mixing technique

If you like your cookies dense, mix the dough by hand. An electric mixer will incorporate more air into your cookie dough, giving it a lighter and crispier texture. Either way, be sure not to mix the cookie dough too much; it will toughen the cookies.

Choosing the right pan

Nonstick coatings are a boon for any cook, but you may find they brown your cookies on the bottom a bit faster than desired. If this is happening to your cookies, lower the oven temperature by 25 degrees, and bake as instructed. If your cookies are still browning too quickly on the bottom, use two cookie sheets (one on top of the other) to create an insulated cookie sheet. If a recipe calls for a greased cookie sheet, don't grease with butter or margarine. Use shortening instead; otherwise the area in between the cookies will burn onto the sheet, and it will be next to impossible to clean. No shortening? Then use a piece of parchment paper instead to prevent them from sticking to the sheet.

When you're baking cookies, be sure you have at least two sheets, so you can scoop out dough while another batch bakes. If you only have one sheet, be sure you let it cool between batches (at least 10 minutes) to prevent the cookie dough from spreading. Cookie dough placed on a hot sheet will begin to melt immediately, resulting in very flat cookies.

Make sure your cookie sheets fit into your oven. You want to be able to leave at least 2 inches around all sides to ensure proper heat distribution while baking. If the cookie sheet is too big, you may find the cookies on the end of the sheet are burning, while the cookies toward the middle are too raw.

Bake only one sheet of cookies at a time so that they bake in the center of the oven where the heat is optimal. If you're pressed for time and need to bake two sheets at once, turn the sheets halfway around and switch the placement of the sheets halfway through baking.

In praise of parchment paper

When I worked in a bakery, we used parchment paper to line our large, industrial baking sheets. Parchment paper, available in many sizes in baking-supply stores and in some supermarkets, is a wonderful tool in the kitchen. It doesn't burn or smoke like waxed paper sometimes can, and it comes in either precut sheets or in a roll. Cut the sheet to fit your pan and scoop the cookies onto it. When the cookies are done, you can slide the whole sheet of parchment paper (with the cookies on them) onto a cooling rack. Parchment paper is great because it keeps your baking sheets clean and mess-free. It also eliminates the need to grease cookie sheets.

Spacing your cookies far enough apart

When scooping cookies onto the baking sheets, be sure to leave enough room for them to spread. Most recipes will tell you the amount of space to leave, but if not, use 2 inches as your general rule. This includes space from the edge of the sheet, too. All the cookies on one tray should be the same size and shape to ensure even baking, otherwise the smaller cookies will burn while the larger cookies are still uncooked.

Always bake a test cookie. A test cookie will let you see what an entire batch of cookies will turn out like before they're baked. That way, if you want to make any adjustments, you won't waste a whole batch of cookie dough in the process. If you find your test cookie has spread too much during baking, add 2 tablespoons of flour and bake another test cookie. Also try chilling the dough before baking for at least 30 minutes — it really works wonders. If you find your cookie is too dry, add 2 tablespoons of milk or water and test again.

Drop Cookies

Like their name suggests, you form drop cookies by dropping the dough onto the baking sheet. Use a regular spoon, not a measuring spoon, to drop the cookies onto the sheet, usually the teaspoons in your silverware drawer are perfect. Use two spoons — one to scoop up the dough and the second to push the dough onto the baking sheet.

When I worked in a bakery, we used spring-handle ice cream scoops to make cookies all the same size and shape (see Figure 7-1). You can use this trick at home. Ice cream scoops are sold by number; this number corresponds to the amount of level scoops you will get out of a quart of ice cream. I suggest choosing a #70 scoop if your recipe calls for dropping the dough by rounded teaspoons. It's a pretty small scoop, but you'll discover how easy it makes scooping out uniform cookies and keeping your hands clean.

If you like rounded cookies and you find your dough is spreading too much in baking, try chilling the dough for an hour or so. To speed this process, you can also scoop out the dough and place it in the refrigerator to chill for at least 30 minutes.

Always check the cookies after the minimum amount of baking time given. Also, you should remove cookies from the baking sheets with a wide spatula so that they don't break once they're done baking, unless the instructions say otherwise. Don't let cookies cool on their sheets. They become harder to remove.

When making drop cookies, make a large batch of dough, form into balls, and freeze on a cookie sheet. When frozen, put them into self-sealing plastic bags and store in the freezer. Later, just remove the amount you need from the freezer, place on cookie sheets, and bake while still frozen — just remember to add an extra 2 or 3 minutes to the baking time.

ice cream scoop

Figure 7-1:
Use an ice cream scoop to make all of your cookies the same size.

An American favorite is born

The invention of the chocolate chip cookie can be attributed to a very smart lady, Ruth Wakefield, owner of the Tollhouse Inn in Massachusetts. Legend has it that, in 1940, she was substituting a chopped-up chocolate bar for the nuts in the butter cookies she was making. She expected the bar to melt evenly throughout the cookie, but instead she was left with a lovely chocolate-studded cookie. A guest at the inn described the cookie to a friend at a Boston newspaper, word got around, and soon the cookie became a local favorite. Then Nestle got involved, bought the recipe, and began marketing chocolate chips, offering Ruth's recipe on each package. And the rest, my friends, is history. So let that story be an inspiration to all bakers — you never know what you may invent!

Crispy Chocolate Chip Cookies

For chocolate chip cookie lovers, the debate is strong. Do you love crispy cookies, perfect for dunking in cold milk? Or do you yearn for the soft, chewy kind that you gobble up right out of the oven? This recipe can do both (see the color section for a photo). If you want a softer chocolate chip cookie, omit the shortening and increase the butter or margarine by ½ cup. Also, remove them from the oven after 10 or 11 minutes of baking. Just let the edges of the cookie brown and don't let them get golden brown all over.

Preparation time: *25 minutes*

Baking time: *10 to 12 minutes*

Yield: *3½ to 4 dozen cookies*

2½ cups flour

2 teaspoons baking soda

1 teaspoon salt

½ cup (1 stick) butter or margarine, softened

½ cup shortening

1 cup light brown sugar, lightly packed

½ cup sugar

2 teaspoons vanilla extract

2 tablespoons milk

2 eggs

2 cups chocolate chips (12 ounces)

1 cup chopped walnuts (optional)

1 Preheat the oven to 350 degrees.

2 Combine the flour, baking soda, and salt. Set aside.

3 In a large mixing bowl, cream the butter, shortening, brown sugar, sugar, vanilla, milk, and eggs together until light and creamy, about 2 minutes. Stop as necessary to scrape down the sides.

4 In three batches, add the flour and mix together well. Stir in the chocolate chips and, if desired, the walnuts.

5 Drop the dough onto ungreased cookie sheets about 2 inches apart. Bake for 10 to 12 minutes, until the edges are a light golden brown. Remove from the oven and transfer the cookies onto a wire rack.

Per serving: *Calories 122 (From Fat 60); Fat 6g (Saturated 3g); Cholesterol 14mg; Sodium 107mg; Carbohydrate 16g (Dietary Fiber 1g); Protein 1g.*

Chocolate Drop Cookies

Thin and crispy, these slightly sophisticated cookies are a chocolate lover's dream.

Preparation time: *15 minutes*

Baking time: *8 to 10 minutes*

Yield: *About 4 dozen cookies*

1 cup semisweet chocolate chips
½ cup (1 stick) butter
½ cup confectioners' sugar
1 egg

2 cups flour
1 teaspoon baking soda
1 teaspoon salt

1 Preheat the oven to 350 degrees.

2 Melt the chocolate chips and butter together over low heat in a small saucepan. Set aside.

3 In a large mixing bowl, beat together the sugar and egg until creamy, about 30 seconds. Add the chocolate mixture and stir. Stir in the flour, baking soda, and salt.

4 Drop the dough by the teaspoonful onto an ungreased baking sheet about 1 inch apart. Bake for 8 to 10 minutes. Let the cookies cool on the baking sheet for a few minutes before transferring them to a rack to cool.

Per serving: *Calories 58 (From Fat 28); Fat 3g (Saturated 2g); Cholesterol 10mg; Sodium 77mg; Carbohydrate 7g (Dietary Fiber 0g); Protein 1g.*

Classic Oatmeal-Raisin Cookies

These cookies are my dad's favorite. To keep the raisins plump, I like to soak them in hot water before adding them to the batter. You can start the soaking 30 minutes before you start the recipe, for plump, moist raisins, if desired.

Preparation time: *15 minutes, plus 30 minutes for chilling*

Baking time: *10 to 12 minutes*

Yield: *About 4 dozen cookies*

1 cup (2 sticks) butter or margarine, softened	*1 teaspoon salt*
1 cup sugar	*1 teaspoon baking soda*
1 cup light brown sugar, firmly packed	*1 teaspoon baking powder*
2 teaspoons vanilla extract	*½ teaspoon cinnamon*
3 eggs	*3 cups rolled oats (not instant)*
¼ cup milk (low-fat is okay)	*1½ cups raisins*
2½ cups flour	*1 cup walnuts (optional)*

1 In a mixing bowl, cream together the butter, sugar, brown sugar, and vanilla. Add the eggs, one at a time, beating well after each addition. Add the milk.

2 In a separate bowl, combine the flour, salt, baking soda, baking powder, and cinnamon. In three batches, add the flour mixture to the butter mixture. Stir in the oats, raisins, and, if desired, the walnuts. Chill the dough for 30 minutes.

3 Preheat the oven to 350 degrees. Drop the dough by the teaspoonful 1 inch apart onto an ungreased cookie sheet. Bake for 10 to 12 minutes. Let the cookies cool for 1 minute before transferring them to a cooling rack.

Vary It! *Jazz up ordinary oatmeal cookies by adding ½ cup chocolate chips, or substitute chocolate-covered raisins in place of regular raisins. Or you can update the classic by using dried cranberries or blueberries in place of the raisins.*

Per serving: *Calories 131 (From Fat 41); Fat 5g (Saturated 3g); Cholesterol 24mg; Sodium 91mg; Carbohydrate 21g (Dietary Fiber 1g); Protein 2g.*

Everything Cookies

The great thing about Everything Cookies is that they have everything in them! They start as peanut butter cookies with oats, chocolate, raisins, and nuts. You can add whatever you like, too. Stir in your favorite candy or nut.

Preparation time: *15 minutes*

Baking time: *10 to 12 minutes*

Yield: *About 3 dozen cookies*

¾ cup (1½ sticks) butter or margarine, softened

1 cup peanut butter (creamy or chunky)

1 cup sugar

1 cup light brown sugar

2 eggs

1 teaspoon vanilla extract

2 cups flour

1 teaspoon baking soda

1 teaspoon salt

¼ cup milk

1½ cups rolled oats (not instant)

1 cup chocolate chips

1 cup raisins

½ cup peanuts or walnuts

1 Preheat the oven to 350 degrees.

2 In a mixing bowl, cream together the butter, peanut butter, sugar, and brown sugar. Add the eggs and beat well for 1 minute, stopping the mixer once to scrape down the sides. Add the vanilla and beat for 15 seconds to combine.

3 Add the flour, baking soda, and salt and blend well. Stir in the milk to blend. Add the oats, chocolate chips, raisins, and peanuts. The mixture will be somewhat thick.

4 Drop rounded teaspoons of dough 1 inch apart on an ungreased cookie sheet. Bake for 10 to 12 minutes, until lightly browned. Let the cookies cool for 1 minute before transferring them to a cooling rack.

Per serving: *Calories 213 (From Fat 95); Fat 11g (Saturated 4g); Cholesterol 22mg; Sodium 142mg; Carbohydrate 28g (Dietary Fiber 1g); Protein 4g.*

Chocolate-Coconut Macaroons

The cream of tartar helps stabilize the egg whites, so you don't want to leave it out. You will need to line the cookie sheets with parchment paper so that they won't stick as you remove them from the sheet. If you don't have parchment paper, you can use waxed paper, but it might smoke a little as you bake the cookies.

Preparation time: *20 minutes*

Baking time: *20 to 25 minutes*

Yield: *3 to 3½ dozen cookies*

¼ cup unsweetened cocoa powder	¼ teaspoon cream of tartar
1 cup confectioners' sugar	¼ teaspoon salt
¼ cup sugar	½ teaspoon almond extract
3 large egg whites	2 cups sweetened coconut

1 Preheat the oven to 300 degrees. Line the cookie sheets with parchment paper.

2 In a small bowl, sift together the cocoa, confectioners' sugar, and sugar.

3 In a mixing bowl, using an electric mixer, beat the egg whites, cream of tartar, and salt together until foamy, about 2 minutes. Beat in the cocoa mixture, about 1 tablespoon at a time, until the egg whites are stiff and glossy.

4 Fold in the almond extract and coconut. Drop the mixture by heaping teaspoonfuls about an inch apart on an ungreased cookie sheet. Bake for 20 to 25 minutes. Cool for 10 minutes and then transfer the cookies to a wire rack to continue cooling.

Vary It! *If you want to skip the chocolate part, omit the cocoa and sugar. If you want to double your pleasure, toss in ½ cup chocolate chips when you fold in the coconut.*

Per serving: *Calories 39 (From Fat 15); Fat 2g (Saturated 1g); Cholesterol 0mg; Sodium 30mg; Carbohydrate 6g (Dietary Fiber 0g); Protein 1g.*

Butterscotch Drops

If you don't like the nuts in this recipe, just leave them out. These chewy cookies are sure to please all age groups.

Preparation time: *15 minutes*

Baking time: *10 to 12 minutes*

Yield: *3 dozen cookies*

2½ cups flour

1 teaspoon baking soda

1 teaspoon salt

2 sticks butter or margarine, softened

1¼ cups dark brown sugar, lightly packed

1½ teaspoons vanilla extract

2 eggs

1 cup butterscotch chips

1 cup pecans

1 Preheat the oven to 350 degrees.

2 Combine the flour, baking soda, and salt. Set aside.

3 In a large mixing bowl, cream the butter, sugar, vanilla, and eggs together until light and creamy, about 1 minute. Stop as necessary to scrape down the sides. In three batches, add the flour and mix well. Stir in the chips and pecans.

4 Drop the dough onto ungreased cookie sheets about 2 inches apart. Bake for 10 to 12 minutes, until the edges are a light golden brown. Remove from the oven and transfer the cookies onto a wire rack to cool.

Per serving: *Calories156 (From Fat 81); Fat 9g (Saturated 5g); Cholesterol 26mg; Sodium 111mg; Carbohydrate 18g (Dietary Fiber 1g); Protein 2g.*

Poppy Seed Cookies

These crispy cookies have a nice crisp lemony snap to them. Because the buttery flavor of the cookie is important for overall flavor, I recommend not using margarine for this recipe.

Preparation time: *10 minutes, plus 30 minutes for chilling*

Baking time: *12 to 15 minutes*

Yield: *2 dozen*

½ cup (1 stick) butter	*1 cup flour*
1 cup sugar	*¼ cup poppy seeds*
1 egg	*Zest of 1 lemon*
½ teaspoon lemon extract	*¼ teaspoon salt*
½ teaspoon almond extract	

1 In a large bowl, cream the butter and sugar together. Add the egg, lemon extract, and almond extract and beat well. Scrape down the sides of the bowl as needed. Mix in the flour, poppy seeds, lemon zest (for instructions on zesting lemons, see Chapter 5), and salt. Mix well. Chill for 30 minutes.

2 Preheat the oven to 350 degrees. Drop heaping teaspoons of the dough 2 inches apart onto ungreased cookie sheets. Bake for 12 to 15 minutes, until the edges are very light colored.

3 Remove the baking sheet from the oven and allow the cookies to cool for 2 minutes before removing them from the cookie sheet. Transfer to a wire rack to cool further.

Tip: *To speed up the softening of cold butter, slice it first; then let stand for about 10 minutes.*

Per serving: *Calories 104 (From Fat 49); Fat 5g (Saturated 3g); Cholesterol 19mg; Sodium 28mg; Carbohydrate 13g (Dietary Fiber 0g); Protein 1g.*

Shaped Cookies

Shaped cookies can be as simple as peanut butter cookies, with the crisscross pattern on top, or as fancy as candy-cane cookies. The dough for shaped cookies is usually richer and softer than drop cookie dough, so chilling the dough before working with it is helpful. If the dough is still too soft after chilling, mix in 2 tablespoons of flour. If it is too soft and crumbly, add 2 tablespoons of water.

The dough for shaped cookies can be rolled out, slid onto a baking sheet, refrigerated, and then cut. Or it can be shaped into a log, wrapped in plastic wrap, and then refrigerated. Use a thin, sharp knife to slice the dough. You also can make the dough ahead of time and freeze it. Thaw it in the refrigerator before using it.

If you're shaping the dough into different shapes, make sure that all the cookies are the same shape and size to ensure even baking.

Make your own slice-and-bake cookies. Properly wrapped dough will last several weeks in the freezer and up to 24 hours in the refrigerator. When you need some quick cookies, they'll be ready to pop into the oven. To make your own slice-and-bake cookies, follow these easy steps:

1. **Shape chocolate chip, peanut butter, sugar cookie, or gingerbread cookie dough in a round log shape.**

   A convenient size is 3 inches in diameter and between 9 and 12 inches long.

2. **Wrap tightly in plastic wrap, with the ends tightly twisted, and refrigerate or freeze.**

3. **When you're ready to bake, bring the dough to room temperature and slice the dough into ¼-inch-thick rounds.**

   The dough should be workable — not too soft or rock hard.

4. **Place the rounds onto a baking sheet and bake according to their instructions.**

Peanut Butter Cookies

Who can resist peanut butter cookies? They make perfect dunkers in milk and seem to be a universal favorite with the younger set. For a really dense, chewy cookie, mix the batter by hand.

Preparation time: *15 minutes*

Baking time: *12 to 15 minutes*

Yield: *About 4 dozen cookies*

1 cup (2 sticks) butter, softened

1½ cups light brown sugar, firmly packed

½ cup sugar

2 eggs

1½ teaspoons vanilla extract

1½ cups peanut butter (smooth or chunky)

3¼ cups flour

1½ teaspoons baking soda

½ teaspoon salt

1 Preheat the oven to 325 degrees.

2 Cream together the butter and both sugars until well blended. Stir in the eggs, vanilla, and peanut butter. Add the flour, baking soda, and salt.

3 Drop the dough by the teaspoonful onto an ungreased baking sheet about 2 inches apart. Flatten the tops of the cookies with the tines of a fork, if desired. (To keep the fork from sticking to the dough, dip it in sugar prior to flattening.) Bake for 12 to 15 minutes. Let the cookies rest on the baking sheet for a few minutes before transferring them to the wire rack to cool.

Vary It! *If you want to go a little wild, throw in 1 cup chocolate chips for that peanut butter cup flavor.*

Per serving: *Calories 150 (From Fat 74); Fat 8g (Saturated 3g); Cholesterol 19mg; Sodium 107mg; Carbohydrate 17g (Dietary Fiber 1g); Protein 3g.*

Crisp Sugar Cookies

I like these cookies because you don't have to roll them out. You just roll the dough into balls and press them with the bottom of a glass. Try to make all the cookies the same shape to make sure that they bake evenly.

Preparation time: *20 minutes*

Baking time: *10 minutes*

Yield: *4 dozen cookies*

1 cup (2 sticks) butter	½ teaspoon salt
½ cup sugar	1½ teaspoons vanilla extract
½ cup confectioners' sugar	1 egg, beaten
½ teaspoon baking soda	2½ cups flour
½ teaspoon cream of tartar	Sugar, for dipping

1 Preheat the oven to 375 degrees.

2 In a large mixing bowl, cream together the butter and both sugars until light and creamy. Add the baking soda, cream of tartar, salt, and vanilla, and mix to blend. Then add the beaten egg and flour.

3 Shape the dough into balls the size of a small walnut and place them on a baking sheet.

4 Dip the bottom of a glass into additional sugar; press on each cookie, flattening to about ¼-inch thickness. Bake for 10 minutes, until lightly brown. Cool on a wire rack.

Per serving: *Calories 73 (From Fat 36); Fat 4g (Saturated 2g); Cholesterol 15mg; Sodium 39mg; Carbohydrate 8g (Dietary Fiber 0g); Protein 1g.*

Gingersnaps

Not only do these cookies make a great snacking treat, but you also can save a dozen or so in the freezer and use them the next time you want to make a crumb crust for a cheesecake. They'll last up to six months frozen.

Preparation time: *15 minutes, plus 1 hour for chilling*

Baking time: *8 to 10 minutes*

Yield: *About 5 dozen cookies*

1 cup sugar

¾ cup (1½ sticks) butter or margarine, softened

¼ cup molasses

1 egg

2¼ cups flour

1½ teaspoons baking soda

¼ teaspoon salt

1 teaspoon cinnamon

½ teaspoon cloves

½ teaspoon ginger

¼ teaspoon nutmeg

Sugar, for rolling

1 In a large bowl, cream the sugar and butter until light, about 1 minute. Add the molasses and egg and continue beating until light and fluffy. Stir in the flour, baking soda, salt, cinnamon, cloves, ginger, and nutmeg. Cover the bowl and chill for 1 hour.

2 Preheat the oven to 350 degrees.

3 Place about ½ cup of sugar on a plate; add more sugar if needed. Shape the dough into 1-inch balls. Roll the balls in sugar and place them on a baking sheet about 2 inches apart. Bake the cookies for 8 to 10 minutes or until set. Cool the cookies on a wire rack.

Per serving: Calories 56 (From Fat 22); Fat 2g (Saturated 2g); Cholesterol 10mg; Sodium 43mg; Carbohydrate 8g (Dietary Fiber 0g); Protein 1g.

Lemon Cookies

Lemon cookies are a favorite of mine because they're a little different than your average cookies. Kissed with lemon and almond, they're perfect with tea or as an afternoon snack.

Preparation time: *15 minutes, plus 1 hour for chilling*

Baking time: *9 minutes*

Yield: *7 dozen cookies*

1 cup butter, softened (margarine is not recommended)	1 egg
½ cup sugar	4 cups flour
½ cup light brown sugar, firmly packed	½ teaspoon baking soda
3 tablespoons fresh lemon juice	1 tablespoon grated lemon zest
	½ cup finely chopped almonds

1 In a large mixing bowl, beat together the butter and both sugars. Add the lemon juice and egg and beat well.

2 Sift the flour and baking soda together and add to the butter mixture. Add the lemon zest and nuts and mix until well blended.

3 Shape into 4 rolls, 2 inches in diameter, and wrap tightly in plastic wrap. Chill until firm, about 1 hour.

4 Preheat the oven to 375 degrees. Cut the dough into ⅛-inch slices and place them about 1 inch apart on a cookie sheet. Bake for 9 minutes or until lightly browned. Cool the cookies on a wire rack.

Per serving: *Calories 56 (From Fat 24); Fat 3g (Saturated 1g); Cholesterol 8mg; Sodium 4mg; Carbohydrate 7g (Dietary Fiber 0g); Protein 1g.*

Apricot-Date Half-Moons

These definitely win for cuteness — their name sounds like *after the date* half-moons. They're so chubby and plump that I find them rather irresistible. Adding cottage cheese to a cookie recipe may sound kind of funny, but it was all I had in the fridge at the time, and it really makes these cookies yummy. For the filling, I find dates and apricots difficult to cut into small pieces, and you don't want a lumpy filling, so I just simmered them for a while in some brandy and sugar and then gave them a few whirls in the food processor until I liked their consistency.

Preparation time: *15 minutes to make; 20 minutes to fill; 2 hours for chilling*

Baking time: *10 to 12 minutes*

Yield: *About 2½ dozen cookies*

⅓ cup confectioners' sugar	½ cup chopped dates
¾ cup (1½ sticks) unsalted butter	½ cup chopped dried apricots
¾ cup small-curd cottage cheese	¼ cup sugar
2 teaspoons vanilla extract	2 tablespoons water
1¾ cups flour	2 tablespoons brandy
Pinch of salt	1 egg, beaten (optional)

1 In a large mixing bowl, cream together the confectioners' sugar, butter, and cottage cheese (it will not get completely smooth like only butter and sugar would). Add 1 teaspoon of the vanilla. Add the flour and salt and continue mixing until the dough just comes together. Gather the dough into a ball and chill for 2 hours.

2 When the dough has almost finished chilling, combine the dates, apricots, sugar, water, and brandy in a small saucepan and cook, stirring frequently, over low heat until thickened. Transfer to the bowl of a small food processor and pulse several times to blend (it will be thick and sticky). Stir in the vanilla.

3 Preheat the oven to 375 degrees. Divide the dough in half and roll out one of the halves to about ¼-inch thickness. Using a drinking glass or a cookie cutter, cut out 2½-inch round circles. Place about ½ teaspoon of the filling in the center of the dough, fold it in half, and pinch closed. Repeat with the remaining dough. Brush each half-circle with the beaten egg, if desired.

4 Bake for 10 to 12 minutes, until golden brown. Transfer to a wire rack to cool.

Vary It! *You can use straight apricots or go wild with dried cranberries, blueberries, or even raisins — whatever you please.*

Per serving: *Calories 99 (From Fat 44); Fat 5g (Saturated 3g); Cholesterol 13mg; Sodium 27mg; Carbohydrate 12g (Dietary Fiber 1g); Protein 2g.*

Poppy Seed Thumbprints

Here's a twist on the classic. Poppy seeds add a great flavor to this cookie. I suggest using raspberry jam, but you can use whatever flavor you like.

Preparation time: *25 minutes*

Baking time: *20 minutes*

Yield: *About 2½ dozen cookies*

1 cup confectioners' sugar	*2 cups flour*
1 cup (2 sticks) butter, softened	*3 tablespoons poppy seeds*
1 egg	*½ teaspoon salt*
1 teaspoon vanilla extract	*½ to ⅔ cup raspberry preserves*

1 Preheat the oven to 300 degrees.

2 In a large mixing bowl, beat together the sugar and butter until light and fluffy, about 1 minute. Mix in the egg and vanilla. Stir in the flour, poppy seeds, and salt.

3 Drop the batter by the teaspoonful onto a baking sheet. Gently press your thumb in the center of the dough to form a depression (do not press all the way through to the baking sheet). Fill each cookie with about ½ teaspoon of preserves.

4 Bake the cookies for about 20 minutes or until the edges turn light brown. Remove from the baking sheet to cool.

Per serving: *Calories 120 (From Fat 61); Fat 7g (Saturated 4g); Cholesterol 24mg; Sodium 44mg; Carbohydrate 14g (Dietary Fiber 0g); Protein 1g.*

Russian Tea Balls

These tea balls are also known as Mexican Wedding Cakes. If you use an electric mixer, don't crank up the speed too quickly. Otherwise, you'll be left in a puff of confectioners' sugar.

Preparation time: *20 minutes*

Baking time: *10 minutes*

Yield: *4 dozen cookies*

1 cup (2 sticks) butter, softened

½ cup confectioners' sugar

1 teaspoon vanilla extract

2¼ cups flour

½ teaspoon salt

¾ cup finely chopped walnuts

Additional confectioners' sugar, for dusting

1 Preheat the oven to 400 degrees.

2 In a large mixing bowl, beat together the butter, confectioners' sugar, and vanilla. Stir in the flour, salt, and chopped nuts.

3 Roll into l-inch balls and place on an ungreased baking sheet. Bake for about 10 minutes, until set but not brown.

4 While the cookies are still warm, roll them in additional confectioners' sugar; let cool on a wire rack. Roll in the powdered sugar again.

Tip: *Finding cookie dough sticking to your hands? Wet your hands with cold water first, and you'll find that they won't be as sticky.*

Per serving: *Calories 72 (From Fat 46); Fat 5g (Saturated 3g); Cholesterol 10mg; Sodium 25mg; Carbohydrate 6g (Dietary Fiber 0g); Protein 1g.*

Anisette Biscotti

These cookies are easy to make and so satisfying, with their distinctive flavor of black licorice. The logs get a bit wider and flatter as they bake, so compensate for this by making them a little narrower before they go into the oven. Using parchment paper is best, but waxed paper will also work, and although it may smoke or steam a bit in the oven, it won't affect the biscotti.

Specialty tools: *an electric mixer*

Preparation time: *25 minutes*

Baking time: *30 minutes, then 30 more*

Yield: *2 to 3 dozen biscotti*

3 eggs

1 cup sugar

½ cup (1 stick) unsalted butter, melted

2 teaspoons anise extract

3 cups flour

¼ teaspoon salt

3 teaspoons baking powder

1 cup coarsely chopped walnuts or almonds, optional

1 Preheat the oven to 350 degrees. Line a baking sheet with parchment or waxed paper.

2 Using an electric mixer, beat the eggs on high speed about 2 minutes, until light and frothy. Keep the mixer on high speed and slowly add the sugar, ¼ cup at a time, and drizzle in the melted butter. Add the anise extract.

3 Reduce the speed to low and add the flour, salt, and baking powder, and mix just until blended (the dough will not be stiff, but rather glossy from the melted butter).

4 Divide the dough in half and form the dough into 10- to 12-inch logs, 2 to 3 inches high. If the dough seems sticky, dust your hands with flour. Place the logs on the baking sheet (they should both fit sideways). Bake for 30 minutes, until firm but not hard. Remove from the oven.

5 Reduce the oven temperature to 300 degrees.

6 Let the logs cool for 20 to 30 minutes before slicing them on the diagonal into half-inch slices. Return the slices to the baking sheet (you will need two sheets for all the slices) and return to the oven for 30 more minutes, or until they're dry and crispy.

Note: *The biscotti will bake all the way through after 30 minutes, and you don't have to re-bake it if you don't want to. It is a lovely, tender cookie baked just once.*

Per serving: *Calories 89 (From Fat 28); Fat 3g (Saturated 2g); Cholesterol 25mg; Sodium 54mg; Carbohydrate 14g (Dietary Fiber 0g); Protein 2g.*

Pressed Cookies

Pressed cookies are a holiday favorite. You can make a large amount of pressed cookies in a short amount of time, so they make holiday baking a breeze. What is a pressed cookie? It's made using a cookie press, which is a device that forces dough down a hollow tube and through a die-cut disk, resulting in shaped cookies. You can come up with many variations by using one standard recipe and simply decorating the cookies in different ways or changing the pressing disk. Shop for a cookie press that's easy to use and clean and that comes with several disk attachments.

Basic Cookie Press Cookies

This is a basic recipe, which I welcome you to embellish to suit your tastes. This dough usually passes well through a cookie press. If you find it too thick, stir in a tablespoon or two of milk. If it has no body to it and doesn't hold its shape, stir in a tablespoon or two of flour. The dough changes quickly, so don't add too much flour or milk at any one time.

Preparation time: *20 minutes*

Baking time: *12 minutes*

Yield: *6 dozen*

1 cup (2 sticks) butter, very soft	*1 teaspoon vanilla extract*
¾ cup sugar	*2⅓ cups flour*
⅓ teaspoon salt	*1 egg, beaten*
2 egg yolks	*Decorating sugar or colored sprinkles*

1 Preheat the oven to 350 degrees. In a large bowl, beat together the butter, sugar, and salt with an electric mixer until light and fluffy. Beat in the yolks and vanilla until smooth. Add the flour gradually, beating the dough until just combined well. The dough will be soft.

2 Pack the dough into a cookie press fitted with the disk of choice and press about 1 inch apart onto ungreased baking sheets. Gently brush the cookies lightly with the beaten egg and sprinkle with decorating sugar.

3 Bake the cookies until the edges are pale golden, for about 12 minutes. Cool the cookies on sheets for 2 minutes and transfer to racks to cool completely.

Vary It! *Divide the dough in half or in thirds and color with a few drops of food coloring. Add a teaspoon of almond or lemon extract to the dough. Decorate your cookies with bits of chocolate, candied fruit, poppy seeds, cinnamon dots, dollops of jam, or sprinkles of sugar before you bake them, if you like.*

Per serving: *Calories 52 (From Fat 25); Fat 3g (Saturated 2g); Cholesterol 16mg; Sodium 10mg; Carbohydrate 6g (Dietary Fiber 0g); Protein 1g.*

Rolled Cookies

When making rolled cookies, you need something to cut the dough with. You don't need cookie cutters. You can use a glass or a clean tuna can with both sides cut out, or you can just cut the dough with a knife. Traditionally, cookie cutters are used to make the job quite easy and fun. When choosing a nontraditional shape, avoid those with intricate designs or lots of "fingers." You run the risk of burning the thinner part of the cookie before the bigger parts have fully cooked.

Making your cookies look mag-ni-fique

Cookies make the perfect gift for special occasions. Whether you're taking them to an informal work function or they are decking the halls at holiday time, there will be times when you will want your cookies to shine a little more than usual. Here are some super-easy tips to dress those masterpieces up when the need arrives:

🗹 If you're going to a picnic and decide to bring cookies for a portable dessert or snack (which is always a good idea), jazz up the presentation by lining the container with clean linen napkins or bandanas.

🗹 Personalize your basic sugar cookie or gingerbread cookie recipe by decorating the dough with cinnamon hearts, chocolate chips, colorful candy-coated chocolates, chopped nuts, or raisins (or even chocolate-coated raisins!) before baking.

🗹 Melt some chocolate and dip half the cookie into it. Set the cookie on a rack until the chocolate hardens. You can even sprinkle some colored sprinkles or finely chopped nuts on top of the chocolate before it hardens.

🗹 Sandwich a scoop of ice cream between two homemade cookies and watch them disappear. (Who doesn't like ice cream sandwiches?)

🗹 Buy some tubes of frosting in the baking aisle in the supermarket and use it to frost your cookies. Any cookie looks good wearing a bit of frosting.

🗹 Press your thumb into the center of each cookie to make a little depression and then fill it with chocolate chips or jam before baking.

🗹 Decorate the plates or trays you serve the cookies on with colorful napkins or pretty doilies.

🗹 Dust the tops of chocolate brownies with confectioners' sugar. Powdered sugar not only makes the brownies look more appetizing but also covers up any imperfections.

🗹 Place a brownie square in the bottom of a bowl, top with ice cream and your favorite sundae toppings, and serve. Brownie sundaes are always a hit.

Rolled cookie dough is much like pastry dough, and it follows many of the same baking principles. Rolled cookie dough usually requires some chilling time to re-harden the butter and to let the dough rest, so it's easier to roll out. When you chill the dough, divide the dough in half or in thirds. Take out a piece of the dough to work with, and leave the remaining pieces in the refrigerator so they stay nice and chilled.

Rolling out cookie dough can be quick and easy if you follow these steps. Make sure that the dough is the right temperature. If it's too cold, it will crack and fall apart. If it's too warm, it will stick to everything in sight. Remove the dough from the refrigerator about 15 minutes before you plan to use it. That will take the chill out of it, but leave it with firmness to give your cookies good shape. The more you practice with rolled cookies, the better you'll become.

1. **Before rolling out your dough, lightly dust the work surface with flour.**

   I like to use a flat, large, nick-free wooden cutting board, but any countertop is fine. You can also lightly dust the work surface with flour and sugar. The sugar does a great job of not allowing the dough to stick, and it will not toughen your cookies the way too much flour will. However, don't be too generous with either ingredient when dusting.

2. **Roll out your dough.**

   Roll out the dough to the same, even thickness so that your cookies will bake evenly.

3. **Cut out your shapes.**

   When you're ready to cut out the shapes, dip your cutter in flour, sugar, or powdered sugar to prevent the dough from sticking to the cutter. Tap off any excess before cutting the dough so that you won't get clumps of flour on your cookies. When you cut through the dough, give the cookie cutter a tiny twist to be sure you've cut all the way through the dough. The twist should be subtle, just a fraction of an inch.

   As you cut out your cookies, try to cut as many as possible out of one sheet. If you have an odd-shaped cookie cutter, such as a candy cane or Christmas tree, sometimes turning the cookie cutter upside down on every other cut or creatively angling the cutter enables you to cut out more cookies by using the whole dough surface.

4. **When you've cut out all your cookies, carefully lift up the scrap dough and put it aside.**

   On your work surface, you'll have all your cutout cookies.

5. **Use a pancake turner or metal spatula to transfer your cookies to a baking sheet.**

   The dough is quite delicate, and you wouldn't want to stretch it or tear it by transferring the cookies by hand. Save all the scraps from each section of dough. Then gather all the scraps together to re-roll again. This will eliminate excessive re-rolling.

Keep in mind when you're rolling out the cookies that the dough will toughen up if you roll it out too many times. That's why you want to cut out as many cookies as possible the first time and then gather up all the scraps and roll it all out again.

If you really need to re-roll scraps of cookie dough, dust the surface with equal parts flour and confectioners' sugar. This will help keep the dough from getting tough.

If you don't have a rolling pin or don't want to be troubled by rolling out the cookie dough, you can "unroll" cookies. Scoop out a heaping tablespoon of cookie dough and roll it into a ball. Place the ball onto a cookie sheet. Dip the bottom of a drinking glass (2-inch diameter) into granulated or confectioners' sugar and gently press down the dough into a ¼-inch-thick round. Repeat until you have filled the tray (9 to 12 cookies) and then bake as directed.

When your cookies have baked, let them cool for a few minutes on the cookie sheet before transferring them to a cooling rack. This will let delicate shapes harden, so no gingerbread people will leave any limbs stuck onto the sheet.

Gifts for cookie lovers

Cookie cutters make great gifts. You can find them in just about every shape and size and for just about every occasion. Check out your local baking-supply or kitchen-supply store to come up with ideas for great cutout cookies. For a really special gift, present the cutter with a recipe and a batch of cookies. I'm sure that the recipient would like to know what nice cookies the new cutter makes.

Gingerbread Cookies with Royal Icing

These cookies are perfect if you want crunchy gingerbread. I recently used this recipe to make a cookie piñata for an edible art show. It was a big hit. It's a good recipe to use if you want to make a gingerbread house; just double it and omit the baking soda so it won't rise. Royal icing dries to a hard, white icing. It is also the "cement" in the food world; you can stick cookies together with it. You can find the glycerin for the icing in baking supply stores or vitamin stores. The recipe doubles or even triples quite well.

Preparation time: *35 minutes (includes rolling and cutting time), plus 2 hours or overnight for chilling*

Baking time: *12 minutes*

Yield: *About 3 dozen 2-inch cookies*

3½ cups plus ¼ cup flour	*¾ cup sugar*
2½ teaspoons ground ginger	*2 eggs*
1 teaspoon ground cinnamon	*1 teaspoon vanilla extract*
¾ teaspoon baking soda	*⅓ cup dark molasses*
¾ teaspoon salt	*Royal Icing (see the following recipe)*
¾ cup vegetable shortening	

1 In a medium bowl, combine the 3½ cups flour, ginger, cinnamon, baking soda, and salt. Stir to combine and set aside.

2 In a mixing bowl, cream together the shortening and sugar, about 30 seconds. Add the eggs and vanilla, stopping once to scrape down the sides of the bowl, about 1 minute. Add the molasses and beat until well blended, about 30 more seconds. Add the dry ingredients and beat on low speed to mix together. The dough should come off the sides of the bowl and hold together. If the dough is too loose, stir in the additional ¼ cup flour, 1 tablespoon at a time, until the dough comes away from the sides of the bowl. (I use a stand mixer, so the dough hangs onto the paddle. If you're using an electric mixer, the results may be different. Do not add more than ¼ cup additional flour.)

3 Gather the dough together into a ball and cut it in half. Wrap each half in plastic wrap. Chill for 2 hours or overnight. Remove the dough from the refrigerator and let stand at room temperature for 15 minutes.

4 Preheat the oven to 350 degrees.

5 Lightly dust your work surface and rolling pin with flour. Roll out the dough until it's ¼-inch thick. Using a cookie cutter or juice glass, cut out the cookies. Place them on the cookie sheets about ½ inch apart. Repeat with the second ball of dough. Gather the scraps and roll out again.

6 Bake the cookies for 12 minutes. Transfer to a wire rack to cool.

Royal Icing

1 egg white

1 cup confectioners' sugar

2 drops glycerin (optional)

In a mixing bowl, beat the egg white until frothy. Add the confectioners' sugar in two batches, beating well after each addition. Mix in the glycerin, if using. Transfer to a small bowl. Cover with a damp paper towel if you won't use it immediately, but don't let it sit for more than 1 hour. Frost the cookies with the icing.

Per serving: *Calories 126 (From Fat 42); Fat 5g (Saturated 1g); Cholesterol 12mg; Sodium 81mg; Carbohydrate 19g (Dietary Fiber 0g); Protein 2g.*

Storing your cookies

Cookies can be stored at room temperature if they'll be eaten within a few days; in the refrigerator if they'll be eaten within a week; or in the freezer for several months (freezing cookies is a good idea so you always have cookies on hand). Some cookies (usually ones with frosting) need to be refrigerated after they're cooled — the recipes will let you know if this is necessary.

Cookies should be allowed to cool completely before they are stored. If cookies are stored in an airtight container while they're still warm, they will give off heat, create condensation, and then become soggy.

Crisp, thin cookies actually do better if they're wrapped in an airtight container. If your crisp cookies soften a bit, re-crisp them by placing them on a baking sheet and popping them into the 250-degree oven for 5 to 7 minutes. Freezing crispy cookies and then defrosting them before eating also helps them retain their crispiness.

Soft, moist cookies should also be stored in an airtight container. You can also put in the container a slice of bread (a trick I learned from my friend Martha) or a slice of an apple (which you need to change daily) to help your cookies stay moist and chewy. You can also microwave cookies to make them tender again. Wrap them in a clean paper towel and heat for 15 to 20 seconds on High.

Frosted cookies should be stored in a single layer or with a sheet of waxed paper between layers, depending on how soft the frosting is. Also, if you have delicate shaped or rolled cookies, consider storing them in single layers or with waxed paper between the layers.

Bar cookies are easy to store — just wrap the top of the baking pan with aluminum foil or plastic wrap, and you're done. They also can be removed from the pan and transferred to a container or serving plate. Seal the container or just wrap the plate with aluminum foil or plastic wrap to keep the brownies or bar cookies fresh.

Tender Sugar Cookies

Kissed with a touch of nutmeg and almond, these sugar cookies are a head above the rest and are great for decorating (see color photo). I like them best coupled with a cup of tea or hot chocolate. To avoid baking frustration, use a cookie cutter that will give you solid shapes and an evenly cut cookie that will bake evenly. Sometimes a cookie cutter that's too detailed results in shapes that won't bake evenly or gets stuck in the mold, which can be very disappointing.

Preparation time: *15 minutes, plus 30 minutes to overnight for chilling*

Baking time: *12 minutes*

Yield: *3 dozen 2-inch cookies*

3½ cups flour	1 cup (2 sticks) butter (not margarine)
1 teaspoon baking soda	1½ cups sugar
2 teaspoons cream of tartar	2 eggs
1 teaspoon salt	½ teaspoon vanilla extract
½ teaspoon ground nutmeg	½ teaspoon almond extract (optional)

1 Sift together the flour, baking soda, cream of tartar, salt, and nutmeg. Set aside.

2 In a mixing bowl, mix together the butter and sugar until light and fluffy, about 1 minute. Add the eggs, vanilla, and, if desired, the almond extract, and continue beating, stopping once or twice to scrape down the sides, about 1 minute more. Blend in the flour mixture, just to incorporate.

3 Gather the dough together and wrap in plastic. Refrigerate for 30 minutes, or up to 24 hours.

4 Preheat the oven to 375 degrees. Have ready two baking sheets.

5 Remove the dough from the refrigerator and let rest for about 10 minutes to take the initial chill off the dough. Lightly dust your work area with flour or sugar (or a combination).

6 Roll out the dough until it is ¼-inch thick. Using a cookie cutter or juice glass, cut out the cookies. Place them on the cookie sheets about ½ inch apart. Gather the scraps and roll out again.

7 Bake for about 12 minutes or until pale golden. Transfer to a wire rack to cool.

Tip: *If you're a purist and only roll once, gather all your cookie dough scraps together and mold it into a 2-inch round log and slice and bake the scraps. The real secret to keeping rolled cookies tender is to use the least amount of additional flour necessary on your work surface.*

Per serving: *Calories 127 (From Fat 50); Fat 6g (Saturated 3g); Cholesterol 26mg; Sodium 104mg; Carbohydrate 18g (Dietary Fiber 0g); Protein 2g.*

Brownies and Bar Cookies

Brownies and bar cookies are different than other cookies because they're baked in one pan and then cut into squares (or whatever shape you desire) before serving.

If you use a glass baking pan rather than metal, remember to reduce the baking temperature by 25 degrees. For more information about baking pans, see Chapter 3.

Always use the correct pan size. If you substitute a larger pan, your brownies will be too thin and may dry out when you bake them. If the pan is too small, it will take a much longer time to bake, and the inside may still be raw when the outside is done cooking.

Cut your bar cookies into their shapes only after they've been cooled completely, unless otherwise instructed. If you cut them when they're too warm, they're difficult to cut cleanly and may crumble much easier than when they have cooled completely. You can also chill them before cutting if you have a really moist top, such as a cream cheese topping.

A great trick for cutting brownies and bars evenly, and eliminating dirty pans, is to line the baking pan with aluminum foil. When the brownies have cooled completely, just lift out the aluminum foil, place them onto a cutting board, and remove the foil. You can then cut the bars and place them on a serving plate or even back into the pan. Another incredibly easy way to slice up bar cookies is to use a pizza cutter rather than a knife.

Dense Chocolate Brownies

In my opinion, people belong in two camps: those who love dense, chocolaty brownies and those who love lighter, cakier brownies. I am a dense, moist brownie lover. This recipe creates brownies that are big with chocolate and light on flour, giving them a dense, deep chocolate flavor. Enjoy!

Preparation time: *15 minutes*

Baking time: *20 to 25 minutes*

Yield: *18 to 24 brownies*

1⅔ cups sugar	1⅓ cups flour
¾ cup (1½ sticks) butter	1 cup cocoa powder
2 tablespoons strong brewed coffee, water, or milk	½ teaspoon baking powder
	¼ teaspoon salt
3 eggs	1½ cups chocolate chips
2 teaspoons vanilla extract	½ cup walnuts (optional)

1 Preheat the oven to 350 degrees. Grease a 9-x-13-inch pan.

2 In a mixing bowl, combine the sugar, butter, and coffee in a large bowl and beat well. Add the eggs and vanilla and mix well, stopping once to scrape down the sides of the bowl.

3 Stir in the flour, cocoa, baking powder, and salt. Stir in the chocolate chips. Pour into the prepared pan and sprinkle the top with the walnuts, if desired. Bake for 20 to 25 minutes. Do not overbake. A cake tester will *not* come out clean. Let cool completely before cutting.

Per serving: *Calories 199 (From Fat 91); Fat 10g (Saturated 6g); Cholesterol 42mg; Sodium 43mg; Carbohydrate 28g (Dietary Fiber 2g); Protein 3g.*

Black-and-White Brownies

The creamy cheesecake oozes on top of and around the brownie in this recipe (see the color section for a photo) — every bite is a delicious combo of the two flavors. Serve them at room temperature, but store them refrigerated in an airtight container.

Preparation time: *30 minutes*

Baking time: *60 minutes*

Yield: *25 servings*

Brownie:

1 cup sugar	*1 teaspoon vanilla extract*
3 eggs	*¾ cup flour*
½ cup cocoa	*½ teaspoon salt*
1 cup (2 sticks) butter or margarine, melted	*½ teaspoon baking soda*

Topping:

2 packages (8 ounces each) cream cheese (Neufchâtel is okay to use)	*2 eggs*
½ cup sugar	*1 teaspoon vanilla extract*

1 Preheat the oven to 300 degrees. Spray a 9-inch baking pan with nonstick cooking spray.

2 In a mixing bowl, beat together the 1 cup sugar and 3 eggs until light and frothy, about 1 minute. Add the cocoa, butter, and 1 teaspoon vanilla, and stir together. Stir in the flour, salt, and baking soda. Pour into the baking pan.

3 In a blender or small bowl, add the cream cheese, ½ cup sugar, 2 eggs, and 1 teaspoon vanilla. Blend until smooth. Carefully spread the mixture on top of the chocolate layer (for easier spreading, chill the bottom chocolate layer first).

4 Bake for about 60 minutes, or until the topping is set. Remove from the oven and cool. Cut into 5-x-5-inch rows. Refrigerate the remaining squares.

Vary It! *If you want to make them double chocolate, melt 2 ounces bittersweet, milk, or German chocolate and stir it into the cheesecake topping.*

Per serving: *Calories 208 (From Fat 134); Fat 15g (Saturated 9g); Cholesterol 82mg; Sodium 140mg; Carbohydrate 16g (Dietary Fiber 1g); Protein 3g.*

Lemon Bars

These lemon bars are tender and a nice combination of sweet and tart. The cookie bottom and moist lemon topping melt in your mouth.

Preparation time: *20 minutes*

Baking time: *40 to 45 minutes*

Yield: *18 to 24 bars*

2 cups plus 4 tablespoons flour

1 cup (2 sticks) butter, softened

½ cup confectioners' sugar

4 eggs

2 cups sugar

1 teaspoon baking powder

Zest from one lemon

Juice from 3 large lemons

1 Preheat the oven to 350 degrees.

2 Mix together the 2 cups flour, butter, and confectioners' sugar. Pat the mixture into the bottom of a 13-x-9-inch baking pan. Bake the crust for 20 minutes.

3 While the crust is baking, beat together the eggs, 4 tablespoons flour, sugar, baking powder, and lemon zest and juice. Remove the crust from the oven and pour in this mixture. Return the pan to the oven and bake for 20 to 25 minutes more, until set. Cool the bars in the pan on a wire rack. Cut them when they have cooled. Garnish with additional confectioners' sugar, if desired.

Per serving: *Calories 197 (From Fat 77); Fat 9g (Saturated 5g); Cholesterol 56mg; Sodium 28mg; Carbohydrate 28g (Dietary Fiber 0g); Protein 2g.*

Chapter 8

Creating Great Cakes

In This Chapter

▶ Getting the lowdown on different types of cakes

▶ Recognizing what happens when a cake bakes

▶ Baking great-looking cheesecakes

▶ Cooling a cake properly

Anyone can bake cakes. There's no magic to it — although you may think that there is when you watch a simple mixture of eggs, butter, flour, and sugar turn into a thick, creamy batter, and then bake into a yummy treat that melts in your mouth. Although magic isn't involved, chemistry and technique are. Both can be explained and mastered. If you're feeling at all apprehensive about making a cake, don't. You can feel like a complete klutz in the kitchen and still turn out a respectable cake. My premise is everyone can, and should, bake cakes.

When you've decided to bake a cake, you need to choose the kind of cake you want to make. In this chapter, I introduce the categories of cakes so that you can size them up for yourself. Whichever you choose, I include lots of tips and hints to help you bake a great cake.

Butter Cakes

The most popular and best-known type of cake is the butter or shortening cake. These are the classic layer cakes, the cakes you associate with birthday parties and festive occasions, loved for their moist sweetness and high-stacking layers filled with delicious frostings and topped with decorations.

What makes butter or shortening cakes different from other varieties of cakes is they have a lot of fat (butter, shortening, or oil) in relation to the number of eggs used. Making a good butter cake isn't difficult, but you do need to know how to correctly mix the ingredients together to produce a silky batter that includes the right amount of air. Butter cakes rise from the air whipped into the batter as well as from the addition of baking powder or soda.

I recommend purchasing cake flour when you bake cakes. It really does make a difference with the final product, and you can freeze flour (label it first!) if you don't use it often.

Because the fat is the essential ingredient in butter cakes, selecting the best fat for your purposes is critical. Many professionals say unsalted butter is the best choice. Salt was originally added to butter as a preservative, but with modern refrigeration we no longer really need the salt. If you bake without it, you have more control over the salt content of your foods. If, however, you have only salted butter on hand, don't worry — it won't affect the flavor of your cake.

An often forgotten ingredient in good butter or shortening cakes is air. Solid vegetable shortening is great for incorporating air into the batter, which gives added volume to cakes and makes them softer and spongier. Solid vegetable shortening is the densest and will cream better than any other fats. Unfortunately, the flavor is not as rich as if you were to use butter (or even margarine), which can be disappointing. In all the butter/shortening recipes, feel free to substitute half shortening and half butter to get the best of both ingredients. For more on fats, see Chapter 5.

If you find your cakes continually come out with domed centers, decrease the flour in your cake recipe by ¼ cup and spread the batter from the center to the sides of the pan. Domed centers are caused by thick batters cooking the edges first, allowing the centers to continue to rise higher than the sides.

A well-prepared butter cake is moist and has a tender crumb. For the best results, make sure the fat you choose is softened. Shortening is ready to go from the can, but if you choose butter, you'll have to let it soften. If the butter yields slightly to your touch, but is still solid and not melted, it's just right. If you have to press hard, it's still too cold. Let it sit out for 15 more minutes and test again. If the butter is melting inside of the wrapper, it's too soft; pop it in the fridge for about 15 minutes to harden slightly before using. Butter taken directly out of the refrigerator should be ready to use in 20 to 30 minutes.

If you are pressed for time and need your butter to soften pronto, cut the butter into 10 to 12 pieces and leave it at room temperature. It will be softened and ready to use in about 5 minutes.

The proper technique for preparing butter cake batter is to have all the ingredients at room temperature. Cream the butter or butter/shortening blend with the sugar until light and smooth. If you use an electric mixer, begin on medium-low speed and then increase to medium speed. This will allow air to be incorporated into the fat without overheating and melting it — an important thing to keep in mind when working with all-butter cakes. Then add the eggs, followed by the dry ingredients, oftentimes alternated with the liquids to keep the batter creamy and smooth. Bake and — voilà! — perfect cakes!

TIP

If your cake falls in the oven, cut it into chunks and dip it in a chocolate fondue. The texture will be uneven, but that won't matter. Or you can use the cake for a custard bread/cake pudding.

Light and Fluffy Yellow Cake

I add ginger to my yellow cake. You don't have to, but it lends a delicate flavor to the cake, and most people love the hint of something special. You can also add ground cinnamon or nutmeg, too. The cover shows this cake with Mocha Frosting (Chapter 9).

Preparation time: *20 minutes*

Baking time: *25 to 35 minutes*

Yield: *16 servings*

2½ cups cake flour	1 cup (2 sticks) butter or margarine
1 teaspoon baking soda	1¼ cups sugar
1 teaspoon baking powder	3 eggs
½ teaspoon salt	2 teaspoons vanilla extract
1 teaspoon ground ginger	¾ cup sour cream, plain yogurt, or buttermilk

1 Preheat the oven to 350 degrees. Grease two 8- or 9-inch cake pans.

2 In a medium bowl, combine the flour, baking soda, baking powder, salt, and ginger. In a separate mixing bowl, cream together the butter and sugar using an electric mixer. Add in the eggs and vanilla. Scrape down the sides of the bowl occasionally.

3 Alternate adding the flour mixture and the sour cream to the butter mixture, beginning and ending with the flour. Stir just enough to combine, but don't overmix. Divide the batter evenly between the pans.

4 Bake until golden brown around the edges and the center springs back when you touch it, 30 to 35 minutes for the 8-inch pans, 25 to 30 minutes for the 9-inch pans. Cool for 10 minutes before removing the cakes from the pan. Cool completely before frosting.

Per serving: *Calories 263 (From Fat 134); Fat 15g (Saturated 9g); Cholesterol 76mg; Sodium 195mg; Carbohydrate 30g (Dietary Fiber 0g); Protein 3g.*

Martha's Chocolate Cake

Martha, who is one of my best friends, told me how she used to sit in her math class when she was in grade school and dream of having a slice of this cake when she got home from school. This cake is so moist and delicious that it will keep you dreaming, too. Flip to Chapter 9 for Martha's Sweet and Creamy Frosting if you want to try the real McCoy! See the color section for a photo of this cake.

Specialty tools: *an electric mixer*

Preparation time: *15 minutes*

Baking time: *25 to 30 minutes*

Yield: *One 9-inch layer cake or one 8-inch layer cake and 6 cupcakes*

2 cups flour	*1 cup vegetable oil*
1 teaspoon salt	*1 cup hot coffee*
1 teaspoon baking powder	*1 cup milk*
2 teaspoons baking soda	*2 eggs*
¾ cup unsweetened cocoa powder	*1 teaspoon vanilla extract*
2 cups sugar	

1 Preheat the oven to 325 degrees. Grease and flour either two 9-inch cake pans or two 8-inch cake pans and 6 muffin cups.

2 Sift together the flour, salt, baking powder, baking soda, cocoa, and sugar into a large mixing bowl. Add the oil, coffee, milk, eggs, and vanilla. With an electric mixer, beat at medium speed for 2 minutes (the batter will be thin).

3 Pour the batter evenly into both 9-inch cake pans or fill the 6 muffin cups halfway with batter and divide the remaining batter between both 8-inch pans. Bake for 25 to 30 minutes, until a wooden toothpick inserted into the center of the cake comes out clean (check the cupcakes after 15 minutes). Let the cakes cool for 15 minutes before removing them from the pans. Let them cool completely on the wire racks before frosting.

Per serving: *Calories 404 (From Fat 186); Fat 20g (Saturated 2g); Cholesterol 38mg; Sodium 458mg; Carbohydrate 53g (Dietary Fiber 2g); Protein 5g.*

Carrot Cake

This is quite a cake — a three-layer beauty. I love carrot cake, so I can never have too much of a good thing. If you don't have three pans, bake two of the layers and then wash and reuse one of the cake pans. Think about making this cake a day in advance. It tastes even better the second day.

Preparation time: *25 minutes*

Baking time: *30 to 40 minutes*

Yield: *12 servings*

1½ cups vegetable oil	*3 teaspoons cinnamon*
2 cups sugar	*2 teaspoons baking soda*
4 eggs, beaten	*1 teaspoon salt*
1 teaspoon vanilla extract	*3 cups grated carrots*
2 cups flour	*1 cup walnuts, coarsely chopped (optional)*

1 Preheat the oven to 325 degrees. Grease and flour three 8- or 9-inch cake pans.

2 In a large mixing bowl, beat together the oil and sugar. Add the eggs and vanilla and mix to combine.

3 Sift together the flour, cinnamon, soda, and salt, and add to the creamed mixture. Stir in the carrots and walnuts, if desired. Pour into prepared pans and bake for 30 to 40 minutes. Let the cakes cool completely on a wire rack before frosting.

Per serving: *Calories 485 (From Fat 263); Fat 29g (Saturated 3g); Cholesterol 71mg; Sodium 435mg; Carbohydrate 53g (Dietary Fiber 2g); Protein 5g.*

Let them eat cake!

Birthday cakes have a long history. The Roman emperors celebrated their birthdays with offerings of cakes to the gods and to the common people. In the Middle Ages, people celebrated with a cake on the feast day of their name saint instead of their birthday.

It is believed that the first birthday cake candles were used in Germany during the Middle Ages as symbols of earlier religious votive candles. The candle in the center of the cake was called the Lebenslicht, or "light of life"; today we call this the "one to grow on."

Applesauce Cake

When fall arrives, my refrigerator is full of apples, and I like to make my own apple-sauce. If you aren't that ambitious, look at your grocery store for the flavorful apple-sauce blends. I have used pear applesauce and even peach applesauce for this recipe.

Preparation time: *20 minutes*

Baking time: *1 hour and 15 minutes*

Yield: *12 to 14 servings*

2 cups flour	*½ teaspoon ground nutmeg*
1 cup sugar	*½ teaspoon allspice*
1 teaspoon baking powder	*½ cup vegetable oil*
1 teaspoon baking soda	*½ cup applesauce*
1 teaspoon salt	*2 eggs*
1 teaspoon cinnamon	*1 cup chopped walnuts or pecans*
½ teaspoon cloves	

1 Preheat the oven to 350 degrees. Grease a 9-x-5-inch loaf pan.

2 Sift together the flour, sugar, baking powder, baking soda, salt, cinnamon, cloves, nutmeg, and allspice into a large mixing bowl.

3 Add the oil and applesauce and mix for 2 minutes. Add the eggs and mix for 2 minutes longer.

4 Fold in the nuts and turn into the prepared loaf pan. Bake the loaf for 1 hour and 15 minutes, or until a toothpick inserted into the center comes out clean. Cool the loaf in the pan for 10 minutes. Remove from the pan and finish cooling on a metal rack.

Per serving: *Calories 304 (From Fat 150); Fat 17g (Saturated 2g); Cholesterol 35mg; Sodium 269mg; Carbohydrate 36g (Dietary Fiber 2g); Protein 5g.*

Banana-Sour Cream Bundt Cake

This is a lovely, dense cake that travels well. If you want, you can throw in a cup of chocolate chips or dress up the cake with a dusting of confectioners' sugar.

Specialty tool: *6½-cup capacity ring mold or Bundt pan*

Preparation time: *20 minutes*

Baking time: *45 minutes*

Yield: *About 12 servings*

½ cup (1 stick) butter, softened

1¼ cups sugar

2 eggs

1 cup mashed very ripe bananas (about 2 bananas)

½ teaspoon vanilla extract

½ cup sour cream

2 cups flour

1 teaspoon baking powder

1 teaspoon baking soda

¼ teaspoon salt

½ cup chopped walnuts

½ teaspoon cinnamon

1 Preheat the oven to 375 degrees. Grease well a 6½-cup capacity ring mold or Bundt pan.

2 In a large bowl, beat the butter until light, about 1 minute. Slowly beat in 1 cup of the sugar. Beat in the eggs, one at a time. Add the mashed bananas, vanilla, and sour cream.

3 Sift together the flour, baking powder, baking soda, and salt. Fold the flour into the creamed mixture, stirring just to blend (do not overbeat).

4 In another bowl, combine the chopped walnuts, the remaining ¼ cup sugar, and cinnamon. Sprinkle half of this mixture over the bottom of the prepared ring mold. Spoon in half of the batter.

5 Sprinkle in the remaining walnut mixture and cover with the rest of the banana and sour cream batter.

6 Bake for 45 minutes or until the cake is brown and starts to pull away from the sides of the mold. Let the cake cool in the pan for 10 minutes before turning it onto a wire rack to cool further.

Per serving: *Calories 308 (From Fat 127); Fat 14g (Saturated 7g); Cholesterol 60mg; Sodium 203mg; Carbohydrate 42g (Dietary Fiber 1g); Protein 5g.*

Pound Cakes

The pound cake got its name because it traditionally contained 1 pound each of flour, butter, eggs, and sugar. It is a staple for bakers because it's easy to make, reliable, delicious, and keeps for a long time. Today's pound cakes are not restricted by the original recipe and can be glamorized with bits of chocolate, poppy seeds, fruits, and raisins, just to name a few. The old-fashioned plain pound cake is still a classic, though.

For a truly dense cake, mix the batter by hand. For a lighter texture, use an electric mixer to cream the butter and sugar, then finish mixing by hand. This is supposed to be a dense cake, so be careful not to overmix the batter by beating it too long with the mixer. Otherwise, it may come pouring over the sides of the pan when it bakes.

 Bake pound cakes in loaf, tube, or Bundt pans, preferably of shiny metal rather than dark steel. Dark pans cause the outside of the cake to brown before the inside is baked through. For more on baking pans, see Chapter 3.

Don't fret if the top of the cake splits — this is normal, caused by steam escaping during baking.

Cooling a cake

Cakes need to cool properly before they're handled. First, allow cakes to cool in their pans for a while. If a cake hasn't cooled enough, it will be quite reluctant to leave the pan — some of the cake may stick to the pan, or half of the cake will come out, and the other half will stay attached. Wire racks are perfect for cakes to cool on after they're removed from baking pans, because the wire racks allow air to circulate all around the cake while it cools. Some kinds of cakes require specific cooling techniques, such as

✔ **Cheesecakes:** Allowing the cheesecake to fully set before removing the springform pan is important. Cool the cheesecake to room temperature. Then cover the top of the pan with plastic wrap and place it in the refrigerator to set for at least four hours; overnight is ideal. After the cheesecake is completely chilled, run a butter knife between the cake and the edge of the pan and gently release the springform ring, bringing it over the top of cake.

✔ **Sponge or angel food cakes:** Sponge and angel food cakes are leavened with air, so they have to cool hanging upside down or they will collapse into themselves. The easiest way is to use a pan that has feet attached to the pan. Just flip around the feet, and turn the cake upside down. If your pan doesn't have feet, don't worry — just turn the pan over onto the neck of a wine bottle or long, heatproof funnel. If those aren't handy, balance the edges of the pan on inverted mugs or cups. Allow the cake to completely cool for several hours. Then remove the pan from the bottle and slide a sharp knife with a long, thin blade between the cake and side of the pan to free any sticking crumbs. Place a plate over the top of the tube pan, flip it over, and remove the pan.

Classic Pound Cake

Not many recipes are easier and more satisfying than a pound cake. This rich, dense cake is perfect on its own, but you also can serve it with a scoop of ice cream, fresh fruit, a drizzle of chocolate sauce, or a sprinkling of confectioners' sugar for a special treat.

Specialty tools: *an electric mixer*

Preparation time: *20 minutes*

Baking time: *55 to 60 minutes*

Yield: *1 loaf (12 to 16 servings)*

1¾ cups flour	¾ cup sugar
¾ teaspoon baking powder	3 tablespoons milk
¼ teaspoon salt	3 eggs
¾ cup (1½ sticks) butter, at room temperature	1½ teaspoons vanilla extract

1 Preheat the oven to 350 degrees. Grease and flour a 9-x-5-inch loaf pan.

2 Sift together the flour, baking powder, and salt in a medium-sized bowl. Set aside.

3 Using an electric mixer, cream together the butter and sugar on medium speed until well incorporated, about 1 minute. Add the milk, eggs (one at a time), and vanilla and continue beating to mix well. Slowly add the flour, about ½ cup at a time, mixing on low speed until just blended.

4 Scrape the batter into the prepared loaf pan. Bake for 55 to 60 minutes, or until a wooden toothpick inserted into the center comes out clean. Let the cake rest for 10 minutes before inverting it onto a cooling rack.

Per serving: *Calories 179 (From Fat 88); Fat 10g (Saturated 6g); Cholesterol 64mg; Sodium 69mg; Carbohydrate 20g (Dietary Fiber 0g); Protein 3g.*

Chocolate Swirl Pound Cake

You make this cake in a Bundt or tube pan. I recommend using butter to achieve the rich flavor you want in this cake. Even without the chocolate swirl, this dense cake is very tasty. Check out the photo in the color section.

Specialty tools: *12-cup Bundt or tube pan*

Preparation time: *25 minutes*

Baking time: *50 minutes to 1 hour and 10 minutes*

Yield: *20 to 24 servings*

3 cups sugar	*3 cups flour*
1½ cups (3 sticks) butter, at room temperature	*1½ teaspoons baking soda*
5 eggs	*½ teaspoon salt*
1 cup sour cream	*1 ounce semisweet or bittersweet chocolate*
2 teaspoons vanilla or almond extract, or 1 teaspoon each	*1 tablespoon butter*

1 Preheat the oven to 350 degrees. Grease and flour a 12-cup Bundt or tube pan.

2 Using an electric mixer, cream together the sugar and the 1½ cups butter, about 1 minute. Add the eggs, sour cream, and vanilla and blend, stopping once to scrape down the sides of the bowl. Stir in the flour, baking soda, and salt. Reserve 1 cup of the batter. Pour the remaining batter into the prepared pan.

3 In a small saucepan over very low heat, melt the chocolate and 1 tablespoon butter. Stir into the reserved cup of batter.

4 Spoon the chocolate batter around the center of the pan. With a knife, gently swirl the two batters together with an *S* motion. Do not overmix.

5 Bake for 50 minutes to 1 hour and 10 minutes, until a wooden tester inserted into the center of the cake comes out clean. Let cool for 15 minutes. Remove the cake from the pan and cool completely.

Per serving: *Calories 302 (From Fat 141); Fat 16g (Saturated 9g); Cholesterol 81mg; Sodium 148mg; Carbohydrate 38g (Dietary Fiber 1g); Protein 3g.*

Cupcakes

Like pound cakes, which originally contained a pound of each ingredient, cupcakes are so-called because all the ingredients were originally measured out by the cup: 1 cup of butter, 2 cups of sugar, 3 cups of flour, and 4 eggs. The individual tins came later, so the name really derived from the recipe, not from the baking pans.

Any recipe for layer, butter, or pound cake makes a fine cupcake. Coffee cake recipes can also be used, as can recipes for fruit cakes, nut cakes, and tea cakes. Cupcakes are baked in muffin pans. As a general rule, the pans are prepared for baking by spreading them with shortening or spraying them with a nonstick coating. They may also be lined with paper or foil baking cups, which ensure that the cakes won't stick to the pan, making cleanup a snap. The liners also help keep moisture in the cakes, keeping them fresher longer.

Flat-bottomed, wafer ice cream cones can be used as baking containers for cupcake batter. Children are particularly fond of them. To make them, fill the cones two-thirds full with batter (about 2 generous tablespoons). Place the filled cones on a flat baking sheet or in muffin tins and bake for about 25 minutes, or until a cake tester inserted in the center of the cupcake comes out clean. Eat the cake and its container.

Testing for doneness

You can do several things to make sure that your cake is thoroughly baked. Some visual clues can tell you whether the cake is done:

✔ The color of the top should be golden brown.

✔ The edges should be just beginning to pull away from the pan.

✔ The cake should appear to be firm and should not jiggle when lightly shaken.

Touch the top surface lightly with your finger; the cake should spring back, and your finger should not make a dent. To be absolutely sure your cake is done, insert a cake tester into the center of the cake. (A product called a *cake tester* actually exists, but save your money — a toothpick, thin wooden skewer, or butter knife will do nicely.) The tester should come out clean and dry, indicating that the cake is done. If the tester comes out wet and covered in batter, bake the cake for a couple more minutes, then retest.

Be sure you set your timer to the minimum baking time given and try not to peek while the cake is baking. As exciting as it is to watch, you make the oven temperature fluctuate each time you open the door, and that could affect the way the cake bakes — in the worst-case scenario, the cake could fall. The only exception to the cake-test rule is cheesecake, which has its own set of rules (see the "Cheesecakes" section).

Chocolate Cupcakes

People can't seem to get enough chocolate, and these cupcakes are the perfect answer when you want just a little something after a meal. These moist little cupcakes will keep you coming back for more. You can frost them with vanilla or chocolate frosting, or just a dusting of confectioners' sugar. Flip to the color section for a photo of these.

Specialty tool: *12-cup muffin tin*

Preparation time: *15 minutes*

Baking time: *20 minutes*

Yield: *12 cupcakes*

½ cup shortening, at room temperature	*½ teaspoon salt*
1 cup sugar	*1 teaspoon baking soda*
1 egg	*½ cup buttermilk*
1½ cups flour	*½ cup hot water*
½ cup unsweetened cocoa powder	*1 teaspoon vanilla extract*

1 Preheat the oven to 375 degrees. Grease or line 12 muffin cups.

2 In a medium-sized mixing bowl, cream together the shortening and sugar until light and creamy, about 1 minute. Beat in the egg.

3 In a small bowl, combine the flour, cocoa, and salt. Stir the baking soda into the buttermilk and stir to dissolve. Add the flour mixture alternately with the buttermilk to the shortening mixture, beginning and ending with flour and mix just to combine.

4 Add the hot water and vanilla. Pour the batter into the muffin tins and bake for 20 minutes or until a toothpick inserted into the center comes out clean. Cool the cupcakes on a wire rack completely before frosting them.

Vary It! *If you like, you can use ¼ cup shortening and ¼ cup butter (½ stick). Just make sure that both are at room temperature.*

Per serving: *Calories 216 (From Fat 87); Fat 10g (Saturated 3g); Cholesterol 18mg; Sodium 146mg; Carbohydrate 31g (Dietary Fiber 2g); Protein 3g.*

Lemon Cupcakes

Delicate lemon cake kissed with a light lemon frosting, these cupcakes are perfect to celebrate springtime. Top them with colored sprinkles, and they'll be too irresistible to pass up.

Preparation time: *30 minutes*

Baking time: *15 to 20 minutes*

Yield: *24 servings*

2 cups cake flour	*⅔ cup milk*
2 teaspoons baking powder	*2 teaspoons lemon extract*
½ teaspoon salt	*½ teaspoon vanilla extract*
⅔ cup (1¼ sticks) butter, at room temperature	*Zest from 1 lemon (about 1 teaspoon)*
1 cup sugar	*Lemon Frosting (see the following recipe)*
3 eggs	

1 Preheat the oven to 350 degrees. Line two 12-cup muffin tins with paper liners.

2 In a small bowl, prepare the cupcake batter: Combine the flour, baking powder, and salt. In a mixing bowl, beat together the butter, sugar, and eggs. Add the milk, lemon extract, vanilla extract, and lemon zest. Scrape down the sides of the bowl occasionally. Stir in the flour mixture.

3 Fill each muffin cup two-thirds full. Bake for 15 to 20 minutes, or until a wooden tester inserted into the center comes out clean. Let the cupcakes cool slightly before removing them from the tin. Cool completely, about 1 hour.

Lemon Frosting

2 packages (8 ounces each) cream cheese	*1 teaspoon lemon extract*
¾ cup (1½ sticks) butter, at room temperature	*1 teaspoon vanilla extract*
¼ cup fresh lemon juice (about 2 lemons)	*1 teaspoon grated lemon zest (optional)*
4½ cups confectioners' sugar	

While the cupcakes are cooling, prepare the frosting: Combine the cream cheese, butter, and lemon juice and beat until smooth and creamy. Add the confectioners' sugar, lemon extract, vanilla, and lemon zest, if desired. Beat until creamy. Chill the frosting until the cupcakes have cooled and are ready to be frosted. Frost the cupcakes and keep them refrigerated until ready to serve.

Per serving: *Calories 316 (From Fat 166); Fat 18g (Saturated 11g); Cholesterol 78mg; Sodium 149mg; Carbohydrate 35g (Dietary Fiber 0g); Protein 3g.*

Sponge Cakes

Sponge cakes are light and airy. The primary reason they rise so high is the air beaten into egg whites. Sponge cakes are both lighter and dryer than butter cakes. They are dryer (in a good way, not like an overbaked cake) because they don't have the fat that adds to the moistness of butter cakes.

Butter cakes blend sugar into the fat to make the air pockets. In contrast, sponge cakes whip the eggs with sugar until light in color (lemon-colored), thick, and at the ribbon stage (when the batter forms a flat ribbon falling back upon itself when the beater is lifted). At this stage, a line drawn with your finger through the batter will remain visible for at least a couple seconds. Whisk-type beaters, not paddles, are always used to make sponge cakes. The air whipped into the egg-sugar mixture at this stage contributes to the rising of the sponge.

When the sponge cake is placed in the oven to bake, the second essential factor is the heat of the oven. Basically, what happens is this: The liquid in the batter becomes steam, which rises and escapes through the foam. The heat also causes the air in these bubbles to expand, which contributes to the rise. This same principle is what makes croissants flaky and puff pastry puffy.

Angel food cake

An angel food cake is a light, fluffy, high-rising cake that is basically a sponge cake without egg yolks or fat. To make a good angel food cake, you just need to know a few basic tricks:

- **Whip the egg whites properly.** Angel food cake is made with a large quantity of egg whites, which are whipped into a foam; this foam provides all the cake's leavening (for instructions, see Chapter 5).

- **Don't grease the cake pan.** The rising batter must cling to the pan sides and hold itself up. The sides of a greased pan will be too slippery for the cake to rise.

- **Preheat the oven.** The cake should not be sitting around waiting to rise, allowing the air cells to deflate while the oven heats up. The oven must also be the correct heat: The ideal temperature is 325 degrees.

- **Test for doneness.** Use something long and thin to test the cake for doneness, such as a clean broom straw, a long thin knife, or a thin bamboo skewer.

- **Invert the pan.** As soon as the cake is done baking, turn the pan upside down and stand it on its feet or hang it upside own over the neck of a bottle or tall funnel. What you want to do is invert the cake until it has completely cooled to ensure it will be firm enough to hold its rise.

✔ **Saw, don't cut.** To cut angel food cake, use a sawing motion with a serrated knife or a pronged *angel-food cutter* (a tool that looks like a row of thin nails attached to a bar). Just remember that if you try to cut the cake with a regular straight-blade knife, you will end up pushing down on the cake, which will flatten it. Freeze it first for easier slicing.

Angel Food Cake

This light and airy cake calls for cake flour. Don't purchase self-rising cake flour by mistake (it will be marked on the package). You can double-check if you aren't sure by reading the ingredients. If any leavening agent, such as baking soda or powder, is present in the flour, it's self-rising and *not* the kind you want.

Specialty tool: *10-inch tube pan*

Preparation time: *15 minutes*

Baking time: *40 to 45 minutes*

Yield: *10 to 12 servings*

1 cup cake flour

1½ cups confectioners' sugar

2 cups egg whites (about 6 to 8 eggs)

¼ teaspoon salt

1 teaspoon vanilla extract

¼ teaspoon almond extract

1 cup sugar

1 Preheat the oven to 350 degrees.

2 Sift the cake flour with the confectioners' sugar twice. Set aside.

3 With a wire whisk or the whisk attachment of an electric mixer, beat the egg whites, salt, vanilla, and almond extract together until they are foamy and just begin to form soft peaks. (See Chapter 5 for instructions on beating egg whites.) Gradually add the sugar, about 2 to 3 teaspoons at a time, and continue beating until stiff peaks form. Do not overbeat.

4 Add the flour mixture to the egg whites in thirds and gently fold with a rubber spatula to combine (about four turns) after each addition.

5 Carefully pour the mixture into a 10-inch tube pan. Bake the cake for 40 to 45 minutes. It will be golden brown and spring back when you touch it. Remove the cake from the oven and turn it upside down over a funnel or the neck of a bottle, or rest it on the feet of the tube pan, if available. Let the cake cool inverted. Remove it from the pan and serve.

Per serving: *Calories 156 (From Fat 0); Fat 0g (Saturated 0g); Cholesterol 0mg; Sodium 76mg; Carbohydrate 36g (Dietary Fiber 0g); Protein 3g.*

Rolling with the jelly rolls

A *jelly roll* is simply a thin sponge cake baked in a broad flat pan and then rolled up around a filling. Typical fillings include jelly or preserves, custard, or mousse. The ever-popular Christmastime treat is the Buche de Noel: a jelly roll filled with buttercream and coated in chocolate.

You want a jelly roll cake to be light and fine-grained, but it should also be a bit elastic and flexible so that it can roll without cracking. You can also use my Angel Food Cake recipe (earlier in this chapter) — just bake it in a jelly roll pan. The texture of the cake is light and flexible enough to make a delicious roll. To ensure that the jelly roll will come neatly out of the pan, spread butter or margarine on the bottom and sides of a pan. Line the bottom of the pan with waxed paper or baking parchment. (See Chapter 5 for more about lining cake pans.)

To assemble a jelly roll, as soon as the cake comes out of the oven to cool, invert the pan over a clean kitchen towel sprinkled with sugar. Lift off the pan and carefully peel off the paper. With a serrated knife, carefully slice off a ⅛-inch strip of the crisp side, which will make rolling the cake easier and prevent cracking. Fold one short end of the towel over the end of the cake, then roll up the cake. Figure 8-1 shows you how this is done.

Rolling up a jelly roll

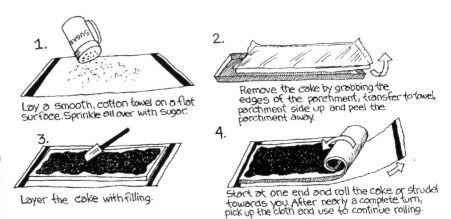

1. Lay a smooth, cotton towel on a flat surface. Sprinkle all over with sugar.

2. Remove the cake by grabbing the edges of the parchment, transfer to towel, parchment side up and peel the parchment away.

3. Layer the cake with filling.

4. Start at one end and roll the cake or strudel towards you. After nearly a complete turn, pick up the cloth and use to continue rolling.

Figure 8-1: Assembling a jelly roll.

Place the cake seam side down to cool. The cake can be left to cool for several hours or even overnight before unrolling and filling it. Once filled, cut the jelly roll with a serrated knife, using a sawing motion. Otherwise, you may press down too hard on the roll and squeeze out the filling.

Jelly Roll

This delicious sponge cake can be served with ice cream or whipped cream. If you want to try a cake without having to frost it, jelly rolls are perfect. You bake, fill, and roll, and then you have a tasty, sophisticated cake to serve.

Specialty tools: *an electric mixer*

Preparation time: *30 minutes*

Baking time: *20 minutes*

Yield: *10 to 12 servings*

¾ cup flour

1 teaspoon baking powder

½ teaspoon salt

4 eggs

¾ cup sugar

1 teaspoon grated lemon peel

6 to 8 ounces raspberry preserves, at room temperature

Confectioners' sugar, for sprinkling

1 Preheat the oven to 375 degrees. Line a 15-x-10-x-1-inch baking pan with parchment or waxed paper. Sprinkle a clean kitchen towel with confectioners' sugar; set aside.

2 In a small bowl, sift together the flour, baking powder, and salt. Set aside.

3 In a medium-sized bowl, beat the eggs with an electric mixer until they thicken slightly and turn a light yellow, about 2 minutes on medium speed. Beat in the sugar, about 2 tablespoons at a time, and continue beating on medium speed for about 5 minutes. Add the lemon peel. Gently fold in the flour mixture and spread the mixture into the prepared pan.

4 Bake for 8 to 10 minutes, until the cake springs back gently when touched. Invert the cake onto the prepared kitchen towel and allow it to cool for just 2 minutes. Remove the pan and carefully peel off the waxed paper. Beginning at the narrow end, roll the cake in the towel and place on a wire rack, seam side down, to cool, about 20 minutes.

5 Unroll the cake, spoon the preserves onto the cake, and spread to cover, leaving a ¼-inch border around the cake's edges. The preserves should be spread about ¼-inch thick. Roll up the jelly roll again and place seam side down onto the cake plate; let rest about 30 minutes. Sprinkle with additional confectioners' sugar before serving.

Vary It! *Instead of using raspberry preserves for a jelly roll, feel free to substitute a butter-cream filling, sweetened whipped cream, pudding, or any flavor of jam or preserve. If you use pudding or whipped cream, be sure to keep the jelly roll refrigerated.*

Per serving: *Calories 176 (From Fat 16); Fat 2g (Saturated 1g); Cholesterol 71mg; Sodium 158mg; Carbohydrate 37g (Dietary Fiber 1g); Protein 3g.*

Cheesecakes

Who can resist the appeal of a rich, creamy, satin-smooth cheesecake? Because this is one luxury that is well within reach, easy to make, and freezes well, it is worth preparing for any occasion.

For a cheesecake to taste smooth and creamy, the batter must be smooth and creamy at all times. The best way to achieve this is to have all ingredients at room temperature before you start baking. Using a mixer with a paddle attachment, beat the cream cheese until it's smooth and soft before adding the other ingredients. If you use a handheld mixer, use it on a low speed so you don't incorporate too much air into the batter, which can cause your cheesecake to crack.

Another popular method is to dump all the ingredients into a blender or food processor and give it a whir for a minute or so; then just pour and bake. This method can incorporate a bit too much air, so if you try it, remove the blender from the motor base and thunk it on the countertop a few times to encourage the air bubbles to rise to the surface and escape.

Whichever method you choose for mixing the batter, stop several times and scrape the sides and the bottom of the container to be sure your batter is lump-free and that no ingredients are stuck to the bottom or sides.

Coping with cracks

Cracks in a cheesecake, whether they happen during baking or cooling, can be caused by several different factors: extreme temperature changes, an oven temperature that's too high, too much air in the batter, baking for too long a time, or being placed in a drafty place to cool. Sometimes cracks just happen, despite your best efforts. But worry not — the taste of the cake won't be affected. If you're serving the cheesecake to guests, and appearance is important, here are a few tips to help disguise those cracks:

✔ **Top the cheesecake with sliced fruit.** Any fresh fruit will do, but f you use bananas or peaches, remember to toss them in a bit of lemon juice to prevent them from browning before serving.

✔ **Spread the top with a thin layer of sour cream.** This will add to the richness of the cheesecake and conceal any imperfections.

✔ **Drizzle melted chocolate on top.** Dip a fork in melted chocolate (see Chapter 5) and drizzle a pattern on top of the cheesecake. It will give the cheesecake a new look. When didn't chocolate make everything a little bit better?

TIP

Cutting the cheesecake

Cutting a cheesecake can be messy. The cake has a tendency to cling to the knife, so making neat slices can be quite a challenge. One solution is to run the knife under hot water after each slice is made. This keeps the knife clean, and the warm knife slices neatly through each piece. Of course, if you're cutting the cheesecake at the table, this method won't work. Instead, use two knives: one to cut the cheesecake and the other to scrape the knife clean after each slice.

A great trick for cutting a cheesecake is to use dental floss or heavy thread. Cut a piece of floss the diameter of the cake, plus enough to wrap around your fingers. Simply pull the thread taut between your hands and press it down all the way through the cake. Release the thread in one hand and pull it out with the other. Repeat, cutting the cake like the spokes of a wheel. It makes a great topic of conversation for your guests.

Baking a great-looking cheesecake

A cheesecake is baked in a springform pan. (Flip back to Chapter 3 to see what one looks like.) It's a good idea to place the springform on a baking sheet with a lip. A springform pan can sometimes leak, despite your best attempt to make sure it's tightly fastened. Placing the pan on a baking sheet will prevent a leaky springform from making a mess in your oven. It's also an easy and safer way to take the cheesecake in and out of the oven, preventing any surprise openings of the springform. If you don't have a baking sheet with a lip, you can wrap the bottom of the springform pan in aluminum foil to seal off any potential leaky cracks.

To tell if your cheesecake is done, observe the top surface carefully. For most cheesecakes, the edges of the cake puff up slightly and may turn faintly golden (a golden brown cheesecake is undesirable). The top should also be dull, not shiny, and when you tap the sides, they should move, but not have the jiggle of liquid. The center should be softer than the edges. The cake will rise slightly during baking, but when it cools, it will settle and solidify. If any cracks appear, they will get smaller as the cake cools and sinks down. You can also carefully run a butter knife around the edge of the cheesecake when it comes out of the oven. Then, as the cake shrinks as it cools, it won't stick to the side of the pan.

You can cool your cheesecake by removing it from the oven, or you can just turn off the oven and crack the oven door. Let the cheesecake cool to room temperature before chilling it in the refrigerator for at least 3 to 4 hours, or preferably overnight, before serving.

Classic Cheesecake

This wonderfully dense cheesecake will have you singing its praises. The flavor is so rich, it is for the true cheesecake lover. Serve with chocolate sauce, fresh fruit, or a dusting of cinnamon. For fewer calories, you can use low-fat cream cheese, but do not use fat-free cream cheese.

Specialty tool: *9-inch springform pan*

Preparation time: *25 minutes, plus 4 hours for setting*

Baking time: *1 hour and 15 minutes*

Yield: *16 servings*

2 cups graham cracker crumbs	*5 eggs*
4 tablespoons (½ stick) butter, melted	*Grated rind of 1 lemon*
2 pounds (four 8-ounce packages) cream cheese, at room temperature	*2 teaspoons vanilla extract*
1½ cups sugar	*¼ cup heavy (whipping) cream or half-and-half*

1 Preheat the oven to 300 degrees.

2 In the bottom of a 9-inch springform pan, combine the graham cracker crumbs and the melted butter. Press into the bottom of the pan and place the pan in the refrigerator until you're ready to fill it.

3 In a large mixing bowl or blender, combine the cream cheese, sugar, eggs, lemon rind, vanilla, and cream, and mix until well blended, about 3 minutes. Stop at least three times to scrape down the bottom and the sides of the bowl with a stiff rubber spatula.

4 Assemble the springform pan and pour the batter into the chilled crust and set on a baking sheet. Bake the cheesecake until the center is barely set, about 1 hour and 15 minutes. Shut off the oven and open it. Let the cheesecake cool like that for 20 minutes, and then finish cooling it on a wire rack. Cover and refrigerate the cheesecake for 4 hours or overnight to set. Serve chilled.

Per serving: *Calories 397 (From Fat 243); Fat 27g (Saturated 16g); Cholesterol 142mg; Sodium 280mg; Carbohydrate 32g (Dietary Fiber 0g); Protein 7g.*

Pumpkin Cheesecake

My former boss, Anne, asked me if there would be a Pumpkin Cheesecake recipe in this book, so here it is. You can use a blender to make this recipe — just be sure to tap the container a few times on the countertop to release any air bubbles before you pour the mixture into the springform pan. This cheesecake is wonderfully rich and very pumpkiny.

Specialty tool: *9-inch springform pan*

Preparation time: *20 minutes, plus 6 hours for chilling*

Baking time: *50 minutes*

Yield: *14 to 16 servings*

Crust:

2 cups graham or cinnamon graham cracker crumbs

5 tablespoons butter, melted

Filling:

2 packages (8 ounces each) cream cheese, at room temperature

1 cup sour cream

1 cup sugar

2 cups (one 16-ounce can) canned or fresh pumpkin (not seasoned pie filling)

½ teaspoon ground nutmeg

¼ teaspoon allspice

2 tablespoons bourbon or maple syrup

1 tablespoon vanilla extract

4 eggs

1 Preheat the oven to 300 degrees.

2 Make the crust: Mix the cracker crumbs and the butter together until the crumbs are moistened and press them into the bottom of a 9-inch springform pan. Your crust should be about ¼-inch thick and a quarter of the way up the side of the pan.

3 In a blender container or large mixing bowl, make the filling: Combine the cream cheese, sour cream, sugar, pumpkin, nutmeg, allspice, bourbon, vanilla, and eggs and mix until well blended, about 2 minutes. Stop the blender or mixer several times to scrape down the sides (cream cheese has a tendency to stick to the sides of the container). Pour the filling into the prepared pan.

4 Bake for 50 minutes or until set and not liquidy in the center. Turn the oven off and crack the door a little. Let the cheesecake cool inside the oven, 30 minutes. When the cheesecake has cooled, remove it from the oven and cover the top with plastic; chill for at least 6 hours or overnight.

Per serving: *Calories 304 (From Fat 172); Fat 19g (Saturated 11g); Cholesterol 100mg; Sodium 200mg; Carbohydrate 28g (Dietary Fiber 2g); Protein 6g.*

Lemon Curd Cheesecake

This is a brandy cheesecake with a lovely lemon topping. It's hard to beat. See the color section for a photo of this delicious cheesecake.

Specialty tools: *9-inch springform pan*

Preparation time: *20 minutes, plus overnight for setting*

Baking time: *45 to 60 minutes*

Yield: *14 to 16 servings*

1½ cups graham cracker or gingersnap cookie crumbs	*3 eggs*
3 tablespoons melted butter	*½ cup sugar or honey*
Two packages (8 ounces each) cream cheese, at room temperature	*¼ cup brandy or lemon juice*
	¼ teaspoon salt
1 cup sour cream	*Lemon Curd (see the following recipe)*

1 Preheat the oven to 325 degrees. Combine the cracker or cookie crumbs and melted butter into the bottom of a 9- or 10-inch springform pan and press into the bottom to make a smooth floor.

2 In a blender, combine the cream cheese, sour cream, eggs, sugar, brandy, and salt and process until smooth. Alternatively, use an electric mixer and blend until smooth. Pour into the prepared springform pan.

3 Bake for 45 to 60 minutes, until set and slightly golden. Remove from the oven and cool.

Lemon Curd

3 eggs	*½ cup sugar*
3 egg yolks	*¼ cup (½ stick) butter, cold, cut into 4 pieces*
½ cup lemon juice (2 large lemons)	

1 Prepare the lemon curd: Combine the eggs, egg yolks, lemon juice, sugar, and butter in a small saucepan and cook, whisking constantly, over medium heat until the butter is melted and the mixture is hot. Reduce the temperature and continue whisking until the mixture begins to thicken (but do *not* let the mixture boil), about 2 minutes. The mixture should be thicker than custard. Pour the mixture into a sieve set over a bowl. Cool the mixture just to room temperature. Refrigerate or place the bowl in a bowl of cold water.

2 Pour the lemon curd over the top of the cheesecake still in the springform pan. Cover and refrigerate overnight. Run a knife around the edge of the cheesecake before removing the springform circle.

Per serving: *Calories 312 (From Fat 197); Fat 22g (Saturated 12g); Cholesterol 171mg; Sodium 222mg; Carbohydrate 23g (Dietary Fiber 0g); Protein 6g.*

Chapter 9

Fabulous Frostings

For some people, cake is just the vehicle for the frosting — frosting can never be too rich, too thick, too sweet, or too chocolaty. Personally, I prefer my frostings to enhance, not overwhelm, the cake I'm eating, but I'm sure I'm in the minority when it comes to cake eaters. Whether you like a little or a lot, when you dress a cake, you generally say you're *frosting* it. This chapter introduces some of the different types of frostings, explains how to frost a basic cake, and provides tips for making it all look great without a lot of fuss.

Finding Out about Frostings

Frostings come in several varieties: buttercream frostings (made predominately with butter, confectioners' sugar and flavoring, they're thick, sweet, and spreadable), icings (usually made with confectioners' sugar and liquid, they're usually poured over a cake and harden), toppings (can be anything from flavored whipped cream to melted chocolate — usually a garnish or thick sauce), glazes (thinner and contain less sugar than icings, they'll set on a cake but not harden), and even fillings (which technically aren't a frosting but can be lumped in with frostings anyway). These types of frosting fall into two general categories:

✔ **Quick frostings:** To make these frostings, you just throw all the ingredients into a bowl and beat until smooth. Quick frostings are self-explanatory. You follow the recipes, making sure that all your ingredients are sifted for the smoothest finish, and then spread the frosting all over the cake.

✔ **Cooked frostings:** Although cooked frostings can be quick, too, they usually require melting something, such as butter, sugar, or chocolate. Cooked frostings need a bit more attention because you'll need to monitor the blend of sugar, cream, butter, and/or chocolate over heat. But they're just as easy to make as "quick" frostings.

Never cook frostings over high heat. For best results, only use very low heat, or a double boiler placed over simmering water, and follow the recipe carefully.

A good frosting has a smooth consistency and a silky appearance. The texture should be spreadable but not runny (unless it is a glaze). Here are some tips to help you get the consistency of your frosting just right:

✔ If the frosting you've made is too thick, add a few drops of milk or water to thin it. Just keep in mind that a small amount of liquid makes a big difference in consistency, so go slowly when adding milk or water.

✔ For the best flavor and most spreadable consistency, use butter or margarine when preparing frostings. However, there are exceptions to this rule (see Martha's Sweet and Creamy Frosting later in this chapter).

✔ Always let your butter soften to room temperature before creaming. Oherwise, your frosting will be lumpy.

✔ If the recipe calls for confectioners' sugar, sift it before incorporating it into the frosting. Even the tiniest lumps will give the frosting a grainy appearance.

Adding a pinch of baking soda to icings prevents hardening and cracking so the icing stays moist.

Knowing How Much to Make

How many times have you been halfway though frosting a cake when you realized that you were running out of frosting? Panic sets in, and you start scraping bits from here or there, spreading it out thinner in spots, or, in sheer moments of desperation, taking off the top layer of cake and scraping out the frosting center. Well, worry no more. Table 9-1 gives you some general guidelines for the amount of frosting you need to adequately cover your cakes. Also, all the frosting recipes give you ample amounts to frost a 9-inch layer cake, so you have no fear about running out. As a general rule, the fluffier the frosting, the more you'll need.

Table 9-1	Frosting Amounts for Various Cakes
Type of Cake	*Amount of Frosting Needed*
8-inch layer cake	2½ cups
9-inch layer cake	3 cups
Bundt, tube, or sheet cake	1 cup glaze; 3 cups frosting
16 large cupcakes	2 to 2½ cups

Making Quick Frostings

As your cake cools, you can put together any of these quick frostings. These frostings are of spreadable consistency, suitable to use as fillings for the cakes and also to frost the sides and tops of the cake. When you have finished applying the frosting, "finish" by using smooth back-and-forth strokes on the top. It will give the cake a nice, even look. Your goal when frosting a cake is apply all the frosting evenly.

Cream Cheese Frosting

This is your classic sweet, creamy frosting. Be sure to refrigerate the cake before using this frosting. Let the cake come to room temperature before serving.

Specialty tools: *an electric mixer*

Preparation time: *5 minutes*

Yield: *3 cups*

1½ packages (12 ounces) cream cheese, at room temperature

¼ cup (½ stick) butter, at room temperature

2½ cups confectioners' sugar

1 teaspoon vanilla extract

1 With an electric mixer, beat the cream cheese and butter together on medium speed until softened. Add the sugar gradually, ½ cup at a time, and beat until blended. Stop the mixer several times during this process to scrape down the sides of the bowl.

2 Mix in the vanilla. Cover and refrigerate if you aren't using it immediately.

Vary It! *Boost the flavor of this frosting with the addition of 1 teaspoon of grated lemon or orange rind.*

Per serving (1 tablespoon): Calories 54 (From Fat 31); Fat 3g (Saturated 2g); Cholesterol 10mg; Sodium 21mg; Carbohydrate 5g (Dietary Fiber 0g); Protein 1g.

Mocha Frosting

Chocolate and coffee combine with cream cheese to make a creamy, delicious frosting. This frosting goes well with a yellow cake (see it pictured on the cover of this book).

Specialty tools: *an electric mixer*

Preparation time: *8 minutes*

Yield: *3 cups*

1 package (8 ounces) cream cheese, at room temperature

4 ounces unsweetened chocolate, melted

¼ cup cold brewed coffee

2 teaspoons vanilla extract

3⅓ cups confectioners' sugar

1 Using an electric mixer, beat the cream cheese on medium speed until smooth. Beat in the melted chocolate, coffee, and vanilla.

2 Add the sugar gradually, ½ cup at a time, and beat until blended. Stop the mixer several times during this process to scrape down the sides of the bowl. Cover and refrigerate if you aren't using it immediately.

Per serving (1 tablespoon): Calories 56 (From Fat 27); Fat 3g (Saturated 2g); Cholesterol 5mg; Sodium 14mg; Carbohydrate 8g (Dietary Fiber 0g); Protein 1g.

Basic Vanilla Buttercream Frosting

This all-purpose buttercream frosting is smooth and sweet. It goes well with just about any cake you make. You can add many different flavors, including almond or lemon extract, or use sour cream instead of heavy cream.

Preparation time: _10 minutes_

Yield: _3 cups_

¾ cup (1½ sticks) butter, softened

5 to 6 cups confectioners' sugar

6 to 7 tablespoons heavy cream or milk, as needed

2 teaspoons vanilla extract

Pinch of salt

1 Cream the butter in a mixing bowl. Slowly beat in 2 cups of the sugar until smooth and creamy. Alternate adding the remaining sugar and the cream in batches, and beat until smooth and creamy, about 2 minutes.

2 Add the vanilla and salt and beat until smooth. Refrigerate the frosting if you're not using it immediately.

Vary It! _Beat in 4 to 6 ounces melted semisweet chocolate with the vanilla and salt if you want a chocolate buttercream frosting._

Per serving (1 tablespoon): _Calories 50 (From Fat 26); Fat 3g (Saturated 2g); Cholesterol 8mg; Sodium 1mg; Carbohydrate 6g (Dietary Fiber 0g); Protein 0g._

Trying Your Hand at Cooked Frostings

Yes, you have to turn on the stove briefly to make these frostings, but they are just as easy to make as the quick frostings and give you a little more variation. Many of these frostings are very sweet and creamy and well worth the extra effort you put into stirring, melting, and, finally, frosting. Start these frostings when your cake is baking. Then, both the frosting and the cake will be ready to use at about the same time.

Sweetened Whipped Cream Frosting

If you simply want to make sweetened whipped cream, see the tip at the end of this recipe.

Preparation time: *5 minutes*

Yield: *3 cups*

1 envelope unflavored gelatin

2 tablespoons cool water

2 cups heavy (whipping) cream

1 cup confectioners' sugar, or more to taste

1 teaspoon vanilla extract

1 Dissolve 1 envelope unflavored gelatin in 2 tablespoons cool water in a small saucepan.

2 Place the saucepan over very low heat and melt until warm. Allow the mixture to cool to lukewarm.

3 Beat the heavy cream with the sugar and vanilla until it begins to thicken. Stir in the gelatin mixture and continue beating until soft peaks form, about 3 minutes with an electric beater. Chill until ready to use, up to 24 hours. Refrigerate the cake once it's frosted.

Tip: *If you want Sweetened Whipped Cream, but you don't need to frost a cake, reduce the amount of cream to 1½ cups. Add the sugar and vanilla, and continue beating until soft peaks form. Do not overbeat, or you will end up with butter.*

Per serving (1 tablespoon): Calories 39 (From Fat 33); Fat 4g (Saturated 2g); Cholesterol 14mg; Sodium 4mg; Carbohydrate 1g (Dietary Fiber 0g); Protein 0g.

Chocolate Frosting

This frosting is really rich. For the best tasting frosting, invest in the highest-quality chocolate available.

Preparation time: *10 minutes*

Yield: *3 cups (enough for an 8- or 9-inch layer cake)*

1 pound semisweet chocolate or one 12-ounce bag semisweet mini chocolate chips	*¼ cup (½ stick) butter*
¾ cup heavy (whipping) cream	*1 tablespoon vanilla extract*

1 Cut the chocolate into small bits and place in a mixing bowl (if you're using chips, you can either chop them up or leave them whole).

2 Combine the cream and butter in a small saucepan and bring to a full boil over medium heat. Remove from the heat and pour it over the chocolate, mixing constantly. Add the vanilla and continue mixing until smooth.

3 Allow the frosting to thicken for about 1 hour in the refrigerator before frosting the cake. If you find the frosting has gotten too hard, just leave it out at room temperature until it softens.

Per serving (1 tablespoon): Calories 67 (From Fat 47); Fat 5g (Saturated 3g); Cholesterol 8mg; Sodium 3mg; Carbohydrate 6g (Dietary Fiber 1g); Protein 1g.

Martha's Sweet and Creamy Frosting

Martha (one of my best friends) says that this frosting is very sweet, and I do too. It requires a bit of time to make, but if you do it while the cake cools, by the time you're finished, the cake will be ready to be frosted.

Preparation time: *40 minutes*

Yield: *About 3 cups*

1 cup milk	*½ cup shortening*
5 tablespoons flour	*1 cup sugar*
½ cup butter, softened	*1 teaspoon vanilla extract*

1 Combine the milk and flour in a 1-quart saucepan and cook, whisking often, until thick and smooth, about 4 minutes. Cover and refrigerate until cool, about 20 minutes.

2 In a mixing bowl, beat together the butter, shortening, sugar, and vanilla until smooth and creamy, about 2 minutes. Add the chilled mixture and beat until creamy, about 10 minutes.

Per serving (1 tablespoon): *Calories 58 (From Fat 38); Fat 4g (Saturated 2g); Cholesterol 6mg; Sodium 3mg; Carbohydrate 5g (Dietary Fiber 0g); Protein 0g.*

Ready, Set, Frost!

Before you frost your cake, you must make sure that the cake has cooled completely. I learned this at a young age. I was so excited to frost my dad's birthday cake that I didn't let the cake cool much, despite my mom's warnings. I just slapped the frosting on the cake and watched as it melted into the cake and disappeared down the sides. I kept piling it on, thinking that eventually the cake would look like it should, but all I ended up with was an inedible birthday cake. So learn from my mistake and let your cake cool completely *before* you frost. Even if it is seems "almost" cool, it won't frost as nicely as if it were totally cool or even popped in the fridge overnight.

If you're frosting a layer cake, first inspect the cake layers carefully. You want the surfaces of both cakes to be as flat as possible, because you will have to balance one layer on top of the other.

A quick and easy solution for a flat surface is to place the bottom layer upside-down, so the rounded side is on the serving plate, leaving you with a perfectly flat frosting surface. The top layer will be placed rounded side up, so the two flat layers are together with the frosting in between.

You can also even out the layers by cutting the domed tops off the cakes. Hold a serrated knife parallel with the top of the cake and gently saw off the domed top, as shown in Figure 9-1. Do this at eye level to be sure you're cutting straight, to ensure a flat top.

Figure 9-1:
Evening
out a cake
layer.

Frosting a cake

Regardless of whether you're frosting a single cake or a multi-layer cake, the best utensil for frosting cakes is a thin, metal spatula with a rounded tip (see Chapter 3 for more on baking tools) or a firm but flexible plastic spatula.

To frost a layer cake, follow these simple steps:

1. **Spread between ½ cup and ¾ cup of frosting (depending on how heavily you like to frost your cake) on top of the bottom layer.**

   Be careful not to spread the frosting with hard strokes, the way you would if you were buttering bread. Using hard strokes will pick up crumbs on the cake's surface and mix it into the frosting, giving you an unevenly textured cake. Instead, gently use the spatula or knife to gently push the frosting where you want it to go. The frosting should be soft and creamy enough to do this easily. Make sure that when you frost a cake, your frosting is at room temperature or just above room temperature and is not too cold. If the frosting is still too stiff, thin it out with just a *few* drops of water or milk.

2. **Place the second layer on the first, cut or domed side up, and brush off any crumbs.**

3. **Frost the sides of the cake with another ½ cup of frosting, or to taste.**

   Begin with a thin layer of frosting to seal in any crumbs. Then, with smooth back-and-forth strokes, frost the sides.

4. **Spread frosting on the top last, using smooth gliding strokes across the cake (see Figure 9-2).**

Figure 9-2:
Spreading frosting on a cake, saving the top for last.

Apply a thin layer of frosting to the cake and then refrigerate until it's set before applying the final, heavier layer of frosting. This will seal in the crumbs, ensuring a clean final appearance.

Is your cake uneven or domed? You can use the frosting to cover up any imperfections in the top of your cake — just spread it a little thicker than on the sides and make it as level as you can.

If you want to frost your cake on the same plate you will be serving it on, but you don't want to dirty up the serving plate as you frost, place narrow strips of waxed paper just around the edge of the plate (not covering the plate entirely). Place the cooled cake layer in the center of the serving plate, so that the edges of the cake overlap the waxed paper strips just a bit. After your cake is frosted, gently pull out the waxed paper strips from underneath the edges of the cake (you might have to give them a gentle tug). Any frosting on the strips will gently slide onto the frosted cake, leaving you with a perfectly clean serving plate.

If you need to refrigerate or store your cake before serving, cover it with either a cake dome or an inverted mixing bowl. Make sure that the bowl is big enough that, when you place it over the cake, it doesn't touch the cake. You don't want to remove the bowl, only to find that your lovely cake has been smashed.

Glazing a cake

Glazing a cake requires a slightly different technique because the glaze is runny, not smooth and spreadable the way frosting is. One cup of glaze is sufficient for one Bundt, tube, or angel cake.

Quick Apricot Glaze

This glaze is delicious over pound cake, angel food cake, or sponge cake. It's also good to use for cake layers if you baked them too long and want to add some moisture back to them.

Preparation time: *7 minutes*

Yield: *1 scant cup glaze*

1 cup all-fruit apricot preserves

Place the preserves in a small saucepan over medium heat. Stir until melted. Cook and stir for about 2 minutes longer, until the fruit is boiling and slightly thickened. It should coat the back of a spoon. Cool slightly and brush over your cake or use as directed. Chill the cake to set the glaze.

Per serving (1 tablespoon): *Calories 48 (From Fat 0); Fat 0g (Saturated 0g); Cholesterol 0mg; Sodium 8mg; Carbohydrate 13g (Dietary Fiber 0g); Protein 0g.*

Classic Sugar Glaze

You can drizzle this mixture over the sides of sponge cakes or over baked sweet breads, quick breads, and coffee cakes.

Preparation time: *5 minutes*

Yield: *About ⅓ cup*

½ cup confectioners' sugar

2 to 3 teaspoons milk, warmed

¼ teaspoon vanilla extract

Combine the ingredients and stir until smooth. Add more milk to thin, if desired.

Vary It! *For a chocolate glaze, melt 4 ounces of semisweet chocolate, cut up or chips, and 3 tablespoons butter over low heat, stirring frequently. Remove from heat and stir in 1½ cups sifted powdered sugar and 3 tablespoons of hot water. Drizzle over cake.*

Per serving (1 tablespoon): *Calories 20 (From Fat 0); Fat 0g (Saturated 0g); Cholesterol 0mg; Sodium 1mg; Carbohydrate 5g (Dietary Fiber 0g); Protein 0g.*

Calling all cake rounds!

Cake rounds are a busy baker's dream. These thick cardboard circles are available in most kitchen-supply stores in a variety of sizes. They hold your cake layers while you're frosting and transporting them from your work area to refrigerator to serving plate. If you can't find cake rounds, just trace a circle, using your cake pan as a size guide, on any heavy, corrugated cardboard and cut it out. Cover your cake rounds with aluminum foil, and they become reusable.

Begin the glazing process by positioning the completely cooled cake on a wire rack over aluminum foil or a baking sheet (to catch the drips). Then follow these steps:

1. **Spoon or pour the glaze, a little at a time, over the top of the cake.**

2. **With a metal spatula or the back of a spoon, spread the glaze into thin areas and to the edge of the cake, allowing some to drizzle over the side.**

3. **Continue spreading the glaze until the cake is well coated and the desired look is achieved.**

Stop spreading the glaze once it begins to set. Otherwise, the smooth finish will be lost. (Don't panic, though. You'll have several minutes before the glaze sets.)

After the glaze is set, carefully transfer the cake to a serving plate. If possible, allow the glazed cake to sit for at least 30 minutes to allow the glaze to set. If it is more than four hours before serving time, cover and refrigerate the cake.

Getting Fancy with a Decorating Bag

Some occasions require slightly fancier cakes. If you want to go beyond frosting and add a decorative frosting pattern, use a decorating bag with different tips to achieve the effect. *Decorating bags,* also called *pastry bags,* are plastic-coated reusable nylon bags. You stuff the frosting into the bag and then squeeze it out again. The tip you select will give you the design you want — a scalloped edge, or a thin line, or maybe a leaf petal.

Pastry bags come in two varieties:

- Ones in which the tip is dropped through the bag and comes out the narrow end

- Ones in which a tube (called a *coupler*) is inserted, and the tips screw on the outside of the narrow end

If you want to purchase a decorating bag, I recommend the second variety (the coupler assembly). With the coupler, you can change the tips (which are usually included in the purchase of the bag) without having to empty the bag of the frosting. With the drop-in tips, you're committed to the tip you have inserted in the bag. If you need to change tips, you have to empty out the frosting, wash the bag, and then reinsert the new tip (unless you purchase several bags) — all of which can become very messy.

Pastry bags come in many sizes; for all-purpose use, get a 16-inch bag. If you're not sure what size you want, remember that a bigger bag is a better choice than a smaller one.

Another type of decorating tool is a metal syringe-type tube. Although this tool is fine for writing (like when you want to write "Happy Birthday" on your cake), I think pastry bags give you more control over the amount of frosting you use and how you decorate.

 When you're planning on decorating your cake, pop the frosted cake in the freezer or refrigerator for several hours to allow the frosting to harden. Then, if you make a mistake while you're decorating, the decoration will be easy to lift off the hardened frosting and you can start all over again without having ruined the frosted cake.

Frostings for decorating

You can use any of the frostings in this book for decorating. If you want to do fancy designs, look for a thicker frosting that will hold its shape for a while. Most people use the same frosting they used to frost the cake when decorating. If you know that you want to decorate, double the recipe or just make 1½ times the recipe to ensure that you'll have enough for decorations on the cake. If you want to add a color to the frosting, choose a vanilla-base frosting so that the color will show.

Tinting frosting

Tinting frosting is not difficult. The best idea is to choose a vanilla buttercream or basic frosting to color. You can tint frosting in one of two ways: with food coloring or with coloring paste, available at baking-supply shops. For all practical purposes, food coloring is the less expensive way to color frosting, but the paste will last a lifetime (that's no exaggeration).

✔ To use food coloring, drop several (no more than five) drops into the frosting you plan on using. Mix thoroughly. Add two additional drops at a time until the desired color is achieved.

✔ To use a coloring paste, dip the tip of a toothpick into the color and add to the frosting you plan on using. Mix thoroughly. Dip the toothpick a second time, if necessary. Coloring paste is *highly* concentrated, so a very little bit goes a long way. Make sure that you mix the frosting to a uniform color and that there aren't any heavy color streaks.

Be *very* careful when using paste food coloring. A very tiny amount will vividly color your frosting. Dip the tip of a toothpick into the paste and then dip that into the frosting. That tiny amount is usually just the right amount of color you'll need for a large bag of frosting. Remember that, as the frosting hardens, the colors will darken. To color frosting, you can use liquid food coloring or paste food coloring, which is available in a baking-supply store.

Choosing a tip

The type of tip you choose determines the decoration you make (see Figure 9-3). Hundreds of tips are available for cake decorating.

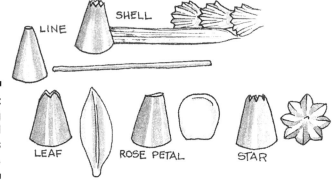

Figure 9-3:
Decorating tips and the designs they make.

The most important thing is to make sure that your tip fits your bag — they come in a variety of sizes for a variety of bags. Then choose the correct tip for the decoration you want to create. The following list presents five of the most popular styles of tips available:

✔ **Drop flower tips:** These tips make the easiest flowers for the beginning cake decorator. The icing is dropped directly onto the cake, either just dropped on or swirled to make it look like a flower. Popular sizes include 107, 129, 190, 217, and 255.

✔ **Leaf tips:** The V-shaped opening in these tips forms the pointed end of the leaf. Leaf tips can make plain, ruffled, or even stand-up leaves. String the leaves together to make an attractive border. Popular sizes include 65, 67, and 352.

✔ **Petal tips:** These tips are for a more-advanced decorator and are used in making roses, violets, carnations, and other flower shapes. You can also use them to make ribbons, bows, swags, and ruffles. Popular sizes include 101, 102, 103, and 104.

✔ **Star tips:** If you were going to get just one decorative tip, I would recommend buying a star tip. This tip enables you to make rosettes, drop flowers, stars, scalloped borders, rope borders, and shells. Popular sizes range between 13 and 22; the larger sizes include 32 and 43.

✔ **Writing tips:** Writing tips are plain, round tips. In addition to writing, you can also make polka dots, stems, vines, or just smooth lines for decoration. They're quite handy to have for decoration. Popular sizes include 1–4 (small), 5–12 (medium), and 1A and 2A (large).

Filling your bag

To fill your decorating bag, place the empty bag (already with the tip in place) in a tall, narrow glass, as shown in Figure 9-4. Fold back about 5 inches of a cuff over the sides of the glass. Using a spatula, fill the decorating bag no more than halfway full with icing. If you fill the bag more than halfway full, the frosting may back up out of the bag. To close the bag, unfold the cuff and gently press all the frosting down toward the tip (don't press so hard that frosting starts to come out the end, though). You just want to get the air pockets out of the bag. When the frosting is pressed down, twist the top of the bag (see Figure 9-4). Continue twisting the end of the bag, being careful not to squeeze it as if it were a tube of toothpaste.

Using your pastry bag

The amount of pressure on the decorating bag, the size of the tip, and the consistency of the icing will determine the amount of icing flowing out of the bag. By increasing the pressure and moving the bag slowly, you can increase the size of the line being piped out. If you don't have a pastry bag, you can make one. See Figure 9-5 to find out how.

Practice your decorations on waxed paper before decorating the cake. This will help you determine the type of decoration you will be making. If your tip gets clogged while you're frosting, give the bag a little extra squeeze over a piece of waxed paper. Avoid doing this over the cake — otherwise you may end up with a big splotch of icing where you don't want it to be. If this doesn't unclog the bag, take a toothpick and poke it into the tip to release the blockage.

Figure 9-4:
Filling and
using a
pastry bag.

FILLING...

.... AND USING A
PASTRY BAG

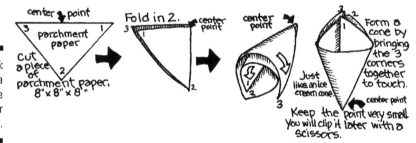

Making a Paper Cone for Decorating

Figure 9-5:
Making a
paper cone
for
decorating.

center point

parchment paper

Cut a piece of parchment paper, 8" x 8" x 8"

Fold in 2.

center point

center point

Just like an ice cream cone.

Form a cone by bringing the 3 corners together to touch.

center point

Keep the point very small. You will clip it later with a scissors.

A turntable or lazy Susan is a cake decorator's best friend. It makes frosting and decorating cakes easier and faster.

Most designs are made by holding the decorating bag at a 45-degree angle to the surface of the cake. Support the bottom of the bag with one hand, and twist the top with the other. Always begin with just a slight twisting pressure on the bag. Don't jerk the bag around too much. Instead, let the frosting just glide out and fall onto the cake.

Before making your design, lightly outline it with a toothpick. If you want to write a message on your cake, you can gently place small strips of sewing thread or dental floss on top of the cake to serve as a straight line on which to write (and then remove them when you're done).

If you make a mistake while decorating, don't panic. Everyone has messed up decorating a cake. The easiest thing to do is to get a metal frosting spatula with a rounded tip and gently lift off the mistake and scrape away any additional coloring. With the tip of the spatula, gently smooth out the area and start over again.

After decorating the cake, clean the tips well in hot, soapy water. Pick out the icing in the hard-to-clean cracks with a toothpick. Always wash your pastry bag and tips by hand. A dishwasher will send your tips flying, and they may become crushed, ruining the delicate tips forever.

If you aren't feeling adventurous enough to try using a decorative bag, see the section on garnishes in Chapter 18 to find ways to add some pizzazz to your cakes without adding stress to your life.

Chapter 10

Perfect Pies and Tarts

In This Chapter

▶ Perfecting a flaky piecrust

▶ Getting ideas for top crust pies

▶ Making decorative crusts

▶ Fixing what went wrong

*E*veryone loves pies, and nothing is more American than a warm pie cooling on the windowsill. Whether that pie is filled with sweet summertime berries, hearty slices of tart apples, or thick pureed pumpkin kissed with brown sugar and cinnamon, pies are satisfying fare. Despite their love of pies, most people shudder at the thought of making the crusts that hold those delectable fillings. Often, they turn to frozen or refrigerated piecrusts to make their baking fuss-free, despite the fact those types of crusts can sometimes be flavorless and thin. But fret no more. In just a few easy steps, you'll have the confidence to make your own dough for incredibly flaky crust.

Pie doughs have simple ingredients: flour, fat (either butter or shortening), and a liquid (either water or milk) to bring everything together. The technique is what you have to master if you want tender, flaky crusts. The best method to achieve perfect pie dough is practice, practice, practice. Before long, you'll wonder why you ever hesitated to make your own.

Picking the Proper Pie Plate

When choosing your pie plate, be sure to use heat-resistant glass or dull-finished metal pie plates for good browning. Never use a shiny pan, because the pan reflects heat, and the pie will have a soggy bottom crust.

Be careful if you choose to use a nonstick pie plate. The Teflon coating doesn't hold the dough in place while it cooks (and the dough contracts), so if your crust isn't secured over the edge of the pie plate, your dough may shrink up quite a bit in the oven.

The most common pie size is 9 inches. Even though pie plates say that they are 9 inches, they can vary dramatically in the amount of filling they can hold. Make sure that your pie plate can hold the amount of filling that's called for. Keep in mind that fruit fillings shrink as they bake, so be generous.

Because crusts have plenty of butter or shortening in them, don't grease the pie plate.

Making Perfect Piecrusts

Making a piecrust doesn't involve many steps. You begin with flour, maybe add a pinch of salt, cut in the butter or shortening, and then add a few drops of water and chill (not you, the dough). By cutting in the butter or shortening, you create little bits of fat mixed in with the flour and held together with water. When you roll out the dough, you'll flatten the butter even more. But when you bake the crust, the butter will melt into the flour, flavoring the flour and leaving behind little pockets where it had once been. And that is how a flaky piecrust is made.

Mixing the dough

Knowing that the butter or shortening melting into the dough and leaving little air pockets gives you a flaky crust, you can understand why overmixing the dough is so bad for a piecrust. It will incorporate the butter into the flour too much, and you won't have little pockets of butter left before the oven has a chance to melt it. Kneading the flour too much also forms gluten, which toughens the dough. If you haven't heard it before, you will hear it now: The secret to flaky piecrusts is less, not more, handling.

Cutting in the fat

Another challenge when making piecrusts is the butter. If you use your fingers to incorporate the butter into the flour, you run the risk of melting it (butter melts at 95 degrees, and your body temp is 98.6 degrees). A pastry blender (see Chapter 3) is a great help in cutting shortening evenly into the flour. If you don't have one, you can also use two knives, cutting parallel with one another, to cut in the butter. Another option is a fork. (See Chapter 5 for tips on cutting fat into flour mixtures.)

No matter which method you use, make sure that your butter is well chilled. You can even cut it into small pieces and toss it in the freezer for a few minutes before you add it to the flour if you like.

Many bakers swear by shortening for a flaky crust. It doesn't melt at the low temperature that butter does, and it's easier to cut into the flour, resulting in less handling of the dough. But I find that shortening falls short when it comes to flavor. If the filling has good flavor, however, it can compensate for lack of flavor in the crust. You can do a mix of half butter and half shortening for the qualities of shortening and the flavor of butter.

The technique I like best for cutting in the fat is the food processor. I chill the metal blade and precut my butter into 10 to 12 pieces before adding it to the flour. After just a few quick pulses (on-and-off blasts — never let it run on the On position), my butter is incorporated into the flour, and I haven't touched a thing. I like to add the water by hand, though. I find the food processor overworks the dough when I use it.

Choosing the right flour

Very little gluten is necessary to hold a piecrust together. The flours with the least gluten are cake flours and Southern flours, such as White Lily brand. You also can find pastry flour, which is low in protein and great for tender crusts. In the bulk section of my whole-foods grocery store, I can purchase whole-wheat pastry flour, so I blend that with cake flour for some of my crusts.

There are advantages to using all-purpose flour — the piecrust will shrink less. Also, Shirley O. Corriher, the doyen of kitchen science, recommends 2 parts all-purpose flour to 1 part cake or instant flour (Wondra or Shake and Blend) for tender crusts. Without a doubt, she knows what she's talking about, so you may want to try that combination if you have the right flours on hand.

Chilling the dough

Chilling the dough is another important step in preparing pie pastry. After the butter or shortening is cut in, the dough needs to return to the refrigerator, well wrapped, for about an hour so the butter can re-harden and the dough can relax, making it easier to handle. If you have made dough for a double-crust pie, split it in half and flatten the halves into disks. Wrap tightly in plastic wrap and then refrigerate. Skimping on this step could have undesirable effects on your finished pastry, so plan accordingly. Pie dough will keep in the refrigerator for up to one week or in the freezer for up to one month. Let the dough come to room temperature before rolling it out.

Before baking the pies, be sure that you've preheated your oven. The initial contrast in temperature aids in the flakiness of your dough.

Rolling out the dough

After you've chilled your dough, let it sit at room temperature for 5 to 10 minutes before you roll it out to take the chill off. It will roll better if it isn't too cold, but don't let it get too warm, either. Pastry cloths, kitchen towels (not terrycloth), and a *rolling stocking* (a mesh or cloth casing that you slip over the rolling pin and gently rub with flour) are wonderful tools to have on hand because they practically eliminate sticking, and you need only a minimum of additional flour. Rubbing flour into your rolling pin and onto your work surface also works fine — just don't use too much. Two tablespoons of additional flour is all you should need. The work surface I like best is a large wooden board, at least 12 x 12 inches. It's flat and hard and gives me plenty of room to spread out.

Instead of using just flour for dusting the work surface when rolling out pastry for sweet pies, use a combination of sugar and flour. The sugar acts like little grains of sand and isn't as easily absorbed into the dough as the flour is. It's a marvelous trick to keep pastry dough from sticking to the work surface, and it won't toughen the dough.

To roll out your piecrust, follow these simple steps:

1. **Begin rolling from the center of the dough outward, lifting and turning the pastry occasionally to make sure the dough isn't sticking.**

   Don't roll the dough from the outside to the center or push the rolling pin back and forth, and don't press down hard when rolling out the dough. Just let the weight of the rolling pin supply all the necessary pressure.

2. **Roll the dough out to ⅛-inch thick or less.**

   It should be at least 2 inches larger than the pie dimensions (if you have a 9-inch pie plate, the dough should be 11 inches in diameter).

   If the dough rips while you're rolling it, don't worry. You can repair it by pressing the two torn sides together. Don't ball it back up and re-roll it. Instead, moisten the edges of the torn pastry and gently press them back together again. If you re-roll the dough, you'll overwork and toughen it.

   If the dough begins to stick, rub more flour into the work surface or rolling pin.

Transferring the crust to the pie plate

After you roll out the crust to the right size, the next step is to delicately transfer it into the pie plate. Doing so is not difficult, but you want to make sure that the pastry doesn't tear. Here are foolproof steps to prevent that from happening:

1. **Gently loosen the pastry from the work surface and fold the pastry in half.**

2. **Place the pie plate right next to the pastry, gently slide the folded pastry into the pie plate, and carefully unfold it.**

   See Figure 10-1. Ease the dough gently into the pie plate and press it against the side of the pie plate so that no air is left between the dough and the plate, which can cause the crust to blister while baking.

Figure 10-1:
Sliding the pastry into the pie plate.

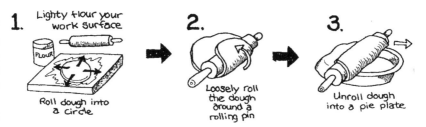

3. **Trim off the excess crust with a knife or kitchen shears and crimp the edges with your fingers, as shown in Figure 10-2.**

Figure 10-2:
Crimping around the edges.

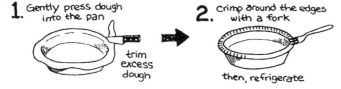

See the section "Making Simple Pastry Edges and Decorations" later in this chapter for more ideas for crimping your crusts.

For juicy fruit pies, brush the bottom unbaked crust with a beaten egg white or melted butter before filling it to prevent the crust from becoming soggy.

Don't prick the bottom crust with a fork if you're filling it with a fruit or custard filling. The liquid filling will make the crust soggy if there are holes in the crust.

Old-Fashioned Pie Dough

This recipe uses a combination of butter and shortening for a buttery flavor and a flaky crust. Use sour cream instead of water for added tenderness.

Preparation time: *15 minutes, plus 2 hours for chilling*

Yield: *One 8- or 9-inch double crust*

2½ cups flour

½ tablespoon sugar

1 teaspoon salt (optional)

½ cup (1 stick) cold unsalted butter, cut into ½-inch pieces

½ cup shortening, chilled and cut into ½-inch pieces

1 egg, beaten

2 tablespoons ice water or sour cream, if necessary

1 In a large bowl, using a pastry blender, combine the flour, sugar, and salt (if desired). Using your fingertips or pastry blender, cut the better and shortening into the flour mixture until it resembles coarse meal. (You will see a few larger or smaller pieces.)

2 Combine the beaten egg and cold water in a small bowl. While stirring lightly with a fork, pour the egg and water into the flour mixture in a fast, steady stream. Continue stirring, occasionally cleaning off the dough that collects on the fork, until the flour is almost completely mixed in but the dough does not form a ball.

3 Empty the dough onto a flat work surface. Pat and shape the dough into a 6-inch disk. Many tiny flecks of butter should be visible.

4 Wrap the dough tightly in plastic wrap or waxed paper and refrigerate it for at least 2 hours or overnight. When you're ready to use it, divide the disk in half and roll each half into an evenly rounded 13-inch circle.

Per serving: Calories 370 (From Fat 228); Fat 25g (Saturated 11g); Cholesterol 58mg; Sodium 10mg; Carbohydrate 31g (Dietary Fiber 1g); Protein 5g.

Stir-and-Roll Pie Pastry

This is another piecrust variation. The texture will be slightly denser and less flaky than a traditional piecrust because you're using oil instead of butter or shortening. One advantage to this crust is that you don't have to let the dough chill before rolling it out and using it. As with all piecrusts, don't overhandle the dough.

Preparation time: *20 minutes*

Yield: *One 8- or 9-inch piecrust*

1½ cups flour

½ teaspoon salt

½ cup vegetable oil

3 tablespoons cold milk or water

1 Mix together the flour and salt in a medium-sized bowl.

2 Pour the oil and milk into a mixing bowl and whisk until frothy. Pour all the liquid at once into the flour. Stir lightly with a fork until mixed and a dough is formed. Gently press the dough together to make a ball.

3 When you're ready to use it, roll out the dough between 2 sheets of waxed paper. Press the dough into an 8- or 9-inch pie pan. Flute the edges and prick thoroughly with a fork.

Vary It! *For a prebaked crust: Preheat the oven to 425 degrees. Bake the crust for 8 to 10 minutes.*

Per serving: Calories 168 (From Fat 85); Fat 9g (Saturated 1g); Cholesterol 1mg; Sodium 148mg; Carbohydrate 18g (Dietary Fiber 1g); Protein 3g.

Prebaking piecrusts

If the pie shell is to be baked without filling, prick the dough all over with a fork. To prevent the pie shell from puffing up and blistering while it bakes, place a sheet of aluminum foil or waxed paper on top of the unbaked piecrust and weigh it down with rice, dried beans, or pie weights (see Chapter 3). Then bake according to the recipe. Remove the weights from the pie shell a few minutes before the baking time is finished so that the bottom will brown a bit.

Getting Double-Crust Pie Ideas

If you're preparing a pie with a top crust, roll out the top crust as directed earlier in this chapter. You can choose from a variety of top crusts.

Solid top crust

Fold the crust in half and make several cuts along the fold, about 1 inch apart. Doing so allows steam to escape while the pie bakes. Gently transfer the folded crust to the pie plate, unfold the crust on top of the filled pie, and trim the top crust to have a 1-inch overhang. Gently press the top crust over the filling, tuck the extra top crust under the bottom crust, and seal the edges.

Lattice crust

Cut ten to fourteen ½-inch strips from the top crust pastry. Place five to seven strips on the filling, about ¾ inch apart. Fold back every other strip halfway and place a strip perpendicular over the unfolded strips. Unfold the strip. Fold back the alternate strips and place another strip ¾ inch from the first. Repeat until you've used up all the strips. (See Figure 10-3 for illustrated instructions.)

A LATTICE CRUST PIE

1. CUT 10 TO 14 ½" STRIPS FROM THE TOP CRUST PASTRY. FOLD BACK EVERY OTHER STRIP HALFWAY AND PLACE A PERPENDICULAR STRIP OVER THE UNFOLDED STRIPS.

2. UNFOLD THE STRIP FOLD BACK THE ALTERNATE STRIPS AND PLACE ANOTHER STRIP ¾" APART FROM THE FIRST.

Figure 10-3:
Making a
lattice crust.

REPEAT UNTIL ALL OF THE STRIPS ARE USED UP *!*

When the whole pie is latticed, attach the strips loosely to the pie edge by moistening the ends and pressing down slightly into the bottom crust edge. Be careful not to pull the strips taut; allow for some shrinkage during baking. Cut off any excess from the strips and seal the edges.

For an easy lattice top, place five to seven strips over the filling, about ¾ inch apart. Turn the pie plate a quarter turn and place the remaining strips at right angles to the first set of strips, about ¾ inch apart. Do not weave the strips.

Cutout top crust

Use a small cookie cutter (no bigger than 1 inch across) to make a cutout pattern in the top crust. Work from the center of the pastry to within 1 inch of the pastry edge (make sure that the pastry is not sticking to the work surface). Gently roll the cutout pastry onto a floured rolling pin and carefully transfer the cutout top over the pie filling. By gently rolling the cutout pastry onto the rolling pin, there's less chance of it ripping while you're transferring the pastry.

Alternatively, you can cover your pie filling with the cutout shapes. A larger cookie cutter works well for this technique. Place the cutout shapes close together over the filling and flute the edges of the bottom pastry. Figure 10-4 shows you how.

Figure 10-4: Making a cutout top crust.

Making Simple Pastry Edges and Decorations

To *flute* (or seal) the edges of the crust means to squeeze the edges of the pastry to make a finished, decorative edge. You want a good seal between the two crusts so that all the pie filling remains inside the pie and doesn't leak out. You can get a good seal in several ways:

✔ **Pinch edge:** This is the classic pie edge decoration. Place your index finger on the outside of the pastry and pinch the thumb and index finger of your other hand to form a *V* shape on the inside of the pastry. Push the pastry into the *V* shape with your index finger, along the entire edge. After you're finished, go around and pinch again to sharpen the edges. When the crusts bakes, the *V* shapes will relax, so you want them as sharp as possible.

✔ **Fork edge:** This edge is the best for beginner bakers. Just flatten the pastry evenly along the rim of the plate with the tines of a fork. To prevent the fork from sticking to the pastry, dip it lightly in flour.

✔ **Cutout edge:** Trim the overhang to the rim of the pie plate. With a tiny cookie cutter, thimble, or bottle cap, cut out decorations from the scraps of pastry. Moisten the edge of the pastry and the bottoms of the cutouts with water and press them into place.

✔ **Twisted edge:** Trim the overhang to the rim of the pie plate. Twist two ¼-inch strips around each other, making the twist long enough to fit around the edge of the plate. Moisten the rim of the pie plate and the bottom of the twist and gently lay it on top. Press it lightly into place. Alternatively, you can loosely braid three ¼-inch strips and lay the braid around the edge.

Creating Tantalizing Pies and Tarts

Baking fresh, flavorful pies and tarts is easier than you imagined. Would you like a slice of classic apple and blueberry pie or luscious banana cream pie? The tempting possibilities go on and on. Remember, practice makes perfect. These recipes will keep you practicing quite a bit.

Fruit and nut pies

Of all the pies out there, fruit pies have to be people's favorites. People love it when fresh pie — juicy, ripe fruits wrapped in a flaky crust — is on the menu. Cherries and berries of any type make a good pie (except strawberries, which don't hold up very well when they're baked). Feel free to mix and match fruits in these recipes. Beyond fruits, pecans also make a great filling for pies, so try your hand at that tasty recipe, too.

Pumpkin Pie

Don't save this delicious pie until Thanksgiving. This pumpkin mixture, laced with cinnamon and ginger, is smooth, creamy, and delicately spiced. Top each slice with a dollop of whipped cream.

Preparation time: *10 minutes*

Baking time: *35 to 45 minutes*

Yield: *One 9-inch pie*

¾ cup light brown sugar, firmly packed	1 teaspoon vanilla extract
½ teaspoon salt	2 eggs
1 teaspoon cinnamon	1 can (15 ounces) pumpkin (not pie filling)
½ teaspoon ground ginger	1 can (12 ounces) evaporated milk
¼ teaspoon ground cloves	1 unbaked 9-inch piecrust

1 Preheat the oven to 375 degrees.

2 Combine all the ingredients (except the piecrust) in a large mixing bowl and blend until smooth.

3 Pour the mixture into the unbaked piecrust and bake until a toothpick inserted into the center comes out clean, 35 to 45 minutes. Cool the pie before serving or refrigerate until ready to serve.

Per serving: Calories 162 (From Fat 52); Fat 6g (Saturated 2g); Cholesterol 45mg; Sodium 206mg; Carbohydrate 24g (Dietary Fiber 2g); Protein 4g.

You'll-Be-Glad-You-Tried-It Apple Pie

The best apple pies are those with just a hint of spice. Check out your local farmers' market or vegetable stand to get a good variety of apples, which will perk up the flavor of any pie. Keep your eyes peeled for varieties like Cortland, Macoun, Ida Red, Stayman, Mutzu, and Gravenstein. Golden Delicious and Granny Smiths are fine, too. Don't use Red Delicious apples, though — they're good for eating but turn to mush if you bake with them.

Preparation time: *30 minutes*

Baking time: *40 to 50 minutes*

Yield: *One 9-inch pie*

Pastry for a 2-crust pie (either recipe in this chapter)

8 cups peeled, sliced apples (about 3½ pounds)

Juice of 1 lemon (about 1 tablespoon)

¼ cup light brown sugar, firmly packed

⅓ cup sugar

3 tablespoons flour

1 teaspoon ground cinnamon

½ teaspoon ground nutmeg

1 teaspoon vanilla extract

2 tablespoons cold butter, cut into little pieces

1 Preheat the oven to 425 degrees. Prepare the pastry for a 9-inch pie plate and line the plate with half the dough, leaving a ½-inch overhang.

2 In a large bowl, toss the apples with the lemon juice. Add the sugars, flour, cinnamon, nutmeg, and vanilla and toss to coat all the apples. Place the apples in the pie plate and scatter the butter pieces over the top of the apples.

3 Roll out the top pastry and carefully lay it over the apples. Pat the pastry over the apples. Fold the edges of the bottom pastry over the top pastry and crimp the edges of the pastry. Cut six to eight slits in the top crust for vents.

4 Place a piece of aluminum foil on a baking sheet (to catch any drips). Place the pie on top of the foil and bake for 40 to 50 minutes, until the crust is golden brown and juice bubbles through the slits in the top crust. Cool the pie on a wire rack before serving.

Per serving: Calories 352 (From Fat 172); Fat 19g (Saturated 8g); Cholesterol 44mg; Sodium 9mg; Carbohydrate 43g (Dietary Fiber 2g); Protein 4g.

Blueberry Pie

Blueberries are in season during the month of July and into August. Get some fresh blueberries when they're in season and put them in your freezer so that you can make fresh blueberry pie in the fall.

Preparation time: *30 minutes*

Baking time: *30 to 40 minutes*

Yield: *One 9-inch pie*

Pastry for a 2-crust pie (either recipe in this chapter)

½ cup sugar

¼ cup flour

½ teaspoon ground cinnamon

¼ teaspoon ground nutmeg

6 cups fresh or frozen blueberries (do not thaw the frozen berries)

1 tablespoon lemon juice

1 tablespoon cold butter, cut into 4 pieces

1 Preheat the oven to 425 degrees. Prepare the pastry for a 9-inch pie plate and line the pie plate with half the dough, leaving a ½-inch overhang.

2 In a large bowl, toss together the sugar, flour, cinnamon, and nutmeg. Add the blueberries and lemon juice and mix to coat. Place the blueberry mixture in the pie plate and scatter the butter pieces over the berries.

3 Roll out the top pastry and carefully lay it over the blueberries. Pat the pastry over the blueberries. Fold the edges of the bottom pastry over the top pastry and crimp the edges of the pastry. Cut 6 to 8 slits in the top crust for vents.

4 Place a piece of aluminum foil on a baking sheet. Place the pie on the foil and bake for 30 to 40 minutes, until the crust is golden brown and juice bubbles through the slits in the top crust. Transfer the pie from the baking sheet to a wire rack to cool.

Per serving: Calories 338 (From Fat 164); Fat 18g (Saturated 8g); Cholesterol 41mg; Sodium 12mg; Carbohydrate 41g (Dietary Fiber 3g); Protein 4g.

Cherry Crumb Pie

Sour cherries combined with a sweet crumb topping make this recipe one of my favorites. It's easy to make and a huge crowd pleaser. Make it in the height of summer when sour cherries are bountiful.

Preparation time: *25 minutes*

Baking time: *40 to 50 minutes*

Yield: *One 9-inch pie*

Pastry for a 9-inch pie (either recipe in this chapter)

¼ cup sugar

¼ cup instant tapioca

6 cups pitted fresh or canned, drained sour cherries

½ teaspoon almond extract

2 tablespoons cold butter, cut into small pieces

Topping:

1 cup flour

¾ cup sugar

½ cup (1 stick) cold unsalted butter, cut into small pieces

½ cup ground almonds

1 Preheat the oven to 400 degrees. Prepare the pastry for a 9-inch pie plate and line the pie plate with half the dough, leaving a 1-inch overhang. Crimp the edges of the piecrust.

2 Toss the sugar, tapioca, cherries, and almond extract to combine. Place the cherry mixture in the pie plate. Scatter the butter pieces over the cherries.

3 Combine all the topping ingredients and blend so that the mixture resembles coarse crumbs (you can do this in a food processor if you want to). Scatter the topping over the cherries.

4 Place a piece of aluminum foil on a baking sheet. Place the pie on the foil and bake for 40 to 50 minutes, until the crust is golden brown and juice bubbles through the top. Cool on a wire rack before serving.

Vary It! *If you don't want the crumb topping, you can make a double crust instead.*

Per serving: *Calories 429 (From Fat 199); Fat 22g (Saturated 7g); Cholesterol 26mg; Sodium 101mg; Carbohydrate 54g (Dietary Fiber 4g); Protein 6g.*

Pecan Pie

Pecan pie is a great Southern tradition. The pecan is one of the few ingredients indigenous to America (blueberries, Concord grapes, and cranberries are a few others). Make this pie to serve at your next barbecue or cookout. Be sure to purchase fresh pecans for this pie.

Preparation time: *20 minutes*

Baking time: *45 minutes*

Yield: *One 9-inch pie*

Pastry for a 9-inch pie (either recipe in this chapter)

3 eggs, separated

½ cup light brown sugar, firmly packed

1 teaspoon vanilla extract

1 cup light corn syrup

1 cup pecans

2 tablespoons butter, softened

2 teaspoons cornstarch or flour

1 Preheat the oven to 350 degrees. Prepare the pastry for a 9-inch pie plate and line the pie plate, leaving a 1-inch overhang. Crimp the edges of the piecrust.

2 In a medium-sized mixing bowl, beat together the egg yolks, brown sugar, and vanilla. Add the corn syrup, pecans, butter, and cornstarch and stir to combine.

3 In a separate bowl with clean, dry beaters, beat the egg whites to stiff peaks. Fold the stiffly beaten egg whites into the egg yolk mixture. Pour the mixture into the unbaked pie shell and place the pie on a baking sheet. Bake for 45 minutes. Cool the pie on a wire rack before serving.

Per serving: Calories 389 (From Fat 172); Fat 19g (Saturated 3g); Cholesterol 71mg; Sodium 182mg; Carbohydrate 53g (Dietary Fiber 2g); Protein 5g.

Cream pies

Cream pie filling is airy and delicate, surrounded by a tender crust. You get a mouthful of goodness when you eat a chocolate cream or luscious banana cream pie. Great for summer, these two chilled desserts are perfect endings to hot summer days.

Chocolate Cream Pie

The sweet flavor of chocolate is particularly satisfying after a rich meal. The only baking this pie requires is the 15 minutes it takes to prebake the crust, making it a great pie to make in the summertime when you don't want to heat up the kitchen. This pie needs to be refrigerated, so it's not a good choice for picnics.

Preparation time: *25 minutes, plus 1½ hours for chilling*

Baking time: *15 minutes (for the pie shell)*

Yield: *One 9-inch pie*

¼ cup cornstarch	3 egg yolks
1 cup sugar	2 tablespoons butter
¼ teaspoon salt	½ teaspoon vanilla extract
2 cups milk, at room temperature	1 prebaked 9-inch pie shell (either recipe in this chapter)
2 squares (1 ounce each) unsweetened chocolate, chopped into small pieces	Whipped cream (optional)

1 In the top part of a double boiler, mix the cornstarch, sugar, and salt. Gradually whisk in the milk. Cook the mixture over simmering water until it thickens, stirring constantly with a whisk, about 10 minutes. Add the chopped chocolate to the thickened mixture and continue stirring until melted through, about 3 minutes.

2 Place the egg yolks in a small bowl and beat them slightly. Slowly add a ladleful (only about ¼ cup) of the hot mixture to the egg yolks. Stir the egg yolk mixture back into the hot mixture in the double boiler. Cook for 5 minutes. Cool. Add the butter and vanilla and stir until the butter is melted and smooth, about 3 minutes.

3 Pour into the cooled baked pie shell and chill until set, about 1½ hours. Top with whipped cream, if desired.

Per serving: Calories 270 (From Fat 121); Fat 13g (Saturated 5g); Cholesterol 64mg; Sodium 171mg; Carbohydrate 35g (Dietary Fiber 1g); Protein 4g.

Banana Cream Pie

This pie is such a treat, especially because bananas are always in season. You make the vanilla pudding for this pie, which makes it special. If you're looking for a shortcut, you can substitute instant vanilla pudding, add some sliced bananas to it, chill it in a pre-baked piecrust, and top it with whipped cream.

Preparation time: *20 minutes, plus 1½ hours for chilling*

Baking time: *20 minutes (for the piecrust)*

Yield: *One 9-inch pie*

¼ cup cornstarch

⅔ cup sugar

¼ teaspoon salt

2 cups milk, warmed

3 egg yolks

2 tablespoons butter

½ teaspoon vanilla extract

3 ripe bananas, sliced

1 prebaked 9-inch pie shell (either recipe in this chapter)

Whipped cream (optional)

1 In the top part of a double boiler, mix the cornstarch, sugar, and salt. Gradually whisk in the milk. Cook the mixture over simmering water until it thickens, stirring constantly with a whisk, about 10 minutes.

2 In a small bowl, lightly beat the egg yolks. Slowly add a ladleful (only about ¼ cup) of the hot mixture to the egg yolks and mix well. Stir the egg yolks back into the milk mixture in the double boiler. Cook for 5 minutes. Cool slightly, stir in the butter and vanilla until the butter melts, and add the banana slices.

3 Pour into the cooled baked pie shell and chill until set, about 1½ hours. Top with whipped cream.

Per serving: *Calories 250 (From Fat 99); Fat 11g (Saturated 3g); Cholesterol 64mg; Sodium 170mg; Carbohydrate 35g (Dietary Fiber 1g); Protein 4g.*

Double-crust pies

Double crusts let you show off the beautiful fillings of your delicious pies. Although they're a little more work than single-crust pies, they're worth the effort. If you need a primer on double-crust pies, be sure to look back a few pages to the section "Getting Double-Crust Pie Ideas" for some thoughts on how to decorate your top or crust. Use either recipe for double-crust pie at the beginning of this chapter for these recipes.

Sour Cherry-Berry Pie

Sweet and tart is how this pie tastes. This pie would look really special with either an easy lattice or traditional lattice top, as shown on the front cover.

Preparation time: *55 minutes if you make the piecrust; 20 minutes if you use refrigerated dough*

Baking time: *50 to 60 minutes*

Yield: *One 9-inch double-crust pie*

Pastry for a 2-crust pie (or 2 sheets refrigerated pie dough)

5 cups fresh or frozen sour cherries (about 2 pounds), pitted

2 cups fresh raspberries or blackberries, or frozen, thawed, and drained berries

¾ cup sugar

2 tablespoons instant tapioca

2 teaspoons fresh lemon juice (½ lemon)

¼ teaspoon vanilla extract

½ teaspoon almond extract

2 tablespoons (¼ stick) unsalted butter, cut into 8 dots

2 to 4 tablespoons water or milk

Coarse or raw sugar (optional)

1 Preheat the oven to 425 degrees. Prepare the pastry for a 9-inch pie plate. Line the pie plate with half the dough, leaving a ½-inch overhang.

2 In a mixing bowl, combine the cherries, raspberries, sugar, tapioca, lemon juice, vanilla, and almond extract. Place in the pie shell. Dot the top of the pie with the butter.

3 Roll out the top pastry and carefully lay it over the cherry filling. (If you have tiny cookie cutters, you can cut out 3 to 4 small shapes to vent the pie before you transfer the crust to the filling, then you won't need to cut the slits in Step 4.) Fold the edges of the bottom pastry over the top pastry and crimp the edges of the pastry.

4 Cut 6 to 8 slits in the top crust for vents if you didn't use the cookie cutters. Brush the top crust with the water and sprinkle with the coarse sugar, if desired.

5 Place a piece of aluminum foil on a baking sheet. Place the pie on the foil and bake for 50 to 60 minutes, until the crust is golden brown and the juice from the fruit is bubbling through the slits in the piecrust. Cool the pie on a wire rack before serving.

Per serving: *Calories 362 (From Fat 172); Fat 19g (Saturated 8g); Cholesterol 44mg; Sodium 9mg; Carbohydrate 45g (Dietary Fiber 3g); Protein 4g.*

Cran-Apple and Pear Pie

Pears add such a nice sweetness to this pie; you'll find yourself turning to it time and again. Because some peeling and chopping are involved, I call for refrigerated pie dough to make this recipe simple. If you're feeling adventurous, go ahead and make enough dough for a two-crust pie and roll the crust out to fit a 9-inch pie plate. Cardamom adds a wonderful spicy-sweetness reminiscent of oranges if used in this pie, but nutmeg works just as well.

Preparation time: *20 minutes*

Baking time: *60 minutes*

Yield: *One 9-inch double-crust pie*

2 refrigerated piecrusts	2 tablespoons flour or instant tapioca
3 apples, peeled, cored, and thinly sliced	¼ cup orange juice
2 small ripe Bosc or Bartlett pears, peeled, cored, and thinly sliced	½ teaspoon cinnamon
1 cup fresh or frozen cranberries	½ teaspoon nutmeg or cardamom
¾ cup sugar	¼ teaspoon salt
	2 tablespoons milk or water

1 Preheat the oven to 425 degrees. Unwrap one of the refrigerated piecrusts. Fix the seam (press the ends together) if separation has occurred. Place the dough in a 9-inch pie plate.

2 In a large bowl, combine the apples, pears, cranberries, sugar, flour, orange juice, cinnamon, cardamom, and salt and mix thoroughly. Pile the fruit mixture in the pie plate.

3 Unwrap the second pastry and fix the seam, if necessary. With a small cookie cutter or a knife, cut out 3 small shapes to vent the pie. Cover the fruit mixture with the pastry dough. Press the edges of the doughs together and flute the crust. Brush the top of the pie with milk or water.

4 Bake for 30 minutes; then reduce the heat to 350 degrees and bake until the crust is browned and the fruit is tender, about 30 minutes more.

Tip: If you shop at your local farmers' market, choose a variety of local apples to make this delicious pie. The only apple I don't recommend for pie-making is Red Delicious.

Per serving: *Calories 253 (From Fat 86); Fat 10g (Saturated 4g); Cholesterol 7mg; Sodium 181mg; Carbohydrate 41g (Dietary Fiber 2g); Protein 0g.*

Making To-Die-For Tarts

Dessert is what guests remember most about the meal you serve them. Tarts are always festive and impressive, and they're perfect for gatherings large and small. This section includes tart recipes that use simple ingredients but convey utterly delectable results. I think you'll enjoy them.

Tart Lemon Tart

You must use freshly squeezed lemon juice for this tart in order for it to be as lip-puckering good as it is. If you like lemon, you'll love this tart. Remember to zest the lemon before you squeeze it for the juice.

Specialty tools: *8-inch springform pan*

Preparation time: *15 to 20 minutes*

Baking time: *20 minutes*

Yield: *One 8-inch tart*

1¼ cups graham cracker or butter cookie crumbs

2 tablespoons butter, melted

½ cup (1 stick) butter

¾ cup freshly squeezed lemon juice (about 4 lemons)

1 cup sugar

4 eggs

1 teaspoon vanilla extract

Zest of 1 lemon

1 Preheat the oven to 350 degrees.

2 Combine the graham cracker crumbs and the 2 tablespoons melted butter in a small bowl and mix to moisten the crumbs. Transfer the crumbs to the bottom of an 8-inch springform pan. Press evenly to cover.

3 In a 1-quart saucepan, combine the ½ cup butter, lemon juice, and sugar. Cook over medium-low heat, stirring constantly, until the butter melts and mixes in with the sugar, 3 to 4 minutes. Stir in the eggs (one at a time), vanilla, and lemon zest. Continue stirring until the mixture just begins to thicken, 2 to 3 minutes. (Don't let it thicken too much — it should coat the back of a spoon.)

4 Remove the mixture from the heat and gently pour it into the prepared pan. Place the springform pan on a baking sheet. Bake for 15 to 20 minutes or until just set (it will not be golden brown). Cool the tart and then refrigerate it for a few hours until you're ready to serve it.

Per serving: Calories 232 (From Fat 113); Fat 13g (Saturated 7g); Cholesterol 97mg; Sodium 98mg; Carbohydrate 28g (Dietary Fiber 0g); Protein 3g.

Wonderful Pear Tart

If you try just one recipe in this book, try this one. It's my absolute favorite tart — plus it's incredibly easy to put together. When you press the batter into the pan, it may not seem like a lot, but as it bakes, it rises nicely. Every time I make this tart, I get rave reviews. I bet you will, too.

Specialty tools: *8-inch springform pan*

Preparation time: *10 minutes*

Baking time: *60 minutes*

Yield: *One 8-inch tart*

¾ cup sugar

½ cup (1 stick) unsalted butter, softened

1 cup flour

1 teaspoon baking powder

2 eggs

2 to 3 pears, peeled, cored, and cut into ¼-inch slices

Juice of ½ lemon

1 teaspoon ground cinnamon, or to taste

1 tablespoon sugar, or to taste

1 Preheat the oven to 350 degrees.

2 In a medium-sized mixing bowl, cream the ¾ cup sugar and butter until smooth, about 1 minute. Add the flour, baking powder, and eggs and mix well.

3 Spoon the batter (it will be thick) into an 8-inch springform pan and spread it around to cover the bottom evenly. Arrange the pear slices on top of the batter in a decorative fashion.

4 Drizzle the lemon juice on top, sprinkle with the cinnamon and sugar, and bake for 1 hour. Cool the tart and remove the springform pan before serving.

Vary It! *You don't have to have pears on hand — tart baking apples, peeled peaches, and fresh apricots (just cut the apricots in half and pit, but don't peel, them) also work well.*

Per serving: *Calories 188 (From Fat 79); Fat 9g (Saturated 5g); Cholesterol 56mg; Sodium 44mg; Carbohydrate 26g (Dietary Fiber 1g); Protein 2g.*

Troubleshooting Common Pie Problems

Despite your best efforts, you're not alone if your piecrusts sometimes just don't live up to your expectations. Table 10-1 provides a quick explanation of what may have happened and why, as well as how to prevent it from happening next time.

Table 10-1	Figuring Out What Went Wrong with Your Crust	
Problem	**Possible Cause**	**Solution**
Pale color	Undercooked	Increase the baking time in 3-minute increments.
	Baked in a shiny pan	Choose a pan with a dull finish or a glass pie plate.
Bottom crust is soggy	Baked at too low a temperature	Increase the temperature by 25 degrees.
	Did not seal with egg white or melted butter	Seal the bottom before filling next time.
Tough, not tender	Overmixed	Handle the dough less next time.
	Too much flour	Use less flour when rolling out the dough.
Too tender	Too much shortening	Decrease the shortening by ½ tablespoon.
	Too little water	Increase the water by 1 teaspoon.
Not flaky	Overworked	Handle the dough less next time
	Cut in the butter too much	Make sure that the dough resembles coarse meal.

Chapter 11

Crisps, Cobblers, and Other Delights

Crisp, cobblers, custard, and crunches (some people call these *crumbles*) — they may sound funny, but they're favorites for many Americans. They're down-home desserts from a slower-paced era, when baking was done on a daily basis and dessert was always a finish to every meal.

Crisps, crunches, and cobblers are perfect for every beginner baker. The essence is the same for most of them: fresh fruit on the bottom and a sweet dough or crumbly topping on top. Messing them up is next to impossible because they were born of being "tossed together."

Puddings and custards are high on the list of favorite comfort foods and easy to make, too. By using basic ingredients, such as eggs, milk, vanilla, and chocolate, you end up with an extraordinary dessert.

Baking with Fruit

With fruit fillings baked warm and bubbly under a flavorful topper, these desserts build on the season's freshest fruits. Although no one is quite sure where the names originated from, they have survived in many families as recipes passed through the generations.

What I love most about these desserts is that they're easy to make, they take advantage of whatever fruit is in season, and they're much easier to put together than pies. Use peaches instead of apples, raspberries instead of blueberries. Get creative and use a little of each. Don't be afraid. They're the most forgiving of desserts. There are no mistakes — that's my favorite tip. There's just no way you can really do these recipes wrong. Like most fruit desserts, these are best if eaten the same day, topped with sweetened whipped cream (see Chapter 9 for the recipe) or vanilla ice cream.

Apple Crisp

This recipe can be made with fresh apples (try a mix-and-match variety) or with just about any kind of pie filling you would like: apple, peach, blueberry, cherry. Make this dish a la mode and top it with whipped cream or vanilla ice cream.

Preparation time: *10 minutes*

Baking time: *40 to 45 minutes*

Yield: *6 servings*

4 medium apples (Golden Delicious, Granny Smith, McIntosh, or a mixture) or 1 can (21 ounces) apple pie filling

⅓ cup light brown sugar, firmly packed

¾ cup flour

6 tablespoons butter, cut into 6 pieces

¼ teaspoon cinnamon

⅛ teaspoon nutmeg

Pinch of salt

1 Preheat the oven to 350 degrees.

2 Peel and slice the apples (you should have about 4 cups) and arrange them in the bottom of an 8-inch square baking dish or pour the pie filling into the baking dish.

3 In a small bowl or the bowl of a food processor, mix together the brown sugar, flour, butter, cinnamon, nutmeg, and salt with a fork or pulse it a few times until it is crumbly (don't overprocess). Sprinkle the crumbly top over the filling. Bake until the top is lightly browned, 40 to 45 minutes. Serve warm.

Per serving: Calories 246 (From Fat 107); Fat 12g (Saturated 7g); Cholesterol 31mg; Sodium 30mg; Carbohydrate 35g Dietary Fiber 2g); Protein 2g.

Blueberry Crunch

The oats and nuts make the topping crunchy. This is great served warm and topped with either whipped cream or ice cream.

Preparation time: *15 minutes*

Baking time: *30 minutes*

Yield: *4 to 6 servings*

3 cups rinsed, fresh blueberries or 1 package (16 ounces) frozen (not packed in syrup)

2 tablespoons lemon juice

⅔ cup brown sugar, lightly packed

½ cup flour

½ cup rolled oats

⅓ cup butter, softened and cut into 6 pieces

¼ cup chopped walnuts or pecans

1 teaspoon cinnamon

½ teaspoon almond or vanilla extract

¼ teaspoon salt

1 Preheat the oven to 375 degrees.

2 Pour the blueberries in the bottom of an 8-inch square baking pan. Toss the berries with the lemon juice.

3 In a small bowl or in the bowl of a food processor, combine the brown sugar, flour, oats, butter, walnuts, cinnamon, almond or vanilla extract, and salt and then mix just to combine or pulse 5 times in the food processor. Sprinkle the mixture over the blueberries.

4 Bake until the topping is light brown and the blueberries are bubbly, about 30 minutes. Serve warm.

Per serving: Calories 322 (From Fat 14); Fat 14g (Saturated 7g); Cholesterol 27mg; Sodium 113mg; Carbohydrate 48g (Dietary Fiber 4g); Protein 4g.

Delicious Baked Apples

Warm and sweet, with a hint of honey, baked apples are a great treat to make in the fall when apples are in season, the evenings are getting cooler, and you want a hot, satisfying dessert. Look around your market for local apple varieties to try with this recipe.

Preparation time: *20 minutes*

Baking time: *45 to 60 minutes*

Yield: *4 servings*

4 baking apples (McIntosh, Rome Beauty, Golden Delicious, or Granny Smith)

Half of a lemon

½ cup raisins

2 tablespoons honey

¾ cup chopped walnuts or pecans

½ cup butterscotch topping

1 Preheat the oven to 325 degrees.

2 Core the apples (don't cut them in half) using an apple corer. Remove the peel from the upper ⅓ of the apple. Rub the peeled part of the apple with the lemon and squeeze a few drops of lemon juice inside each cut apple. In a small bowl, combine the raisins, honey, and 2 tablespoons of the chopped nuts. Stuff each apple with the raisin mixture. Place the apples in a 9-inch square baking dish. Pour a little bit of water in the bottom of the pan, about ¼ inch deep.

3 Bake, uncovered, until the apples are tender, from 45 to 60 minutes, depending on the size of the apples. Let the apples cool for about 10 minutes before serving. Place each apple on a serving plate. Drizzle each apple with some of the sauce in the pan, the butterscotch topping, and the remaining nuts.

Per serving: Calories 426 (From Fat 138); Fat 15g (Saturated 2g); Cholesterol 0mg; Sodium 150mg; Carbohydrate 76g (Dietary Fiber 7g); Protein 5g.

Peach Cobbler

A cobbler gets its name from the appearance of the cobbled dough on the top. It tastes best the day it's made. And having a touch of whipped cream or a bit of peach ice cream on top never hurts.

Preparation time: *20 minutes*

Baking time: *30 minutes*

Yield: *4 to 6 servings*

Filling:

4 cups sliced, peeled peaches	*1 tablespoon lemon juice*
1 cup sugar	*½ teaspoon ground nutmeg*
2 tablespoons butter	*¼ teaspoon salt*
1 tablespoon cornstarch	

Topping:

3 tablespoons butter, cut into 3 pieces	*½ teaspoon ground cinnamon*
1 cup flour	*¼ teaspoon salt*
1 tablespoon sugar	*⅓ cup buttermilk*
1½ teaspoons baking powder	

1 Preheat the oven to 400 degrees.

2 Prepare the filling: Mix together the peaches, sugar, butter, cornstarch, lemon juice, nutmeg, and salt and place in the bottom of an 8-inch square baking pan.

3 Prepare the topping: In a mixing bowl or food processor, use a fork or pastry cutter to cut the butter into the flour, sugar, baking powder, cinnamon and salt (or pulse several times) until the mixture resembles coarse crumbs. Stir in the buttermilk. Drop the dough onto the filling by the tablespoonful (you can leave a little space between the drops because it spreads as it bakes).

4 Bake until golden brown, 30 minutes. Serve hot or warm.

Tip: *To peel peaches, make a small, light X (don't cut through the flesh, only the skin) on the bottom of each peach. Dunk the peach in boiling water for 30 seconds. Remove from the water with a slotted spoon and plunge into iced water. The skin should slip off easily. If some is still resisting, return the peach to the water for 15 more seconds and try again.*

Per serving: *Calories 359 (From Fat 91); Fat 10g (Saturated 6g); Cholesterol 26mg; Sodium 305mg; Carbohydrate 66g (Dietary Fiber 3g); Protein 4g.*

Custards and Puddings

In truth, custards and puddings aren't much more than eggs, milk, and flavoring cooked together, then baked, thickening it into a delicious satiny creamy dessert. This is comfort food at its best.

The recipes in this section are basic, but you should be aware of what you're doing scientifically, to avoid some pitfalls. Simply put, you're combining your ingredients and baking them until they solidify. However, baking them too long or at too high a temperature can make them dry or grainy or expel their moisture.

To avoid this, you bake custards in a water bath, which helps control the heat of the oven. Although this may sound complicated, it isn't. All you need is a baking pan with a wire rack that fits in it (try a cooling rack or a roasting pan with the rack that your turkey sits on) that comfortably fits the custard cups (see Figure 11-1).

Figure 11-1: Custard cups in a water bath.

You can also cover the custard cups with aluminum foil to prevent water from sloshing into the cups as you transport them to and from the oven. This also serves as an additional heat regulator, allowing the custards to cook slowly and minimizing cracking.

If finding a rack that fits your pan is too troublesome, forget it. You can place a clean kitchen towel, folded in half, in the bottom of the baking pan and place the custard cups on top. Essentially, your goal is to place the custard cups in the pan so they don't touch the walls of the baking pan (and that includes the bottom). I find it much easier to arrange the custard cups on the rack in the water bath pan, place the pan in the oven, pour the hot water around the cups, and bake. Others prefer to add the water first and then carefully transfer the ensemble to the oven to bake. You decide which method works best for you.

Bake the custard just until the center is a bit shaky, but no longer liquid. It should shake like gelatin. You can also insert a knife into the center about halfway in. If it comes out clean or with a small smear of custard, it's done. If liquid is on the knife, bake it longer. If it's too firm, then it's likely overbaked.

If you're afraid that you cooked your custard too long, don't fret. Just remove it from the oven and transfer the cups into a cool water bath to stop the cooking (don't make the water *too* cold or else you may crack the custard cups). Then refrigerate the custard.

Pumpkin Custard

Custard is baked in a water bath. If you're worried about pouring hot water into the custard cups, just fill the baking pan about one-third full of hot water, then add the custard cups. The water should be 1 inch deep. Top these little beauties with some whipped cream just before serving.

Preparation time: *15 minutes*

Baking time: *30 to 45 minutes*

Yield: *8 servings*

1 can (16 ounces) pumpkin puree (not pie filling)

½ teaspoon salt

1⅓ cups evaporated milk

4 eggs

⅔ cup sugar

2 tablespoons butter, melted

1 teaspoon cinnamon

¼ teaspoon ground ginger

¼ teaspoon ground nutmeg

¼ teaspoon ground cloves

1 Preheat the oven to 350 degrees.

2 In a mixing bowl, combine all the ingredients and mix well. Divide the mixture into 8 custard cups or small ramekins (they look like miniature souffle dishes). Place the cups on a rack in a baking pan to fit. Pour very hot water around the cups to the depth of 1 inch.

3 Bake for 30 to 45 minutes, or until a knife inserted into the center comes out clean. Cool. To serve, invert the custard cups onto a serving plate and remove the cup.

Tip: *If you have a turkey baster, use it to adjust the water level of the water bath. You can add or subtract just the right amount of hot water without burning yourself or spilling any water into the custard cups.*

Per serving: *Calories 208 (From Fat 77); Fat 9g (Saturated 5g); Cholesterol 129mg; Sodium 230mg; Carbohydrate 26g (Dietary Fiber 3g); Protein 7g.*

Custard 101

The word custard is derived from "crustade," which is a tart with a crust. After the 16th century, fruit creams became popular, and it was about this time that custards were made in individual dishes rather than a filling in a crust.

Rich Chocolate Pudding

There is nothing like delicious homemade pudding. If you don't have custard cups, you can use any ovenproof material, such as ceramic mugs or small Pyrex bowls. Don't overbake the pudding or else it may burn. If you want to make butterscotch pudding, substitute butterscotch chips for the chocolate.

Preparation time: *20 minutes*

Baking time: *20 minutes*

Yield: *4 to 6 servings*

4 ounces semisweet chocolate or ¾ cup chocolate chips

1 cup heavy (whipping) cream

3 tablespoons sugar

3 eggs

1 tablespoon vanilla extract

Boiling water

1 Preheat the oven to 350 degrees.

2 Chop the chocolate into small bits (if using the squares). In the top part of a double boiler placed over simmering water, melt the chocolate and cream together, stirring often. After the chocolate has melted, stir in the sugar. Set aside to cool.

3 Beat the eggs and vanilla together. Gently stir ¼ cup of the chocolate mixture into the egg mixture. Slowly add the egg mixture to the remaining chocolate, stirring constantly. Carefully pour the chocolate mixture into 4 or 6 little custard cups. Cover each cup with foil. Set the custard cups on a rack in a large baking pan, and carefully pour the boiling water into the baking pan until the water comes halfway up the side of the dishes.

4 Bake for about 20 minutes or until set. Remove from the oven and let cool.

Tip: *If you're afraid to pour the boiling water into the pan, you can always use a ladle and carefully transfer the water from the pot to the baking pan. Don't pour the water on top of the custard cups.*

Per serving: *Calories 293 (From Fat 222); Fat 25g (Saturated 14g); Cholesterol 161mg; Sodium 47mg; Carbohydrate 17g (Dietary Fiber 1g); Protein 5g.*

Chapter 12

Quick Breads, Muffins, and Biscuits

. . . .

In This Chapter

▶ Great ideas for tasty quick breads

▶ Muffins for any time of the day

▶ Savory and delicious breads

▶ The secret for tender muffins

. . . .

Although everyone loves tender coffee cakes, muffins, and hot biscuits, oftentimes people find themselves buying them from the bakery, from the deli, or in the refrigerated sections of the grocery store for convenience. If this sounds famil-iar, maybe it's because you think you don't have the time or talent to whip up a batch from scratch. As you prepare to discover the joys of home-baked goods, quick breads and muffins are the perfect introduction. The batters are not difficult to put together, most can be done in less than 15 minutes, and you can find a recipe that's right for any occasion.

Quick breads, such as banana bread, are popular favorites for many people. In this chapter, I let you know how to whip up batters for these breads. You discover how easy jazzing up quick breads with ingredients such as nuts, raisins, dried cranberries, chocolate chips, and dried fruits can be. I also offer advice on making a variety of muffins, plus give you helpful hints for making tender, flaky biscuits.

Quick Tips for Quick Breads

Quick breads are quite popular because they're a snap to put together and can satisfy either a sweet or a savory desire. Because they're leavened with baking soda or baking powder, they don't require the rising time yeast breads do, which means they're fast and easy to make. Just make sure your leaveners are fresh, so they'll have optimal rising power.

What I like best about quick breads is that they're relatively indestructible when it comes to add-ins. If you want to experiment, try adding ½ cup of any of the following:

- ✔ Nuts
- ✔ Dried fruit
- ✔ Chocolate chips
- ✔ Coconut

What differentiates quick breads, muffins, and biscuits is the proportion of liquid to fat, flour, and eggs — quick breads having the most moisture and biscuits having the least.

Quick breads are generally baked in metal loaf pans. Shiny pans are best, but if you have dark, nonstick pans or glass pans, lower the oven temperature by 25 degrees if you find the breads are browning too quickly. Grease only the bottoms of the loaf pans for nut or fruit quick breads; the ungreased sides give the batter something to cling to as it rises and give you a nicely shaped loaf with a gently rounded top. For more on baking pans, see Chapter 3.

Overmixing the batter can toughen the bread, so just mix until the ingredients are combined, unless specified otherwise by the instructions. You may even want to consider mixing the breads by hand to avoid toughening the dough.

If your bread develops a large crack lengthwise down the center of the loaf, don't worry that you've done anything wrong. The crusts of quick breads are usually thinner and have a tendency to crack. I think it gives the bread a great homemade look.

I find that many quick breads taste even better the second day, although they don't always stick around until then! You can wrap the cooled loaves in plastic wrap and store them in the freezer for up to one week. Check out Chapter 17 for more tips on storing your baked goods.

Sweet breads

Sweet quick breads are usually made with fruits or vegetables (banana, zucchini, and so on) and are redolent with spice. They can be served for breakfast, an afternoon snack, or even as a not-so-sweet dessert at the end of a meal. They are great to bring as housewarming gifts and share with co-workers. They are also great batters that can easily be enhanced with chocolate chips, raisins, nuts or other such treats.

Amish Applesauce Bread

If you're looking for a moist, dense apple-y Fall bread, look no further. I like to serve slices of this bread, toasted with butter, and my favorite butternut squash soup. They go together perfectly.

Preparation time: *15 minutes*

Baking time: *50 minutes to 1 hour*

Yield: *12 to 14 servings*

2 cups all-purpose flour	*½ cup (1 stick) butter, softened*
1 teaspoon baking powder	*¾ cup sugar*
1 teaspoon salt	*2 eggs*
1 teaspoon baking soda	*1 teaspoon vanilla extract*
1 teaspoon ground cinnamon	*1 cup applesauce*
½ teaspoon ground nutmeg	*½ cup walnuts, chopped (optional)*

1 Preheat the oven to 350 degrees. Grease a 9-x-5-inch loaf pan.

2 In a medium bowl, sift together the flour, baking powder, salt, baking soda, cinnamon, and nutmeg.

3 In a separate mixing bowl, cream together the butter and sugar. Beat in the eggs and vanilla.

4 Gradually add the dry ingredients to the creamed butter. Stir in the applesauce and, if desired, the walnuts, mixing just enough to blend all the ingredients.

5 Pour the batter into the prepared pan. Bake for 50 minutes to 1 hour, until a toothpick inserted into the center comes out clean. Cool the loaf on a wire rack for 10 minutes before removing from the pan to finish cooling.

Tip: *Look for an all-natural or homemade variety of applesauce for this bread. It really makes a difference in taste.*

Per serving: *Calories 215 (From Fat 79); Fat 9g (Saturated 5g); Cholesterol 56mg; Sodium 343mg; Carbohydrate 31g (Dietary Fiber 1g); Protein 3g.*

Banana Bread

This is a great recipe to use when you want to use up over-ripe bananas. Don't use underripe bananas for this recipe. The mushier and riper the banana, the better the banana flavor.

Preparation time: *20 minutes*

Baking time: *55 minutes*

Yield: *12 to 14 servings*

1¼ cups sugar	*½ teaspoon salt*
½ cup vegetable oil	*¼ teaspoon baking soda*
2 eggs	*2 medium-size ripe bananas, mashed*
1 teaspoon vanilla extract	*½ cup brewed coffee, warm or cold*
2¾ cups all-purpose flour	*½ cup buttermilk*
2 teaspoons baking powder	*1 cup chopped walnuts*

1 Preheat the oven to 350 degrees. Grease just the bottom of a 9-x-5-inch loaf pan.

2 In a large bowl, beat together the sugar, oil, eggs, and vanilla until light and creamy, about 2 minutes. Add the flour, baking powder, salt, and baking soda and stir together just to moisten the flour.

3 Combine the bananas, coffee, and buttermilk in a separate bowl and stir into the batter. Fold in the nuts. (For information about folding, check out Chapter 5.)

4 Pour the batter into the prepared loaf pan. Bake for 55 minutes or until a wooden toothpick inserted into the middle of the loaf comes out clean. Remove from the pan and cool on a wire rack.

Per serving: *Calories 375 (From Fat 153); Fat 17g (Saturated 2g); Cholesterol 36mg; Sodium 209mg; Carbohydrate 52g (Dietary Fiber 2g); Protein 6g.*

Cranberry-Orange Bread

Fresh cranberries usually appear in markets from late October through December. These tart berries keep very well in the freezer, so stock up when they're in season, and you'll always have some on hand to make this moist, tasty bread. See the color section for a photo.

Preparation time: *15 minutes*

Baking time: *60 minutes*

Yield: *12 to 14 servings*

2 cups all-purpose flour	¼ teaspoon salt
1 cup coarsely chopped fresh cranberries	1 egg
¾ cup sugar	1 teaspoon grated orange zest (peel)
½ cup coarsely chopped pecans or walnuts	½ cup orange juice
2 teaspoons baking powder	½ cup vegetable oil

1 Preheat the oven to 350 degrees. Grease and flour a 9-x-5-inch loaf pan.

2 In a large bowl, mix together the flour, cranberries, sugar, nuts, baking powder, and salt.

3 In a small bowl, mix together the egg, orange zest, orange juice, and oil. Stir the wet ingredients into the dry ingredients and mix until just blended.

4 Pour the batter into the prepared pan and bake for 60 minutes, or until a toothpick inserted into the center of the loaf comes out clean. Cool the loaf for 15 minutes before removing it from the pan. Finish cooling the loaf on a wire rack.

Tip: *The easiest way to chop cranberries is to place them in the bowl of a food processor and give them a few pulses, no more than three or four. You can use the same technique for the nuts.*

Per serving: *Calories 254 (From Fat 120); Fat 13g (Saturated 1g); Cholesterol 18mg; Sodium 118mg; Carbohydrate 31g (Dietary Fiber 2g); Protein 3g.*

Crumbcake

Looking for an easy recipe to share with others? Tender, moist cake topped with crumbly cinnamon and nuts, this is always a crowd pleaser, especially on Mondays when co-workers are missing their weekends.

Preparation time: *20 minutes*

Baking time: *45 minutes*

Yield: *24 2-inch squares*

Topping:

1 tablespoon all-purpose flour

½ cup brown sugar, firmly packed

2 tablespoons butter, cut into four pieces, softened

½ cup chopped walnuts or pecans

1 teaspoon ground cinnamon

½ teaspoon ground nutmeg

Cake:

½ cup (1 stick) butter, softened

1 cup sugar

1 teaspoon vanilla extract

3 eggs

2 cups all-purpose flour

1 teaspoon baking powder

1 teaspoon baking soda

½ teaspoon salt

1 teaspoon ground allspice

1 cup sour cream or plain yogurt

1 Preheat the oven to 350 degrees. Grease a 13-x-9-inch baking pan.

2 In a small bowl, combine the 1 tablespoon flour, brown sugar, 2 tablespoons butter, walnuts, cinnamon, and nutmeg for the topping. Mix well and set aside.

3 Prepare the cake: In a large mixing bowl, cream together the butter, sugar, and vanilla until light and fluffy, about 1 minute.

4 Add the eggs, one at a time, mixing well after each addition.

5 Sift together the flour, baking powder, baking soda, salt, and allspice and add to the butter mixture. Mix in the sour cream.

6 Pour the batter into the prepared pan. Sprinkle the top of the batter evenly with the topping.

7 Bake for 45 minutes or until a toothpick inserted into the center of the cake comes out clean. Cool in the pan on a wire rack before cutting.

Vary It! *Try folding 1 cup of fresh blueberries into the batter before you pour it into the pan.*

Per serving: *Calories 178 (From Fat 83); Fat 9g (Saturated 5g); Cholesterol 44mg; Sodium 133mg; Carbohydrate 22g (Dietary Fiber 1g); Protein 3g.*

Sweet Chocolate Chip Pull-Apart Bread

Some people call this monkey bread. I find it a lot of fun to make and to eat, and who can resist the goodness of chocolate? This sweet, chocolaty bread drizzled with butter and cinnamon is hard to resist. Instead of cutting it, you pull it apart with your hands — make sure to lick them clean when you're done!

Preparation time: *20 minutes*

Baking time: *30 minutes*

Yield: *16 balls*

2 cups all-purpose flour

¾ cup sugar

1 tablespoon baking powder

½ teaspoon salt

5 tablespoons cold butter, cut into 5 pieces

1 cup semisweet chocolate chips

⅔ cup milk

1½ teaspoons ground cinnamon

3 tablespoons melted butter

1 Preheat the oven to 350 degrees. Grease an 8-inch-square baking pan.

2 In a mixing bowl or in a food processor, combine the flour, ½ cup of the sugar, baking powder, and salt.

3 Using a pastry blender or a few pulses of the food processor, cut the cold butter into the flour mixture until the mixture resembles coarse meal. See Chapter 3 for tips on using a pastry blender. Stir in the chocolate chips and milk to combine.

4 Divide the dough into 16 balls and place in the prepared baking pan (the balls will touch).

5 Combine the remaining ¼ cup sugar and the cinnamon. Drizzle the balls with the melted butter and sprinkle them with the cinnamon-sugar mixture.

6 Bake for 30 minutes, until light brown. Cool in the pan set on a wire rack before removing from the pan.

Per serving: Calories 205 (From Fat 85); Fat 9g (Saturated 5g); Cholesterol 17mg; Sodium 150mg; Carbohydrate 29g (Dietary Fiber 1g); Protein 2g.

Savory breads

Savory breads are usually served with a meal instead of as dessert or a sweet treat. Savory quick breads are perfect for the hurried cook who wants to offer homemade bread without fussing with yeast breads. Boston Brown Bread is nice with a hearty bowl of chili or soup, and the Southern Corn Bread goes well with baked or barbecued chicken.

Boston Brown Bread

The whole-wheat flour, cornmeal, and dark molasses make this a rich, satisfying bread.

Preparation time: *15 minutes*

Baking time: *1 hour*

Yield: *24 servings*

1½ cups all-purpose flour

¾ cup sugar

1½ teaspoons baking soda

1½ teaspoons salt

½ cup cornmeal

2 cups whole-wheat flour

¾ cup dark molasses

1 egg, lightly beaten

2 cups milk

½ cup (1 stick) butter, melted

1 teaspoon vanilla extract

1 Preheat the oven to 325 degrees. Grease two 9-x-5-inch loaf pans.

2 Sift together ½ cup of the all-purpose flour, sugar, baking soda, and salt into a large mixing bowl. Stir in the cornmeal and whole-wheat flour. Add the remaining 1 cup all-purpose flour, molasses, egg, milk, melted butter, and vanilla, mixing only until all the flour is moistened.

3 Pour into the prepared pans. Bake for 1 hour or until a toothpick inserted in the center of the loaf comes out clean. Remove the bread from pans and cool on a wire rack.

Vary It! *Stir in 1 cup of raisins or walnuts (when you add the flour) to add extra flavor.*

Per serving: *Calories 174 (From Fat 45); Fat 5g (Saturated 3g); Cholesterol 22mg; Sodium 241mg; Carbohydrate 30g (Dietary Fiber 2g); Protein 3g.*

Southern Corn Bread

Looking for a tender, sauce-sopping bread for your next barbecue? Down South, they preheat the pan the corn bread goes into. If you have a 10-inch cast-iron skillet, by all means break it out for this recipe.

Preparation time: *10 minutes*

Baking time: *20 minutes*

Yield: *One 8- or 9-inch corn bread*

2 tablespoons butter or vegetable oil	1½ teaspoons salt
2 cups finely ground cornmeal	1½ cups buttermilk
4 teaspoons baking powder	1 egg, lightly beaten

1 Preheat the oven to 450 degrees. Place the butter or vegetable oil in the bottom of an 8- or 9-inch square baking pan (or a 10-inch cast iron skillet) and place it in the oven while it heats for about 3 minutes (if you're using butter, keep an eye on it to make sure it doesn't burn).

2 In a large bowl, combine the cornmeal, baking powder, and salt.

3 In a separate bowl, mix together the buttermilk and egg and add it to the cornmeal mixture. Stir just to combine; do not overmix.

4 Pour the batter into the preheated skillet or pan and bake for about 20 minutes, until a knife inserted into the center comes out clean. Cool the corn bread in the skillet for 20 minutes before serving.

Tip: If you can only find coarsely ground cornmeal, you can use 1 cup of all-purpose flour and 1 cup of the coarse cornmeal in place of the finely ground cornmeal.

Per serving: Calories 120 (From Fat 27); Fat 3g (Saturated 2g); Cholesterol 24mg; Sodium 456mg; Carbohydrate 19g (Dietary Fiber 2g); Protein 4g.

Making the Perfect Muffin

Making a tender, moist muffin is really quite simple, but not knowing the proper technique can result in tough, smooth-topped muffins. The secret to bumpy rounded muffin tops and a moist inside is to avoid overmixing the dough and to use only a bowl and a spoon for mixing. Don't use a handheld or stand mixer. When you combine the flour mixture with the liquids, just give it a few (no more than five) good turns with a sturdy wooden spoon. There will be, and should be, a tiny bit of unmixed flour in your batter, and that's okay. Believe it or not, the batter will "finish mixing" in the oven, and the unmixed flour will not be present in the muffin.

If you blend your batter until it's smooth and uniform, you'll have made a cakelike batter, which will result in tougher muffins with peaked or smooth tops — not desirable for most muffins. You want to have slightly rounded, bumpy-topped muffins baked to a golden brown.

Preparing the pans

The easiest way to prepare muffin tins is to use paper liners. Just pop the liners in and fill three-quarters full of batter. You don't need liners in order to make muffins, though. Just grease only the bottoms of the muffin cups (the sides of the cup should be left ungreased), unless the recipe calls for the entire cup to be greased. Not greasing the sides actually gives you a better-shaped muffin.

When you're filling muffin cups, fill the cup only three-quarters full of batter. Overfilling muffin tins will result in the batter spilling on top of the muffin tins — plus, your muffins will be oddly shaped. You may even have batter drip to the floor of the oven, which is always an unpleasant mess. Wipe off any batter that has spilled onto the top of the muffin pan before baking them.

As soon as the muffins are done baking, let them sit for just one minute to set and then remove them from the muffin pan. They should just tumble out when the pan is inverted; however, if some of the muffins are reluctant to come out, just run a butter knife or a thin metal spatula around the cup to loosen the muffin. If you leave muffins to cool in their cups, they will become a bit soggy from the trapped steam.

Going mini

The standard muffin cup is 2½ x 1¼ inches; however, almost every muffin, cake, and quick-bread recipe can be baked in mini-muffin, mini-Bundt, or mini-loaf pans. To determine the amount of baking time needed for these sizes, measure the volume of your baking pan as follows:

1. **Fill the pan to capacity with water.**

   For muffin tins, fill just one cup.

2. **Pour the water into a glass measuring cup and measure the liquid.**

   The amount of water equals the capacity of your baking pan.

When you use alternative baking pans, you not only have to adjust the amount of batter you use in each pan, you must also alter the baking time of your recipe. Table 12-1 presents some guidelines. Bake your mini creations at 350 degrees, and always check them after the minimum time given.

Table 12-1	Adjustments for Alternative Pans	
If Your Pan Holds . . .	*Use This Much Batter*	*And Bake For . . .*
¼ cup	3 tablespoons	10 to 15 minutes
⅓ cup	¼ cup	15 to 20 minutes
½ cup	⅓ cup	15 to 20 minutes
¾ cup	½ cup	20 to 25 minutes
1 cup	¾ cup	30 to 35 minutes

Magnificent muffins

The recipes in this section are sure to become favorites.

Blueberry Muffins

Tender muffins are studded with juicy blueberries in this recipe, which comes from my grandmother's sister, Liz. She used it when she was a pastry chef in a little café. I modified it a bit to make these muffins very easy to put together. You only need one bowl and a spoon for mixing. See the color section for a photo.

Preparation time: *15 minutes*

Baking time: *20 minutes*

Yield: *24 muffins*

2 cups all-purpose flour

2 teaspoons baking powder

1 cup sugar

½ cup (1 stick) butter, melted

½ cup milk

1 teaspoon vanilla extract

2 eggs, lightly beaten

2½ cups blueberries, fresh or frozen (not packed in syrup)

1 Preheat the oven to 400 degrees. Grease or line two 12-cup muffin cups.

2 In a small bowl, combine the flour and baking powder; set aside.

3 In a large mixing bowl, combine the sugar, butter, milk, vanilla, and eggs. Mix to combine.

4 Slowly add the flour mixture to the sugar mixture and stir just to moisten the dry ingredients. Fold in the blueberries just to combine. Don't overmix.

5 Fill the muffin cups three-quarters full of batter. Bake (both pans side by side is okay) for 20 minutes or until golden brown. A wooden toothpick inserted into the center of the muffins will come out clean when the muffins are done. Let the muffins rest for 5 minutes on the cooling rack before removing them from the pan.

Tip: *If you have greased all of your muffin cups and then find your batter does not fill all of them, pour a few tablespoons of water into the greased empty cups to prevent them from burning while you bake. Just remember, when it's time to remove the muffins from the pan, not to invert the pan to release them or the water will spill out, too!*

Per serving: *Calories 122 (From Fat 41); Fat 5g (Saturated 3g); Cholesterol 29mg; Sodium 41mg; Carbohydrate 19g (Dietary Fiber 1g); Protein 2g.*

Corn Muffins

Little bits of corn enhance the flavor of these muffins. They're great for a picnic or to serve with a piping-hot bowl of chili. Split a muffin in half and smear it with butter for a real treat.

Preparation time: *10 minutes*

Baking time: *15 to 20 minutes*

Yield: *12 muffins*

1 cup milk	*3 tablespoons brown sugar*
⅓ cup vegetable oil	*1½ teaspoons baking powder*
2 eggs	*¾ teaspoon salt*
1¼ cups cornmeal	*1½ cups corn kernels, frozen or canned (drain if canned)*
1¼ cups all-purpose flour	

1 Preheat the oven to 400 degrees. Grease or line 12 muffin cups.

2 In a large bowl, beat together the milk, oil, and eggs with a wire whisk. Stir in the cornmeal, flour, brown sugar, baking powder, and salt until the dry ingredients are just moistened. Fold in the corn kernels. For folding tips, see Chapter 5.

3 Divide the batter evenly among the muffin cups — they should only be three-quarters full. Bake the muffins for 15 to 20 minutes, until a wooden toothpick inserted into the center comes out clean. Remove the muffins from the pan and cool on a wire rack.

Per serving: *Calories 206 (From Fat 72); Fat 8g (Saturated 1g); Cholesterol 38mg; Sodium 216mg; Carbohydrate 29g (Dietary Fiber 2g); Protein 5g.*

Gingersnap Muffins

Full of molasses and cinnamon flavor, these muffins are delicious with marmalade or make a terrific snack when eaten plain. They also go well with pumpkin or squash soup.

Preparation time: *20 minutes*

Baking time: *14 to 18 minutes*

Yield: *30 muffins*

¼ cup sugar

¼ cup brown sugar, firmly packed

½ cup (1 stick) unsalted butter, softened

⅔ cup light molasses

1 egg

1½ teaspoons baking soda

1 teaspoon cinnamon

1 teaspoon ground ginger

½ teaspoon ground cloves

2 teaspoons grated lemon peel

2½ cups flour

1 cup sour cream

Powered sugar, for garnish (optional)

1 Preheat the oven to 375 degrees. Grease or line muffin cups.

2 In a large mixing bowl, combine the sugar, brown sugar, butter, molasses, egg, baking soda, cinnamon, ginger, cloves, and lemon peel. Beat until well mixed, 2 to 3 minutes.

3 Add the flour and sour cream. Stir with a spoon until the ingredients are moistened and just combined.

4 Spoon the batter into the muffin cups, about two-thirds full. Bake for 14 to 18 minutes or until a toothpick inserted into the center comes out clean. Let cool for 5 minutes before removing from the pan. Garnish with a sprinkling of powdered sugar, if desired.

Vary It! *Make minis! Reduce baking time to 11 minutes. The yield will be 4 dozen.*

Per serving: *Calories 117 (From Fat 45); Fat 5g (Saturated 3g); Cholesterol 19mg; Sodium 73mg; Carbohydrate 17g (Dietary Fiber 0g); Protein 2g.*

Lemon Poppy Seed Muffins

In my mind, nothing says good morning like these tender, sweet lemon poppy seed muffins. When zesting the lemon, be sure to avoid the white pith, which will lend a bitter flavor to the muffin if used.

Preparation time: *10 minutes*

Baking time: *15 minutes*

Yield: *12 muffins*

⅓ cup buttermilk	1¾ cup all-purpose flour
¼ cup vegetable oil	¼ cup poppy seeds
1 egg, lightly beaten	1 tablespoon grated lemon peel
⅔ cup sour cream	2½ teaspoons baking powder
2 tablespoons fresh lemon juice	½ teaspoon baking soda
1 teaspoon lemon extract	½ teaspoon salt

1 Preheat the oven to 400 degrees. Grease or line 12 muffin cups.

2 In a large mixing bowl, combine the buttermilk, oil, egg, sour cream, lemon juice, and lemon extract. Add the flour, poppy seeds, lemon peel, baking powder, baking soda, and salt and mix with a spoon just until moistened.

3 Fill the muffin cups about three-quarters full. Bake for about 15 minutes or until a tooth-pick inserted into the center comes out clean. Remove from the pans and cool the muffins on a wire rack.

Per serving: Calories 160 (From Fat 83); Fat 9g (Saturated 2g); Cholesterol 24mg; Sodium 249mg; Carbohydrate 16g (Dietary Fiber 1g); Protein 4g.

Biscuit Basics

Fresh, hot, fluffy biscuits are a dinnertime dream for me. I went to college in North Carolina, and living in the South for four years taught me a thing or two about biscuit-making, such as using flour made from soft winter wheat to produce a more tender and lighter biscuit than those made with all-purpose flour. If you want to taste the difference, look for White Lily brand flour (or call 423-546-5511 for ordering information). You can also use cake flour in place of all-purpose flour, measure for measure, for a lighter biscuit.

Mixing biscuit dough

Biscuits are a lot like pie pastry in that too much handling will toughen the dough, and the biscuit won't be as delicate. Because you don't want to over-mix your biscuit dough, working efficiently when making biscuits is important. Two basic steps are involved with mixing biscuit dough:

1. **Cut the fat into the flour so that it resembles coarse crumbs.**

   Cutting-in is a mixing method in which solid fat is incorporated into dry ingredients, resulting in a coarse texture. Do this by using a pastry blender, a fork, or two knifes. See the section on pastry blenders in Chapter 3 for tips on cutting fats into flour mixtures.

2. **Add the liquid ingredients to the flour mixture.**

   Mix these with a fork until they have just come together and the dough leaves the sides of the bowl. It's okay if your biscuits are still damp.

That's all the mixing your biscuit dough needs. Any more mixing, and you'll get tough biscuits.

The rise of the biscuit

Biscuits come from the French words meaning "twice cooked" *(bis cuit)* and are a far cry from the light fluffy treats we're familiar with today. They began as dry, hard crackers — the hard tack that sailors took with them on long sea voyages because the biscuits would last a long time without spoiling. Later, shortening was added to the recipe, but the biscuits were still hard because cooks mixed the batter for a long time. Ultimately, with the invention of baking powder, biscuits began their rise, and soon tender and fluffy became the norm for the biscuit.

Forming your biscuits

There is an art to a well-formed biscuit. Working with the dough too much will make your biscuits less tender. Steam is a powerful leavener for biscuits, so it's okay if your biscuits are a bit moist when you roll them out. Don't over-flour the dough to make it easier to handle. Just pat out the dough, cut it with a cookie cutter, then place the biscuit on a baking sheet.

1. **Turn your biscuit dough out onto a floured surface and either gently roll out the dough with a rolling pin or pat it out with your hands into a circle about ½ inch thick.**

2. **Use a 2-inch round cookie cutter to cut out your biscuits.**

   You can also flour the rim of a drinking glass and use this instead of a cookie cutter. The key is the thickness of the dough.

3. **Gather the scraps, pat the dough out again, and cut a few more biscuits.**

   Try not to roll out the dough any more than absolutely necessary because overhandling the dough results in tougher biscuits.

If you want biscuits with soft sides, place them in the pan so their sides are touching. If you want them to have crusty sides, place them about an inch apart on the baking sheet.

Storing your biscuits

Biscuits are really best when eaten hot — fresh out of the oven. However, you can make them a day ahead if you need to, but not much more in advance than that. Store your biscuits in an airtight container when they've cooled completely.

You can also make the biscuits, cut them out, and refrigerate them for up to 2 hours before baking, so that you can serve them piping hot without doing everything at the last minute.

Buttermilk Biscuits

The buttermilk gives these biscuits incredible tenderness. They are easy to make — the perfect biscuit for beginners. White Lily is the most popular brand of Southern flour, but if you can't find it, you can use all-purpose flour.

Preparation time: *15 minutes*

Baking time: *10 to 12 minutes*

Yield: *About 16 biscuits*

2 cups White Lily brand soft white flour or cake or all-purpose flour

¼ teaspoon baking soda

1 teaspoon baking powder

1 teaspoon salt

Pinch of sugar

6 tablespoons cold butter, cut into 6 pieces

¾ cup buttermilk

1 Preheat the oven to 425 degrees.

2 Sift together the flour, baking soda, baking powder, salt, and sugar into a large mixing bowl. Cut in the butter with a pastry blender until the texture resembles coarse meal. Add the buttermilk and mix until just moistened.

3 Pat out the dough onto a lightly floured surface until it is about ½-inch thick. Cut the dough into 2-inch circles (use a drinking glass or cookie cutter). Gather up the scraps and pat them out again. Place biscuits on an ungreased baking sheet.

4 Bake until just light brown, for 10 to 12 minutes. Serve hot.

Per serving: Calories 100 (From Fat 41); Fat 5g (Saturated 3g); Cholesterol 12mg; Sodium 249mg; Carbohydrate 13g (Dietary Fiber 0g); Protein 2g.

Cheese Biscuits

Handle the dough as little as possible and barely stir in the buttermilk. Trust me on this. The dough will be lumpy, but it'll work itself out in the oven and you'll have delicious, tender biscuits.

Preparation time: *15 minutes*

Baking time: *16 minutes*

Yield: *About 12 biscuits*

2 cups White Lily brand soft white flour, cake flour, or all-purpose flour

1 to 2 cloves garlic, crushed (optional)

1 tablespoon sugar

2 teaspoons baking powder

¼ teaspoon baking soda

¼ teaspoon salt

1 teaspoon black pepper

6 tablespoons (¾ stick) chilled unsalted butter, cut into small pieces

1¼ cups grated extra-sharp Cheddar cheese

½ cup grated Parmesan cheese (about 1½ ounces)

1 cup chilled buttermilk

1 Preheat the oven to 425 degrees. Lightly butter two 9-inch cake pans.

2 Combine the flour, garlic (if desired), sugar, baking powder, baking soda, salt, and pepper in medium bowl to blend. Cut in the butter until mixture resembles coarse meal. Add the Cheddar and Parmesan cheese and toss to coat well.

3 Gradually mix in the buttermilk and stir just to moisten the dough.

4 Drop the dough by ¼-cupfuls (or use a 2-inch ice cream scooper) onto the prepared pans (6 for each pan); they will be touching.

5 Bake the biscuits until golden on top, about 16 minutes. Transfer to a platter. Serve warm or at room temperature.

Per serving: Calories 196 (From Fat 101); Fat 11g (Saturated 7g); Cholesterol 32mg; Sodium 311mg; Carbohydrate 17g (Dietary Fiber 0g); Protein 7g.

Chapter 13

Yeast Breads

In This Chapter

▶ Understanding the whats and hows of bread-making

▶ Paying attention to the ingredients that go into bread and knowing the roles they play

▶ Kneading and shaping dough

▶ Getting bread to rise

Many people get nervous about baking bread from scratch, thinking that you have to have some secret talent to make it rise or come out tasting good. And because bread is so readily available and such a staple for many people, picking up a loaf at a local grocery store or bakery is much easier than making your own from scratch. Although I'm not suggesting that you *never* pick up another store-bought loaf, I must say that, from all the baking I've done over the years, there is nothing better than baking your own bread. Making your own bread is deeply satisfying yet simple. From the relaxing repetition of kneading the dough to the slow, quiet rise to the shaping of the loaves and the heavenly smell of it baking in the oven . . . there's nothing quite like it.

Bread is not overstated, nor is it decadent. It's simple and basic and has played a major role in history for thousands of years. With the invention of the bread machine, you can make homemade loaves in no time. But to truly experience the wonderful experience of bread-making, everyone should bake at least one loaf of bread in her life. Try it once using one of the recipes in this chapter. I'm sure that the loaf you make won't be your last.

Understanding the Role of Yeast Bread Ingredients

Whole books have been dedicated to the art of bread-making, and there are hundreds of different techniques and doughs that you can bake. Instead of overwhelming you with too much information, I just want you to know the basics, to lay a good solid foundation upon which you can build your bread-baking knowledge. When you feel comfortable with the mixing, kneading, and rising of basic bread doughs, you can move on to fancier types of loaves and rolls. First, you need to know how all the ingredients work together, in order to have a better understanding about the making of bread.

Yeast

Yeast is the ingredient that makes bread rise. It's a live plant, which, when dissolved in warm water (no more than 110 degrees) and given something to eat, becomes active. Yeast needs food to stay alive. Generally, the sweetener (usually sugar or honey) added to the dough is the yeast's initial food. When the bread is kneaded, more sugar is made in the starch from the flour, which sustains the yeast until it finally dies when it's baked in the oven.

To ensure that your yeast stays fresh for as long as possible, store it in the refrigerator.

Several different types of yeast are available:

- ✔ **Active dry yeast:** I like to use active dry yeast because it has a longer shelf life and is easier to store than fresh compressed cake yeast. It's available in foil packs or jars coded with an expiration date. One package of active dry yeast contains 1 scant tablespoon (*scant* means "barely"), so if you don't have yeast in the premeasured packages, measure out 1 level tablespoon and then gently shake back just a little.

- ✔ **Bread machine yeast:** Bread machine yeast is designed to dissolve thoroughly when used in conjunction with a bread machine. If you're baking your bread without the use of a bread machine, don't use bread machine yeast.

- ✔ **Compressed cake yeast:** Compressed cake yeast is fresh yeast; its cells are not dried. Of all the yeasts, it is the powerhouse for rising and making wonderful breads. You can substitute 1 square of fresh compressed cake yeast (available in 0.6-ounce squares) for one ¼-ounce package of active dry yeast.

  Do not use compressed cake yeast without proofing it first. (See the sidebar "Oh yeah? Proof it" for details on this technique.) Because fresh yeast has a considerably shorter shelf life than active dry yeast, you may find that it's already dead even though the expiration date printed on the wrapper hasn't passed. Bakery supply stores sell the freshest cake yeast.

If you're shopping for yeast, you may come across brewer's yeast, which is available in most health-food stores. This yeast is *not* for bread-making and should not be substituted for active dry yeast.

Yeast likes to be snug and warm, but not hot. The most common mistake that first-time bread makers make is to kill the yeast by overheating it. One of the first steps in bread-making is to dissolve the yeast in warm water — sometimes a temperature is given (not over 110 degrees). How can you tell if the water temperature is correct? The most accurate way is to use a thermometer. If you don't have one, you can measure the temperature almost as accurately by feel. Your body temperature is about 98.6 degrees, so if you run the hot water until it's just slightly warm to the touch, but not uncomfortable, that should be about right.

Oh yeah? Proof it!

Proofing yeast — dissolving it in warm water, sometimes with a little sugar — was once an essential step in baking bread. The foam and distinct odor the yeast produced were "proof" that the yeast was still alive. Because yeast now comes packaged with an expiration date, much of the guesswork is eliminated, but beginning bread bakers may want a sure thing. Feel free to proof your yeast if you want to make sure that it's alive. If you use fresh cake yeast, you must proof it. Because fresh yeast has the shortest shelf life and the most punch, it's easy to proof, and finding out right from the start that the yeast is no longer alive will save you a lot of heartache later.

Don't proof rapid-rise or quick-rise yeast. Because they're designed to make dough rise faster, the proofing stage can use up a lot of their energy and leave them without enough oomph for the rising stage of the dough.

To proof yeast, follow these steps:

1. Combine 1 tablespoon yeast with ¼ cup warm water (not over 110 degrees) and ½ teaspoon sugar.

2. Stir well to dissolve the yeast and sugar; then let it rest for about 5 minutes or until it becomes bubbly and foamy.

   This bubbling foam is proof that the yeast is alive. Proceed with your recipe.

If you decide not to proof your yeast but discover, after many attempts to coax your bread to rise, that the yeast is dead — the dough just lies in the bottom of the bowl, unchanged — don't despair! You can save your bread by adding new yeast. This time, proof the yeast as just described and then knead it into your dead dough. You'll probably have to add some additional flour (just a couple of tablespoons) to get the right consistency again. Knead the dough for a couple of minutes and then set it in a warm, cozy place to rise again. This time, it should work.

Flour

Flour is the main ingredient in bread. Flours made from wheat contain proteins that, when liquids are added and the dough is kneaded, form gluten. This gluten gives the dough its elasticity, allows the dough to stretch as it traps the gases released by the yeast, and causes the bread to rise. The different varieties of flour that are made from wheat have different amounts of gluten-making proteins, so it's good to know a little about your choices for bread-making.

✔ **All-purpose enriched white flour:** This type of flour is by far the most common, although it isn't always the best choice for making yeast breads. A mix of hard and soft wheats, this flour has been chemically bleached, which aids in some of the loss of its nutrients and is why it is then enriched with additional vitamins. Because it is *all-purpose,* it's a good flour to have around if you want to make a cake, bread, or cookies, although the results may not be as good as if you chose a flour specifically intended for each purpose (cake flour for cakes and bread flour for bread).

✔ **Bread flour:** Bread flour is protein-rich white flour made from hard wheat. It's a good choice for bread-making because it's a gluten-rich flour that makes a good, elastic dough and gives good volume when your bread rises. Loaves made with bread flour are likely to be a bit tastier, lighter, and better risen than those made with all-purpose flour.

Bread flour absorbs more liquid than all-purpose flour, so you may need less flour if your recipe calls for all-purpose flour and you're using bread flour instead.

✔ **Self-rising flour:** This flour is all-purpose flour with salt and baking soda mixed in it. I don't recommend it for yeast breads.

✔ **Unbleached white flour:** Unbleached flour is a mixture of hard and soft wheats and has not been chemically whitened. It has a slightly higher protein content and contains more nutrients than all-purpose flour, making it a good choice for baking bread.

✔ **Whole-wheat flour:** Commercial whole-wheat flour is milled to include the flour, bran, and germ of the wheat. If a recipe calls for white flour and you want to use whole wheat, try substituting whole-wheat flour for half the amount of white flour. I've had great success substituting half whole-wheat flour for white flour in traditional loaves of bread.

Whole-wheat flour produces a much denser loaf of bread and absorbs more liquid than white flour, so if you're substituting whole-wheat flour for white flour, add the minimum amount of flour called for in the recipe and then continue to add more slowly to make sure that you don't toughen the dough.

A final word about flour: Flours (even the same type and brand) can vary in the amounts of moisture they absorb and contain. That's why you see many bread recipes give a general amount of flour (4 to 6 cups) and leave it up to you to determine how much flour to use that day. Believe it or not, even the weather — whether it's dry or humid outside — can affect how much flour you use in your bread! So pay more attention to how your dough looks than to the cup amount of flour you're adding to your dough. Good dough should have the following characteristics:

✔ It should be smooth and elastic.

✔ It should not stick to the sides of the bowl, nor should it stick to your hands or the countertop.

✔ It should give when it's kneaded.

✔ It should not be tough.

Don't pack flour into your measuring cup. Instead, spoon it into the cup to measure it. And always add flour slowly; don't dump all of it in at once.

Sweeteners

The usual sweeteners you find in bread-making are sugar and honey. Although the sweetener typically doesn't make the bread sweet like a cake, it does add some flavor and feed the yeast. When the yeast eats the sugar, it begins a fermentation process, which produces the gases that cause the bread to rise. The sweetener also browns during baking, which helps produce a bread with a nice texture and golden-brown crust.

All flour is not created equal

If you've eaten biscuits both above and below the Mason-Dixon line, you may have noticed that the texture of the biscuits made in Pennsylvania differs from the texture of the biscuits made in North Carolina. That's because they're made with different types of wheat. Hard wheat contains more gluten-forming proteins, making it good for yeast breads. It's mostly grown in the United States in Montana, the upper Midwest, and the Southwest. Soft wheat has less gluten but more starch, making it a better choice for biscuits, quick breads, and special fine-textured cakes. It's grown in milder climates in the middle and eastern United States.

Salt

Salt is quite important in baking bread. It adds flavor, controls yeast growth, and prevents overrising. Salt was always the final ingredient added to the brioche dough we made in the bakery, and I have to admit that, on more than one occasion, we would forget to add it. Although the omission wasn't apparent, when we went to put the dough into the bowl to rise overnight, the next morning we would come in to find dough pouring out over the sides of the bowl and a rather flavorless, weakly structured dough. So learn from my mistakes and don't forget to add the salt. That said, don't overdo it, or the salt will inhibit the proper growth of the yeast. Just use the amount called for in the recipe.

Fat

Fat in bread recipes adds to the tenderness and texture of the bread. Fats are also flavor carriers and act as natural preservatives, helping your loaf retain its moisture and stay mold free. Butter adds a bit of color, but you can substitute shortening or lard for butter measure for measure. Some recipes also use vegetable or olive oil.

Eggs

Eggs are not essential to bread-making, but some recipes call for them. The addition of eggs produces a richer dough and gives the dough a lovely pale yellow color.

Liquids

The liquid in a bread recipe moistens the flour, which activates the gluten. It also can feed the yeast. Typical liquids found in bread recipes are water, milk, and buttermilk. Water gives bread a brown, crisp crust. Milk gives a velvety, creamy texture to the bread. Buttermilk adds a nice tangy flavor. Yeast dissolves a bit more slowly in milk than in water.

If you use milk or buttermilk, warm it slightly (so that it's warm to the touch) to remove the chill of the refrigerator before dissolving the yeast in it.

Mixing and Kneading Breads

When you get ready to make bread, it's important to get all your ingredients assembled on the workspace. Typically, a recipe calls for you to dissolve the yeast in a liquid and then add several other ingredients (butter, salt, and sugar) to the yeast. Then you add the flour.

You can mix doughs in two ways: with a mixer with a dough hook or by hand. Either way, adding the flour slowly is very important. The first 2 to 3 cups will be absorbed quickly into the dough, making a wet, loose batter. Then you start adding the flour in ½-cup intervals and continue mixing until the dough starts to come away from the sides of the bowl.

If you have a sturdy mixer with a good motor, using it is the easy way to mix bread dough. If you're using a mixer with a dough hook attachment, knead the dough for about 5 minutes on medium speed. Remove the dough from the bowl and finish kneading by hand on a lightly floured surface.

Don't use a handheld mixer to mix yeast bread dough. The dough will become too heavy for the motor, and you may burn it out. Unless you have a heavy-duty stand mixer with a dough hook attachment, I recommend mixing the dough by hand. Or, if you have a large enough bowl and a dough blade, you can mix it in a food processor.

Mixing bread dough by hand is a little more work, but it has its rewards. When the dough comes away from the sides of the bowl, turn the dough out onto a lightly floured surface. A large wooden cutting board, a clean counter-top, or a large slab of marble makes a good kneading surface.

Before you begin kneading, make sure that your work surface is completely dry and that no obstacles are in your way. Put away all your ingredients except the flour, clear off a space, clean it if necessary, make sure that it's dry, and then lightly dust it with flour. Also, rub your hands with a little flour to keep the dough from sticking to them.

If you're kneading bread on a wooden board and you find that it's slipping or moving on the counter, wet a dishrag and place it between the board and the countertop. That should help steady the board.

Kneading dough develops the gluten and incorporates tiny air pockets into the dough, all of which helps with the rising of the bread and its texture and look. As you knead the dough, you may notice that it still feels a bit sticky or tacky. If so, lightly dust the surface of the dough with additional flour and continue kneading — and dusting — until your dough is finished.

Follow these simple steps to knead dough by hand like a pro:

1. **Turn the dough onto a lightly floured surface.**

2. **Dust the top of the dough with flour (don't use more than a tablespoon or two of flour for each dusting).**

3. **Press the heels of your hands into the top of the dough.**

   You need to use some arm strength, so lean into the dough and push the dough hard into the kneading surface. Sometimes, I link my fingers together, one hand on top of the other, as if I'm giving CPR to the dough. It increases my kneading strength.

4. **Fold the dough in half toward you and press down again with the heels of your hands.**

5. **Give the dough a quarter turn, fold it again, and continue the pushing and kneading with the heels of your hands, always turning the dough and folding it so that all the dough gets worked.**

6. **Continue to lightly dust the dough if it sticks to the board or your hands.**

   Keep up the kneading process for about 10 minutes (3 to 5 minutes if you've used a mixer). If you're kneading by hand, it's unlikely that you'll overwork the dough.

Kneading is a very important step in good bread-making, so don't cut corners here. If you get tired and need to rest, that's okay. Just cover the dough with a clean dish towel and rest for 5 minutes. The dough will be glad to rest, too. You'll know you're done when your dough is smooth, elastic, and a bit satiny. If you press into the dough and it springs back, you've done the job correctly. Figure 13-1 shows kneading in action.

Kneading is actually fun. You can smack, punch, toss, hammer, slam, or abuse your dough however you choose — and it will reward you with good shape and texture. Bread dough is a good thing to take your aggressions out on, and if you make it often enough, you may find that your arms are a bit more toned, and you gain arm strength (hey, maybe there's an idea for a new type of gym class!). If you're a more peaceful-minded baker, you may find yourself in a pleasant rhythmic motion that gives you time to let your mind wander, look out the window, sing along to music, or just sing to yourself.

Kneading Dough

Figure 13-1:
Kneading
bread
dough by
hand.

Encouraging Bread to Rise

After you've finished kneading, it's time to set the bread aside to rise. I find that the best bowl for bread rising is a large, heavy ceramic bowl. Ceramic bowls seem to be good insulators. Metal or glass bowls may fluctuate with the exterior temperature, but you can use them if you want. Yeast rises best when it's cozy warm, so preheat your bowl by rinsing it out with warm water and drying it thoroughly. Then generously grease the inside of the bowl with softened butter, margarine, or even shortening (just don't use oil).

To increase the chances of your bread dough rising sufficiently, follow these steps:

1. **Form the dough into a ball and place it in the bowl.**

2. **Turn the dough once around the bowl to grease the dough itself.**

3. **Dampen a *clean* dish towel with warm water and drape it over the top of the bowl.**

   If you don't have any clean dish towels available, which I often find to be the case, you can just dampen five or six paper towel squares (don't separate them into individual sheets) and double that over the top of the bowl. You also can very loosely cover (but don't seal) the top of the bowl with plastic wrap. The purpose of the cover is to keep the dough draft-free and prevent anything from entering the dough as it rises, but the dough also needs to breathe, so you don't want to seal it off from air.

Many cooks agree that the best place to let dough rise is in a gas oven, turned off. The heat that the pilot light gives off creates the perfect cozy spot for bread to rise, and the oven itself should be draft-free. If you have an electric oven, you can place your bread to rise there as well. If you have two racks in your electric oven, place a pan of hot water on the bottom rack and the bowl with the bread dough on the upper rack. This creates a slightly warmer environment than the average kitchen countertop. The microwave oven, if it's large enough, is also a good, draft-free choice. First, make sure that the bowl you choose fits in there. You also can place a cup of hot water in the corner of the microwave oven, if it fits, to add a bit of warmth, but doing so is not necessary. Of course, the kitchen countertop is fine, too.

The dough needs to double in size, which usually takes 1 to 1½ hours. Always check it after the minimum amount of time. If you're using rapid-rise yeast, check it after 30 to 40 minutes.

You'll know that your bread has finished rising when you can poke your finger about ½ inch into the dough and the indentation stays. If it springs back, continue letting it rise. Don't allow the dough to more than double in size. If a recipe calls for a second rising, literally punch down the dough, give it a few quick turns in the bowl, re-cover the bowl, and allow the dough to rise again.

If you're going to shape the dough into loaves, punch down the dough and turn it out onto a lightly floured board. Knead the dough again for 2 to 3 minutes. Then divide the dough, if necessary, into the portions you need, letting the dough rest for about 5 minutes before shaping the loaves.

Shaping and Baking the Loaves

If you're making two loaves of bread from one batch of dough, pat or roll the dough out into a rectangle slightly shorter than the loaf pans. Fold the dough in thirds, like a letter, or roll it up like a jelly roll. Tuck the ends under and place it seam side down into the prepared loaf pan, as shown in Figure 13-2. Cover and allow the bread to rise until it just comes up to the side of the pan.

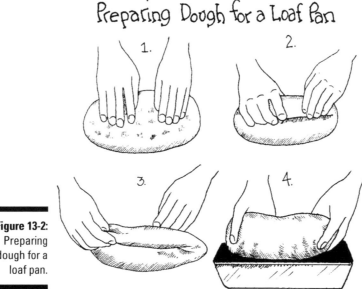

Preparing Dough for a Loaf Pan

Figure 13-2:
Preparing dough for a loaf pan.

You also can braid bread dough (see Figure 13-3). Divide the dough into three equal portions. Roll out each portion to look like a long snake, a few inches longer than the loaf pan, and braid the three portions together. Tuck the ends under and place the braid into the prepared bread pan to rise.

In the first 15 or so minutes of baking, you'll discover that your bread has an amazing growth spurt during which the yeast gets really active and pushes up the bread before the crust begins to set. Always account for this sudden spurt of growth by not allowing your bread to rise over the top of the pan during the second rising time.

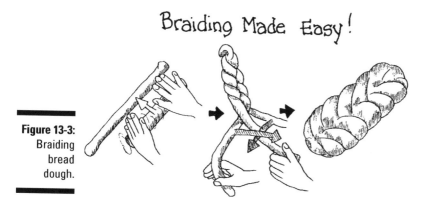

Braiding Made Easy!

Figure 13-3:
Braiding
bread
dough.

Always bake your bread in a preheated oven. Usually, the baking time given for a recipe is accurate, but if you're unsure, give a thump on the bread (watch out, it will be hot!). If it sounds hollow, it's finished. If you still aren't sure whether it's done, you can go ahead and insert a long wooden skewer into the middle of the loaf. If it comes out clean, your bread is finished. Don't judge doneness by the color of the loaf. If you find that your bread is browning too quickly, cover it with aluminum foil for the last 15 or 20 minutes of baking.

Turn the bread out of the pans onto cooling racks when you remove them from the oven. They should slip out easily. If you want a soft crust, you can brush the top with melted butter.

Let the bread cool for at least 30 minutes before you slice it; otherwise, you run the risk of ruining the bread you've worked so hard to make. If you cut it too soon, the center will be gummy, and the bread will not be set enough to cut and can taste doughy. Always use a serrated knife — a straight edge will press and squash the loaf. If you have trouble making even slices, turn the bread on its side and cut it by using very light pressure. Pressing too hard will crush the loaf.

Yeast Bread Recipes

Yeast breads are some of the most satisfying foods you can bake. Few things are as welcoming as a home filled with the aroma of freshly baked bread. Try your hand at some of the breads in this section, and you'll discover how satisfying and agreeable bread-baking can be.

Yeast breads do require a time commitment — usually you need to put aside a few hours to allow for the rising and baking.

Loaves

Loaves are the easiest breads to make; just shape the dough into a loaf shape and voilà! But if you want to get fancy, this section also contains a recipe for a lovely braided egg bread.

Basic White Buttermilk Bread

Try this recipe if you want an uncomplicated, tender, tasty white bread. It is excellent toasted or fried as French toast. If you don't have buttermilk on hand, you can substitute whole milk.

Preparation time: *25 minutes, plus 1½ hours for rising*

Baking time: *35 minutes*

Yield: *2 loaves (about 24 servings)*

¼ cup warm water (not above 115 degrees)	2 cups buttermilk, at room temperature
1 package active dry yeast	5 to 6 cups bread flour
2 tablespoons sugar	1 teaspoon salt
¼ cup (½ stick) butter, melted and cooled to lukewarm	¼ teaspoon baking soda

1 In a large mixing bowl, combine the water, yeast, and sugar. Stir with a whisk to dissolve the yeast. Add the melted butter to the buttermilk and mix it into the yeast mixture.

2 In a separate bowl, mix together 5 cups of the flour, the salt, and the baking soda; mix it into the yeast mixture to form a dough (add up to 1 cup additional flour, if necessary).

3 Knead the dough on a lightly floured surface until smooth and elastic, about 10 minutes.

4 Place the dough in a buttered bowl, cover, and set it in a warm place to rise until doubled, about 1 hour. (You can find tips for doing this in the "Encouraging Bread to Rise" section earlier in this chapter.)

5 Grease two 9-x-5-inch loaf pans. Punch down the dough and knead it again for about 1 minute. Divide the dough in half and shape it into two loaves. Place them in the prepared pans, cover, and let rise in a warm place until the dough just barely reaches the edge of the pan, about 30 minutes.

6 Preheat the oven to 350 degrees. Bake the bread until it's browned and crusty, about 35 minutes. Cool the bread on wire racks.

Per serving: Calories 100 (From Fat 17); Fat 2g (Saturated 1g); Cholesterol 4mg; Sodium 99mg; Carbohydrate 17g (Dietary Fiber 1g); Protein 3g.

Braided Egg Bread

If you're looking to try just one bread recipe, this should be the one. I've been making this recipe for years. It's so versatile and durable that it would be hard to make a mistake. You can braid this loaf for a lovely appearance, or you can place it in loaf pans for sandwich bread. For a shiny loaf, beat an egg with a little water and brush it over the top of the loaves just before they go into the oven. See the color insert for a photo of this bread.

Preparation time: *30 minutes, plus 1½ hours for rising*

Baking time: *40 minutes*

Yield: *2 small loaves (about 16 to 18 servings)*

2½ cups warm water (not above 115 degrees)	2 eggs
1 package active dry yeast	1 tablespoon salt
½ cup honey or sugar	7 to 8 cups bread flour
4 tablespoons butter, melted	

1 Place the water in a large bowl and sprinkle in the yeast. Whisk to dissolve. Whisk in the honey or sugar, butter, eggs, and salt. Slowly add the flour, stirring with the whisk until it gets too thick; then use your hands until a kneadable dough forms (add up to 1 cup additional flour, if necessary).

2 Transfer the dough to a lightly floured surface and knead until the dough is smooth and elastic, adding flour when necessary.

3 Place the dough in a buttered bowl, cover, and let it rise in a warm place until it doubles in bulk, about 1 hour and 15 minutes.

4 Punch down the dough and knead it for 1 minute more. Divide the dough in half. Then divide each half into 3 equal pieces. Let the dough rest for about 5 minutes.

5 Roll out the pieces into logs about 1½ inches thick.

6 Braid three of the logs together (refer to Figure 13-3). Repeat with the remaining three logs so that you end up with two braids. Tuck the ends under and set the braids on a greased baking sheet, as shown in Figure 13-3. Let rise for another 30 to 40 minutes.

7 Preheat the oven to 350 degrees. Bake the bread for about 40 minutes, until golden brown. When you thump it, it should sound hollow. Cool the loaves on wire racks. Let them cool for at least 30 minutes before serving.

Vary It! If you don't want to braid your bread, shape the two halves into loaves and place them in greased 9-x-5-inch loaf pans. Cover and let rise until the dough just reaches the edges of the pans, about 30 minutes. Then bake as directed.

Per serving: *Calories 142 (From Fat 20); Fat 2g (Saturated 1g); Cholesterol 17mg; Sodium 223mg; Carbohydrate 26g (Dietary Fiber 1g); Protein 4g.*

Honey-Oatmeal Bread

When I worked as a cook during the summers, we served oatmeal for breakfast, and we always had a lot left over. Because we didn't like to waste anything, we incorporated it into the bread we made. Whether you have some leftover oatmeal or you need to make some from scratch, give this bread a try.

Preparation time: *45 minutes, plus 1½ hours for rising*

Baking time: *35 minutes*

Yield: *2 loaves (about 24 servings)*

2 cups simmering water	½ cup warm water (not above 115 degrees)
1 cup quick-cooking oatmeal (not instant)	¾ cup honey or maple syrup
2 tablespoons butter	5 to 7 cups flour
1 package active dry yeast	2 teaspoons salt

1 Combine the water, oatmeal, and butter in a small bowl and let stand until it's cool to the touch, about 30 minutes.

2 In a small bowl, combine the yeast, warm water, and honey or maple syrup. Stir to dissolve and let stand for about 5 minutes (the water should be foamy).

3 Measure 5 cups of the flour and the salt into a mixing bowl. Add the oatmeal and yeast mixture and stir, adding more flour if necessary, until the mixture forms a kneadable dough (add up to 2 cups additional flour, if necessary).

4 Knead the dough on a lightly floured surface, adding more flour if the dough gets sticky, until the dough is smooth and elastic and springs back when you touch it, about 10 minutes.

5 Place the dough in a buttered bowl, cover, and set in a warm place to rise until doubled, about 1 hour.

6 Grease two 9-x-5-inch loaf pans. Punch down the dough and knead it again for about 1 minute. Divide the dough in half and shape into two loaves. Place them in the prepared pans, cover, and let rise until the dough barely reaches the edges of the pans, about 30 minutes.

7 Preheat the oven to 375 degrees. Bake the bread until it's browned and crusty, about 35 minutes. Cool the bread on wire racks.

Per serving: Calories 112 (From Fat 10); Fat 1g (Saturated 1g); Cholesterol 2mg; Sodium 146mg; Carbohydrate 23g (Dietary Fiber 1g); Protein 3g.

Jeff's Potato Bread

Mashed potatoes in bread? Yesiree! This substantial bread, inspired by a real baker named Jeff, is much like the person it was named for: tender yet dense and a little flaky.

Preparation time: *35 minutes, plus 1½ hours for rising*

Baking time: *35 to 45 minutes*

Yield: *2 loaves (about 24 servings)*

1 package active dry yeast	*1 cup warm mashed potatoes (instant is okay)*
½ cup lukewarm water (not above 115 degrees)	*½ cup shortening, melted and cooled*
½ cup plus 1 teaspoon sugar	*2 eggs, beaten*
1 cup milk, warmed (not above 115 degrees)	*2 teaspoons salt*
	6 to 7 cups bread flour

1 Dissolve the yeast in the warm water with 1 teaspoon of the sugar and let stand for about 10 minutes.

2 In a large mixing bowl, combine the warm milk with the mashed potatoes and shortening. Add the beaten eggs to the potato mixture. Add the yeast mixture and stir to combine. Add the ½ cup sugar and the salt to the mixture. Mix in enough flour to make a kneadable dough.

3 Knead the dough on a lightly floured surface until it is smooth and elastic, adding additional flour if the dough gets sticky, about 10 minutes. Place the dough in a buttered bowl, cover, and set it in a warm place to rise until doubled, about 1 hour.

4 Grease two 9-x-5-inch loaf pans. Punch down the dough and knead it again for about 1 minute on a lightly floured surface. Divide the dough in half and shape it into two loaves. Place the loaves in the prepared pans, cover, and let rise until the dough barely reaches the tops of the pans, about 30 minutes.

5 Preheat the oven to 350 degrees. Bake the bread until it's browned and crusty, 35 to 45 minutes. Remove the loaves from the pans and cool on wire racks.

Per serving: Calories 150 (From Fat 39); Fat 4g (Saturated 1g); Cholesterol 15mg; Sodium 171mg; Carbohydrate 24g (Dietary Fiber 1g); Protein 4g.

Rolls

In this section, you can find recipes for a variety of rolls, from basic dinner rolls to sticky-sweet cardamom rolls. Yum!

Molly's Sweet Cardamom Rolls

Cardamom, a spice often used in Scandinavian and East Indian cooking, has a wonderful taste reminiscent of spicy oranges. This recipe was inspired by a cardamom bread my Great-Aunt Molly used to make.

Preparation time: *45 minutes, plus 2 hours for rising*

Baking time: *15 to 20 minutes*

Yield: *3 dozen rolls*

2 packages active dry yeast	*1¼ teaspoon ground cardamom*
¼ cup lukewarm water	*9 to 10 cups flour*
2 cups sugar	*1 cup (2 sticks) butter, melted and cooled*
2 cups milk, slightly warmed	*½ cup brown sugar, lightly packed*
½ cup instant mashed potato flakes	*1 tablespoon ground cinnamon*
5 eggs, slightly beaten	*Additional melted butter or beaten eggs, if desired*
1 teaspoon salt	

1 Grease two 13-x-9-inch glass baking dishes.

2 Dissolve the yeast in the lukewarm water. Add ¼ cup of the sugar. Let stand for 8 to 10 minutes. Add the yeast mixture to the warm milk in a large, warm bowl. Add the remaining 1¾ cups sugar, potato flakes, eggs, salt, 1 teaspoon of the cardamom, and half the flour (the dough will be very loose). Cover and let stand until doubled, about 30 to 45 minutes.

3 Add the remaining flour, 1 cup at a time, and ½ cup of the butter. Knead the dough on a lightly floured surface until it's smooth and elastic, about 10 minutes. Place the dough in a buttered bowl, cover, and let rise until doubled again, about 1 hour.

4 In a small bowl, combine the brown sugar, cinnamon, and the remaining ¼ teaspoon cardamom.

5 Sprinkle your work surface lightly with flour. Divide the dough into 3 parts. Roll the dough into a large rectangle, about 12 x 18 and ¼ inch thick. Brush with some of the remaining melted butter; sprinkle with 2½ tablespoons of the brown sugar mixture. Fold the dough over and cut it into twelve 1-inch thick strips. Take one end of the strip in each hand and twist. Then take each twisted strip and twist it around so that it looks like a round sticky bun.

6 Place the bun in the prepared baking dishes. Repeat with the remaining pieces of dough; you should fit three rows of six with sides of the rolls touching. Let them rise until doubled, about 30 minutes.

7 Preheat the oven to 350 degrees. Brush the tops of the rolls with any remaining melted butter or beaten egg, if desired. Sprinkle the rolls with any remaining sugar mixture before baking. Bake until golden brown, about 15 to 20 minutes.

Per serving: Calories 236 (From Fat 59); Fat 7g (Saturated 4g); Cholesterol 45mg; Sodium 84mg; Carbohydrate 40g (Dietary Fiber 1g); Protein 5g.

No-Fail Rolls

These are very sturdy rolls — easy to put together and hard to mess up. If you're looking for a delicious roll recipe but feel intimidated by yeast breads, try these.

Preparation time: *20 minutes, plus 1 hour and 20 minutes for rising*

Baking time: *10 to 15 minutes*

Yield: *2 to 3 dozen rolls*

1 package active dry yeast	*1 teaspoon salt*
1 cup warm water (not above 115 degrees)	*⅓ cup oil or melted shortening*
2 eggs, beaten	*3½ to 4½ cups bread flour or all-purpose flour*
⅓ cup sugar	

1 In a large bowl, dissolve the yeast in the warm water. Mix in the eggs, sugar, salt, and oil. Mix in the flour, 1 cup at a time, and stir well until a kneadable dough is formed. Knead the dough on a lightly floured surface, about 10 minutes, until it is smooth and elastic. Place the dough in a buttered bowl, cover, and let rise until doubled in size, about 1 hour.

2 Punch the center of the dough to let the air out. Form the dough into 24 to 36 rolls by pinching off pieces of dough about the size of a walnut and rolling them lightly on a floured surface. Place them about 2 inches apart on ungreased baking sheets. Cover and let rise until doubled in size, about 20 minutes.

3 While the rolls are rising, preheat the oven to 400 degrees.

4 Bake the rolls until golden brown, about 10 to 15 minutes. Serve warm.

Per serving: Calories 116 (From Fat 34); Fat 4g (Saturated 0g); Cholesterol 18mg; Sodium 103mg; Carbohydrate 17g (Dietary Fiber 1g); Protein 3g.

Crescent Rolls

These rolls are great to make for a party because they're fancy looking. If you have children, they'll love to help you roll the crescents into their shapes.

Preparation time: *30 minutes, plus 1 hour and 40 minutes for rising*

Baking time: *12 minutes*

Yield: *3 dozen rolls*

1 package active dry yeast	*¼ cup (½ stick) butter, cut into 4 pieces*
¼ cup lukewarm water (not above 115 degrees)	*5 to 6 cups bread flour or all-purpose flour*
1 cup milk	*2 eggs*
½ cup sugar	*6 tablespoons melted butter, for brushing the dough*
1 teaspoon salt	

1 Dissolve the yeast in the warm water with a pinch of sugar. Set aside for 5 to 10 minutes to proof, until the surface becomes a little frothy. (For more on proofing, see the sidebar "Oh yeah? Proof it!" earlier in this chapter.)

2 While the yeast is proofing, warm the milk (do not boil) in a 2-quart saucepan. Remove the pan from the heat and pour the milk into a large mixing bowl. Stir in the sugar, salt, and ¼ cup butter. Cool the mixture to lukewarm, about 3 minutes. Add about 1½ cups of the flour to the milk to make a thick batter. Mix well. Add the yeast mixture and eggs to the flour mixture and stir well. Add enough of the remaining flour to make a soft dough.

3 Turn the dough out onto a lightly floured surface; knead until smooth and satiny, about 10 minutes. Place the dough in a buttered bowl, cover, and let it rise in a warm place until doubled in size, about 1 hour.

4 When the dough has finished rising, punch it down and knead it for about 1 minute more. Turn out the dough onto a lightly floured board. Divide the dough into 3 equal pieces. Let the dough rest for about 10 minutes (this makes it easier to roll out the dough).

5 Roll each piece into a 12-inch circle. If you find that the dough is shrinking and won't hold the shape you roll it into, let the dough rest for 5 minutes more. Brush the dough lightly with melted butter and cut it into 12 pie-shaped pieces. Roll up tightly, beginning at the wide end. Seal the points firmly.

6 Place the rolls on greased baking sheets, with points underneath, about 2 inches apart. Curve to form crescents; cover. Let rise in a warm place until doubled in bulk, about 30 minutes.

7 Preheat the oven to 400 degrees. Brush the crescents lightly with the melted butter. Bake until golden brown, about 12 minutes.

Per serving: Calories 117 (From Fat 36); Fat 4g (Saturated 2g); Cholesterol 21mg; Sodium 72mg; Carbohydrate 17g (Dietary Fiber 1g); Protein 3g.

Fluffy Dinner Rolls

Don't be intimidated by making risen bread; this dough is very forgiving. Just remember that the water you use should be only slightly warmer than your body temperature. Brush the tops of the rolls with melted butter before baking them for a very tender crust.

Preparation time: *30 minutes, plus 1½ hours for rising*

Baking time: *30 to 40 minutes*

Yield: *About 2 dozen*

6 to 7 cups flour	1 package active dry yeast
6 tablespoons sugar	2¼ cups warm water (not above 115 degrees)
1¼ teaspoons salt	3 tablespoons vegetable oil

1 In a large mixing bowl, combine 6 cups of the flour, 5 tablespoons of the sugar, and the salt.

2 In a medium-sized mixing bowl, dissolve the yeast and the remaining 1 tablespoon sugar in the warm water. Let stand for about 5 minutes until the top gets a bit foamy. Stir in the vegetable oil. Slowly add the yeast mixture to the flour mixture and mix until it's thoroughly incorporated.

3 Remove the dough from the bowl and knead, adding the remaining cup of flour if the dough gets sticky, and kneading until the dough is smooth and satiny and springs back when you touch it, about 10 minutes.

4 Place the dough in a large buttered bowl. Cover and let rise in a warm place until the dough has doubled in bulk, about 1 hour.

5 Punch down the dough and knead it for about 1 more minute. Pinch off enough dough to make a 1½-inch ball. Roll the dough into a ball and place it in a greased 13-x-9-inch baking pan. Repeat with the remaining dough until you have about 24 balls. They can touch each other in the pan and fit snugly against the sides. Cover and let rise until doubled in bulk, about 30 minutes.

6 Preheat the oven to 350 degrees. Bake the rolls for about 30 to 40 minutes, until golden brown and fluffy.

Per serving: Calories 143 (From Fat 18); Fat 2g (Saturated 0g); Cholesterol 0mg; Sodium 122mg; Carbohydrate 27g (Dietary Fiber 1g); Protein 4g.

Sesame-Topped Rolls

Little knots kissed with sesame seeds, these rolls make a great addition to any dinner. If you desire, pinch off slightly larger pieces of dough and make sandwich buns instead.

Preparation time: *30 minutes, plus 1 to 2 hours for rising*

Baking time: *20 minutes*

Yield: *4 dozen rolls*

1 package active dry yeast (do not use rapid rise yeast)	½ teaspoon ground ginger
1 cup warm water (not above 115 degrees)	2 eggs, beaten
1 cup warm milk	⅓ cup sugar
7 to 8 cups bread flour	⅓ cup shortening, at room temperature
1 tablespoon salt	Melted butter or beaten egg for brushing
	Sesame seeds for garnish

1 In a large mixing bowl, dissolve the yeast in the water and warm milk. Let stand for 5 minutes. Stir 3 cups of the flour, the salt, and the ginger into the yeast mixture. Beat well; let stand covered for 20 minutes (it will be foamy).

2 Add the beaten eggs, sugar, shortening, and the remaining flour, mixing to make a kneadable dough (the dough will be somewhat soft). Knead the dough on a floured surface, adding a little more flour if it becomes sticky, until it's smooth and elastic, about 10 minutes. Place the dough in a large buttered bowl, cover, and let it rise in a warm place for about 1 hour.

3 Punch down the dough, turn it onto a floured board, and knead it for 1 minute. Put it back in the bowl and let it rise a second time, about 40 minutes. Punch down the dough again, turn it out onto the floured board, and knead it again for about 1 minute.

4 Preheat the oven to 350 degrees. Grease two baking sheets.

5 Pinch off pieces of dough slightly larger than a walnut. Roll out each piece into a rope, 6 or 7 inches long, and tie it into a loose knot; place the ropes on the prepared baking sheet about 2 inches apart. Brush the tops of the rolls with melted butter or beaten egg. Sprinkle with sesame seeds. Cover and let rise until doubled, about 20 minutes.

6 Bake for 20 minutes. Serve warm.

Per serving: Calories 102 (From Fat 22); Fat 3g (Saturated 1g); Cholesterol 15mg; Sodium 152mg; Carbohydrate 16g (Dietary Fiber 1g); Protein 3g.

Chapter 14

Savory Baked Goods

In This Chapter

▶ Making soufflés that rise to the sky

▶ Turning out chicken potpies just like Grandma's

▶ Creating custom-made pizzas and calzones

*W*hen most people think of baked goods, cakes and pies generally come to mind. However, savory baked goods offer a host of options for the baker. Soufflés, potpies, and pizza are a perfect start into savory baking — they're comfort foods for some, and long-standing favorites for others. What's great about all the recipes in this chapter is that they're basic templates for a grander foray into savories. You can enhance many of the recipes by adding whatever ingredients are your favorites. (I make a few suggestions in the recipes where appropriate, to get you started.)

Soufflés

If you've never made a soufflé, you should try it at least once. It isn't hard — I promise! The only special equipment you need is a straight-sided soufflé pan and an electric beater to whip up the egg whites. I used to think that it took some major talent to make a soufflé. Then I practiced a few times and made several mistakes, and now the soufflé always comes out great. I soon discovered that the soufflé is a forgiving dish — plus, it's impressive for company and inexpensive to make.

Soufflé, in French, means "to blow," which explains how soufflés "rise." The egg whites capture air, and that air expands when it's heated. The straight sides of the pan allow the soufflé to rise straight up and be quite an impressive sight. If the bubbles grow too much, the soufflé can collapse on itself (the walls of the bubbles will break down and not hold its shape), but that rarely happens. However, every soufflé will deflate after it's taken out of the oven. It won't happen immediately, but if it sits out for 10 to 15 minutes, it will deflate — but it still tastes good!

In France, they say that people wait for the soufflé, but the soufflé waits for no one. This is true, so be sure that everyone is assembled around the table before taking your soufflé from the oven.

You can hold a prepared soufflé up to 2 hours in the refrigerator before you bake it.

Be sure to grease the dish well or half your dish will be ruined because it will stick to the sides of the pan. You can use flour or bread crumbs to dust the inside of the soufflé dish for extra protection against sticking. One last thing: When you stir in the egg yolks and cheese, the mixture will be a little lumpy because the cheese won't melt entirely. That's okay. You want it that way.

Unless you have two soufflé dishes, I don't recommend doubling soufflé recipes. They'll overflow and make a huge mess in your oven (trust me, I've tried it, and it's a big stinky mess).

Cheese Soufflé

This is a recipe for a basic cheese soufflé. If you want to add some other ingredients to it, that's fine. Spinach, bacon, cooked onion, or even pureed pumpkin can be added to the egg yolk mixture and folded into the egg whites. Just make sure that the onion and bacon are chopped finely and the spinach is wilted, squeezed dry, and chopped before you stir them in. You can add about ¼ to ½ cup of the ingredient you desire.

Specialty tools: *Soufflé dish*

Preparation time: *20 minutes*

Baking time: *45 minutes to 1 hour*

Yield: *3 to 4 servings*

3 tablespoons butter

3 tablespoons flour

1 cup milk, at room temperature

5 eggs, separated

¾ cup grated Swiss cheese, lightly packed

1 teaspoon plus a pinch of salt

½ teaspoon black pepper

½ teaspoon ground nutmeg

1 Preheat the oven to 350 degrees. Oil a 2-quart soufflé dish.

2 In a 2-quart saucepan, melt the butter over medium heat. When the butter has melted, whisk in the flour to absorb the butter. Continue whisking for 1 minute (this will cook out any flour taste; it's okay if the flour browns a little).

3 Slowly add the milk in a thin stream, whisking constantly. If the mixture gets lumpy, keep whisking until smooth and the milk begins to thicken, about 2 minutes. Remove the pan from the heat. Stir in the egg yolks, cheese, 1 teaspoon salt, pepper, and nutmeg. Set aside.

4 In a large bowl, beat the egg whites with the pinch of salt until they hold stiff peaks. (See Chapter 5 for information on whipping egg whites.) Transfer about one-quarter of the egg whites to the cheese mixture and stir it in to lighten up the mixture. *Fold* the remaining egg whites into the cheese mixture (don't stir or else you'll deflate the whites) and transfer the mixture into the prepared soufflé pan (see Figure 14-1).

5 Bake for 45 minutes to 1 hour, until the soufflé has risen and a thin straw inserted into the center of the soufflé comes out clean.

Per serving: Calories 308 (From Fat 204); Fat 23g (Saturated 12g); Cholesterol 316mg; Sodium 779mg; Carbohydrate 9g (Dietary Fiber 0g); Protein 16g.

How to Fold Egg Whites into a Soufflé Base

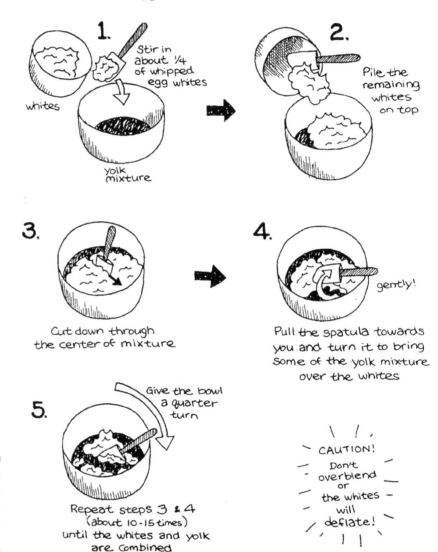

1. Stir in about ¼ of whipped egg whites

whites

yolk mixture

2. Pile the remaining whites on top

3. Cut down through the center of mixture

4. gently!

Pull the spatula towards you and turn it to bring some of the yolk mixture over the whites

5. Give the bowl a quarter turn

Repeat steps 3 & 4 (about 10-15 times) until the whites and yolk are combined

CAUTION! Don't overblend or the whites will deflate!

Figure 14-1: Folding egg whites into soufflé batter.

Potpies

Potpies seem to be back in fashion with the revolution of comfort foods. Potpies can be custom-made to your liking. Simply add the veggies and meat you like and make a savory sauce. The crust bakes on top. You have a hearty, filling meal without much work.

Chicken Potpie

Tender chicken, flavorful vegetables, and a creamy sauce that is kissed with a touch of rosemary — it just doesn't get much better than this. Using prepared puff pastry and only a top crust makes this recipe easy to pull together.

Preparation time: *25 minutes*

Baking time: *45 minutes to 1 hour*

Yield: *4 to 6 servings*

½ cup (1 stick) butter	1 small potato, peeled and chopped
½ cup flour	2 cups cooked chicken, shredded
1½ cups buttermilk	½ cup frozen peas
2 cups chicken broth	½ cup frozen corn
1 tablespoon olive oil	1 teaspoon chopped fresh or dried rosemary
1 medium onion, diced	1 teaspoon black pepper
1 clove garlic, crushed	1 teaspoon salt
3 carrots, peeled and sliced on the diagonal	½ package (17¼ ounces) frozen puff pastry (1 sheet), thawed
2 ribs celery, diced	

1 Preheat the oven to 375 degrees.

2 In a large saucepan, melt the butter over medium heat. Stir in the flour with a whisk and continue whisking for 1 minute; it is okay if the flour browns a little. Turn off the heat.

3 Slowly pour in the buttermilk, followed by the chicken broth, whisking constantly, until smooth. Cook over medium heat, whisking occasionally, until the mixture begins to thicken, about 5 minutes.

4 While the sauce is thickening, heat the oil in a large skillet over medium heat. Add the onion, garlic, carrots, celery, and potato. Cook, stirring often, until the onions are just tender, about 5 minutes (the carrots and potato will still be firm).

5 In a 3- or 4-quart casserole, combine the chicken, peas, corn, rosemary, pepper, and salt, with the vegetables from the skillet. Stir to combine. Pour the thickened sauce over the chicken mixture and stir to combine.

6 Unwrap the puff pastry, roll it out, and cut it to fit the casserole, leaving a 1-inch overhang (this will anchor the crust in place). Cover the casserole top with the puff pastry. Cut slits in the top for vents. Bake for 45 minutes to 1 hour, until the pastry is brown and the potpie is bubbly. Cool for 10 minutes before serving.

Tip: If you want to make the recipe even easier, you can use a 10-ounce package of frozen vegetables instead of the carrots, peas, and corn.

Per serving: *Calories 636 (From Fat 369); Fat 41g (Saturated 14g); Cholesterol 84mg; Sodium 978mg; Carbohydrate 44g (Dietary Fiber 4g); Protein 23g.*

Potato-Beef Potpie

This recipe is like a tender beef stew that you bake. Instead of pastry crust, this potpie is topped with slices of potato. Slow cooking is the secret to its tenderness.

Preparation time: *30 minutes*

Baking time: *1½ hours*

Yield: *8 to 10 servings*

¼ cup vegetable oil	3 tablespoons cold water
1½ pounds chuck steak, cut into ½-inch pieces	½ cup frozen peas
1 medium onion, chopped	½ cup frozen corn
½ cup chopped celery	½ cup frozen green beans
2 medium carrots, sliced ¼ inch thick	1 teaspoon black pepper
1 cup red wine	1 teaspoon salt
2 cups beef broth or water	2 large baking potatoes, peeled and sliced thick (½ inch)
3 tablespoons cornstarch	

1 Preheat the oven to 300 degrees.

2 Heat the oil in a large ovenproof Dutch oven over medium-high heat. Add the steak in batches (do not crowd the pan) and brown, about 3 minutes per batch. Remove the steak from the pan, place in a bowl, and set aside. Repeat with the remaining beef.

3 Using the same pot, reduce the heat to medium and cook the onion, celery, and carrots until just tender, about 7 minutes. Add the wine and beef broth.

4 Dissolve the cornstarch in the cold water. Slowly add the cornstarch mixture to the broth mixture and bring to a boil. Reduce the heat and stir until thickened, 4 to 5 minutes.

5 Stir in the browned beef with any accumulated juices, the peas, corn, green beans, pepper, and salt. Arrange the potato slices on top of the beef mixture. Cover and bake for 45 minutes. Remove the cover and bake for 45 minutes longer.

Tip: *Ovenproof means that the cookware can be used on top of the stove as well as in the oven. If you don't have an ovenproof Dutch oven, prepare the recipe as directed using a large saucepan or Dutch oven but before baking, transfer the contents to a 3- to 4-quart casserole dish to bake.*

Per serving: *Calories 285 (From Fat 151); Fat 17g (Saturated 5g); Cholesterol 47mg; Sodium 485mg; Carbohydrate 17g (Dietary Fiber 2g); Protein 17g.*

Calzones and Pizzas

Pizzas and calzones are easy to make. You may find that they're perfect to serve if you're inviting a group of people over who all like a variety of different things. If you have the ingredients ready, it's so simple to have all your guests make their own pizzas or calzones. You'll save yourself a bunch of work, and everyone will love what they've created. Consider using some of the following:

- ✔ Sautéed vegetables, such as mushrooms, bell peppers, onions, broccoli, zucchini, or eggplant
- ✔ Black and green olives
- ✔ Marinated artichoke hearts
- ✔ Sun-dried tomatoes packed in oil
- ✔ Steamed spinach
- ✔ Gorgonzola or feta cheese
- ✔ Fresh tomato slices
- ✔ Diced cooked ham, sliced pepperoni, cooked ground beef, or shredded cooked chicken

Believe it or not, you can also freeze the pizza dough. Let it rise once, punch it down, and then wrap it in an airtight wrap. Then, when you want to make pizza, let the dough thaw in the refrigerator or at room temperature, and you'll have fresh pizza whenever you want it.

Defrost a 1-pound loaf of frozen bread dough if you don't want to make your own pizza dough. Or you can even purchase a ready-made crust and just add the toppings.

Make-Your-Own Pizza Dough

Everyone loves pizza, and what could be better than custom-making your own pizza? This dough is easy to put together. You just have to allow time for it to rise.

Preparation time: *20 minutes, plus 1 hour for the dough to rise, or until doubled in size*

Yield: *Enough dough for l large pizza*

1½ cups warm water (not above 115 degrees)	*4 cups flour*
1 package active dry yeast	*½ teaspoon salt*
1 teaspoon honey	

1 In a large bowl, combine the water, yeast, honey, and 4 teaspoons of the flour. Stir to combine. Cover the bowl and let stand in a warm place for 15 minutes or until foamy.

2 Add the remaining flour and salt and knead for 10 minutes, adding small amounts of flour if sticky, until the dough is smooth and elastic. Transfer the dough to a large buttered bowl, cover, and let rise in a warm place until doubled in size, about 45 minutes.

3 Punch the dough down, knead it again for about 1 minute, and roll it out to fit a 16-inch pizza pan or a large baking sheet.

Per serving: *Calories 232 (From Fat 6); Fat 1g (Saturated 0g); Cholesterol 0mg; Sodium 147mg; Carbohydrate 49g (Dietary Fiber 2g); Protein 7g.*

Calzones

Calzones are kind of like pizza pockets, without the sauce. They're pretty easy to make. This one, which is stuffed with cheese and broccoli, with a touch of pesto, is delicious.

Preparation time: *20 minutes*

Baking time: *20 to 30 minutes*

Yield: *6 to 8 servings*

1½ cups ricotta cheese (or a mix of cottage cheese and ricotta cheese)

1 cup shredded mozzarella cheese

¼ cup grated Parmesan cheese

2 eggs

1 box (10 ounces) frozen chopped broccoli, thawed (optional)

¼ cup pesto

1 clove garlic, diced

1 teaspoon black pepper

1 teaspoon salt

Make-Your-Own Pizza Dough (see recipe earlier in this chapter) or 1-pound frozen bread dough, thawed

1 Preheat the oven to 425 degrees.

2 In a mixing bowl, combine the all the ingredients except the pizza dough. Set aside.

3 Divide the pizza dough into 6 to 8 pieces. Roll each piece out on a lightly floured surface to about ¼ inch thick.

4 Divide the filling evenly among the dough circles. Fold in half by stretching the dough across the top. Pinch the edges closed to seal.

5 Place the calzones on a baking sheet and bake for 20 to 30 minutes. Wait about 10 minutes before serving. The filling will be hot.

Vary It! *Add these other fillings to the cheese mixture (you can omit the pesto, too): sautéed zucchini, mushrooms, garlic, and onions; steamed spinach; salami cut into thin strips; cooked Italian sausage; and shredded cooked chicken.*

Per serving: *Calories 441 (From Fat 143); Fat 16g (Saturated 8g); Cholesterol 94mg; Sodium 677mg; Carbohydrate 54g (Dietary Fiber 3g); Protein 21g.*

Quiches

Quiches are a delicious blend of eggs and cheese, with veggies and meat mixed in, that are usually baked in some type of crust. The following recipe uses a delicious potato crust, but you can substitute any crust, including a refrigerated or frozen one.

A great way to prevent a soggy crust is to put a layer of cheese between the dough and the egg mixture. It acts as a watertight barrier between the crust and egg custard.

Avoid watery quiches by baking them long enough that the center is set. You can vary the fillings or leave them out entirely. Remember: If you use mushrooms, cook them first to release some of the water. Otherwise, they may water down your custard too much, and then it won't set.

Broccoli and Cheese Quiche with Potato Crust

I love the potatoey crust of the quiche. Quiches are incredibly easy, filling dishes to put together. If you don't want a potato crust, substitute the Old-Fashioned Pie Dough (see Chapter 10 for the recipe) and bake the crust for 8 minutes before filling.

Preparation time: *25 minutes*

Baking time: *60 minutes*

Yield: *8 to 10 servings*

3 medium-sized russet potatoes, peeled if desired, and cut into 1-inch cubes	4 eggs, beaten
	¼ cup sour cream
2 tablespoons butter	¼ cup yogurt
1 large onion, chopped	½ cup milk or buttermilk
2 cups chopped broccoli	1½ tablespoons salt
1 cup shredded Cheddar cheese, firmly packed	1½ tablespoons pepper

1 Preheat the oven to 350 degrees. Grease a deep-dish 9-inch pie plate.

2 Place the potatoes in a large saucepan and cover with water. Bring to a boil over medium-high heat and cook until tender, about 15 minutes. Drain the potatoes and set aside to cool.

3 While the potatoes are cooking, melt 1 tablespoon of the butter in a medium-sized skillet over medium heat. Add the chopped onion and cook, stirring occasionally, until softened, 5 to 7 minutes. Remove half of the onions from the pan and set aside.

4 Add the broccoli to the remaining onions in the skillet, return to the heat, and continue cooking until the broccoli changes color to a bright green and is tender-crisp, about 5 minutes more (do not overcook the broccoli; it will continue to cook in the oven).

5 When the potatoes are cool enough to handle, add the remaining 1 tablespoon butter and the reserved onion and mash (you don't have to make the mixture perfectly smooth). Press the potato mixture evenly into the prepared pie plate.

6 Pat the cheese on top of the potatoes. Sprinkle the broccoli and onion mixture on top of the cheese.

7 In a mixing bowl, combine the eggs, sour cream, yogurt, milk, salt, and pepper, and beat well. Pour on top of the broccoli. Place the pie plate on a baking sheet and transfer to the oven. Bake the quiche for 1 hour, or until the quiche is set. Let the quiche cool for 10 minutes before serving.

Vary It! *You can fill a quiche with just about anything you like: Try cooked ham, sautéed mushrooms and red onions, shredded zucchini, or bell peppers.*

Per serving: *Calories 165 (From Fat 89); Fat 10g (Saturated 6g); Cholesterol 108mg; Sodium 464mg; Carbohydrate 12g (Dietary Fiber 2g); Protein 8g.*

Chapter 15

Baking with Mixes and Premade Doughs

*B*aking mixes and refrigerated or frozen doughs can be a baker's best friend. Tasty and quick, they come already mixed with the right amounts of flour and leavener, and all you need to do is add the fat and liquid and — presto! — you have a perfect cake.

As the days seem to grow shorter and my to-do list longer, I've become a great fan of quick and easy recipes. Incorporating refrigerated doughs and box mixes into your baking life will allow you to still create a delicious baked good while reducing the need to have many ingredients on hand, not to mention the time it takes to make it.

Cakes and other homemade goodies are a source of comfort. Plus, they can be associated with celebrations and special times. Unfortunately, they are sometimes viewed as a challenge to make and a mess to clean up. Using mixes, however, can make preparation easier and the results more predictable. And a cake from a mix can be made on the spur of the moment.

Maybe you're one of those people who is too busy to bake everything from scratch or hasn't gained a tremendous amount of confidence in the kitchen. The best part about working with box mixes and frozen or refrigerated doughs is that they're sure-fire confidence builders.

You can find premade doughs in funny places throughout the supermarket. The following table gives a brief rundown of where I find my products. While your grocery may not shelve things identically, you at least have an idea of where to start looking.

What You're Looking For. . .	Where to Find It . . .
Cake mixes	In the baking aisle
Jiffy brand corn mixes	In the baking aisle, near other flours and pancake mixes
Frozen bread dough	Frozen foods section, usually found with pretzels and near frozen pizzas and other frozen bread products; sold in multi-packs of 1-pound loafs
Refrigerated pie dough, refrigerated crescent rolls	In the refrigerated section, near the butter and eggs
Puff pastry/phyllo dough	In the frozen foods section, found with other desserts (frozen layer cakes and pies) and frozen fresh fruit

The more comfortable you become with baking cakes and breads by using these ingredients, the more likely you will be to venture a few steps farther and start baking completely from scratch. I love the collection of recipes that follow because they are easy and tasty and will surely become part of your everyday recipe group.

Baking with Mixes

You can use any brand of cake mixes, but you need to know about a couple differences between mixes and cakes from scratch:

- ✔ The pudding-in-the-mix brands produce a heavier cake that has a lot of moisture. The plain mixes produce a slightly lighter cake and have what I would consider a classic cake texture. They both are good, so you just need to choose which works best for the cake you want to make.

- ✔ Size doesn't matter when it comes to box cakes. Cake mixes vary in weight from brand to brand. I tested all my cake recipes with a variety of brands, so you can choose the brand you like and be ensured good results.

If you're an experienced box-cake maker, you may realize that sometimes the cakes rise a lot in the middle but the sides are not so high. You may also notice that your cake tunnels or has lots of air pockets. To avoid tunnels and puffy centers in your baked cake, either sharply tap the filled cake pan several times on the kitchen counter before you place it in the oven or run a knife through the batter in an *S* pattern to pop the bubbles. Also, spread the batter evenly in the pans after you pour it in.

One drawback to baking with mixes is that you aren't working with all-natural ingredients. Most cake mixes have artificial flavoring. You can combat the fake taste of cake mixes by using nice natural flavors or extracts. Orange juice, lemon zest, almond extract, or even chocolate chips or peanut butter chips can disguise "artificial" flavors when stirred into a mix. Mixes also contain *emulsifiers,* which bind together the fat and liquid and prevent them from separating. This can be helpful because box cakes stay fresh longer than those made from scratch, but it is another artificial ingredient you wouldn't have if you baked from scratch.

Mixed goods

The following recipes use box mixes but taste just like you made them from scratch. Having cake mixes on hand can really simplify your life when you want to bake on the spur of the moment. Box mixes make baking easier because you don't have to worry whether you have all the little ingredients on hand. You may find yourself baking more often because baking with mixes is easy, fun, and really, really tasty.

Baking outside the box

It may come as a big surprise to you, but you can tinker quite a bit with cakes and breads, and they still come out great. I encourage you to doctor up your own cake mixes. Here are some suggestions to go out of the box for delicious box cake results:

✔ Use whole eggs instead of just the whites. Your cake will benefit from the yolks, giving it a richer flavor and a tender texture.

✔ Instead of adding oil, substitute half the oil with melted butter for a better taste and texture.

✔ Instead of flouring cake pans with flour, use cocoa when making chocolate cakes.

✔ Try adding ½ cup toasted coconut to the batter of a yellow or angel food cake

✔ For an almond edge, add 1 teaspoon almond extract to the batter, or if you prefer a peppermint taste, simply add 2 tablespoons peppermint schnapps.

✔ Coffee and chocolate go hand in hand. Replace half of the liquid called for with brewed and cooled coffee or espresso.

Super Chocolate Cake

Rich chocolate cake with chocolate frosting studded with chocolate chips. Does it get any better than this? Leave the milk on the counter; you'll want a few glasses with this recipe. Yum!

Specialty tools: *an electric mixer*

Preparation time: *25 minutes*

Baking time: *30 minutes*

Yield: *12 servings*

1 package (18½ ounces) chocolate cake mix	*½ cup water*
½ cup (1 stick) butter, room temperature	*1 tablespoon grated lemon peel*
6 eggs	*Chocolate Chip Frosting (see following recipe)*
½ cup whipping cream	

1 Preheat the oven to 350 degrees. Grease two 9-inch cake pans.

2 Prepare the cake: Combine the cake mix, butter, eggs, whipping cream, water, and lemon peel in a large mixing bowl. Beat with an electric mixer on low speed for 1 minute. Increase the speed to medium-high and beat an additional minute.

3 Divide the batter evenly into the pans. Bake for 30 minutes, or until a wooden tester inserted in the center comes out clean. Remove the cakes from the pans and allow to cool completely on a wire rack.

Chocolate Chip Frosting

2½ cups chilled whipping cream	*1½ cups miniature semisweet chocolate chips (about 8 ounces)*
10 tablespoons sugar	
6 tablespoons unsweetened cocoa powder	

1 Using an electric mixer, beat the whipping cream, sugar, and cocoa in large bowl until stiff peaks form, 3 to 5 minutes. Fold in the chocolate chips.

2 Frost the cake with the frosting.

Per serving: Calories 652 (From Fat 411); Fat 46g (Saturated 24g); Cholesterol 209mg; Sodium 416mg; Carbohydrate 60g (Dietary Fiber 2g); Protein 8g.

Crazy-Good Pineapple Upside-Down Cake

If you love pineapple cake, you will love how easy this cake is. You can have it in the oven ten minutes after you start. The cake is tender and buttery and has a hint of pineapple flavor throughout.

Preparation time: *10 minutes*

Baking time: *30 to 35 minutes*

Yield: *12 to 16 servings*

1 box (18½ ounces) yellow cake mix

¾ cup sour cream (low-fat is okay)

2 eggs

2 tablespoons vegetable oil

1 teaspoon vanilla extract

1 teaspoon cinnamon

1 can (20 ounces) pineapple slices in its own juice

1 cup light brown sugar, firmly packed

6 tablespoons (¾ stick) butter, melted

10 maraschino cherries (optional)

1 Preheat the oven to 375 degrees. In a mixing bowl, combine the cake mix, sour cream, eggs, oil, vanilla, cinnamon, and ½ cup pineapple juice from the slices. Mix well with a whisk. If the batter is too thick, add 1 tablespoon more of the pineapple juice.

2 Combine the brown sugar, melted butter, and the remaining pineapple juice (it should be 2 to 3 tablespoons) in the bottom of a 9-x-13-inch baking pan. Mix together well. The sugar should be pretty well dissolved.

3 Arrange the pineapple slices in the bottom of the pan on top of the sugar mixture. (You should have three rows: four slices in one row and three in the other two rows. You could even it out by eating one slice.) Dot the centers of the pineapples with cherries, if desired. Pour the batter evenly on top of the pineapple slices.

4 Bake for 30 to 35 minutes, until a toothpick inserted into the center comes out clean. Remove from the oven and let cool about 10 minutes.

Tip: *When you preheat the oven, place the pan in the oven with the unmelted stick of butter in it. When the oven reaches the right temperature, remove the pan (the butter will be melted) and stir in the brown sugar and remaining pineapple juice. The sugar dissolves really easily, and you have one less bowl to wash. Just be careful! The pan will be hot.*

Vary It! *Mix in ⅓ cup sweetened coconut and ¼ cup chopped pecans with the melted butter and sugar mixture. Don't limit yourself to canned pineapple. Try peaches, apricots, or even pears. It's heavenly!*

Per serving: Calories 301 (From Fat 115); Fat 13g (Saturated 5g); Cholesterol 44mg; Sodium 235mg; Carbohydrate 45g (Dietary Fiber 1g); Protein 3g.

Deluxe Corn Bread Casserole

This recipe will be your sanity saver on Thanksgiving, because you can make this dish in no time flat, and it's popular with adults and kids alike. It's somewhere between really moist corn bread and a cheesy spoonbread and is the perfect accompaniment to chicken, turkey, and even meat loaf. If you're short on oven space at holiday time, you can bake it for the first 30 minutes and then set it aside for a few hours. Just pop it in the oven with the cheese on top 15 minutes before you're ready to eat. Try this once, and it will be on your short list of favorites.

Preparation time: *5 minutes*

Baking time: *45 minutes*

Yield: *8 to 10 servings*

1 box Jiffy brand cornbread mix	1 cup sour cream
1 can (14½ ounces) creamed corn	¼ cup butter or margarine, melted
1 can (15 ounces) whole corn kernels, drained	¼ to ½ cup shredded Cheddar cheese
2 eggs	

1 Preheat the oven to 350 degrees. In a large mixing bowl, mix together the cornbread mix, creamed corn, corn kernels, eggs, sour cream, and butter. Transfer to a 13-x-9-inch greased baking dish.

2 Bake for 30 minutes or until the center is firm. Remove from the oven (you can let cool, if you want to serve it later). Sprinkle the cheese on top. Return to the oven and bake for 15 more minutes. Serve immediately.

Per serving: *Calories 277 (From Fat 132); Fat 15g (Saturated 8g); Cholesterol 69mg; Sodium 531mg; Carbohydrate 33g (Dietary Fiber 3g); Protein 6g.*

Baking with Refrigerated and Frozen Dough

I must admit, I am a huge fan of refrigerated pie dough. It makes putting a pie together as simple as . . . well, pie. Essentially, it eliminates the need to chill and roll the dough, which are the two most time-consuming tasks of making pie. Although I think the piecrust companies could stand to make the circles just an inch larger, I am generally happy enough with the results of the pie dough that I highly recommend it to beginning bakers. You can even get creative with the pie dough — cut out small shapes or even cut it into 1-inch strips and make a lattice piecrust.

Frozen bread dough has many purposes:

- ✔ You can roll the dough out into logs, shape it like a pretzel, dip it in butter, and bake it.

- ✔ You can roll the dough out thin to use it as a pizza crust.

- ✔ You can shape the dough into a loaf (round or square) or small balls for rolls and bake it for fresh bread for your table.

You can really doctor up bread doughs — with a few add-ins, you can make cinnamon-raisin bread or French bread. The ideas are endless. I highly recommend experimenting with a frozen loaf or two. The recipes in this section are designed to get you thinking about ways to use premade doughs. Then, when you have the time, you'll be better able to branch out and start making doughs from scratch.

Super-Easy Veggie Party Pizza

Looking for something tasty and incredibly easy that's a little different? Try this pizza, made with crescent rolls, the next time the gang is coming over. The secret to a flavorful pizza is a mixture of cheeses. If this is for adults, I suggest getting fresh Asiago cheese; it adds a depth of flavor that is quite popular with a more mature palate.

Specialty tools: *1 pizza stone or baking sheet*

Preparation time: *10 to 15 minutes*

Baking time: *30 minutes*

Yield: *8 slices (4 servings)*

1 tube (8 ounces) refrigerated crescent roll dough

3 tablespoons olive oil

1 clove garlic, crushed

1 teaspoon dried basil

1 teaspoon dried oregano

½ teaspoon salt

½ teaspoon ground black pepper

2 cups sliced vegetables (choose from fresh mushrooms, green and red bell pepper, chopped red onion, fresh broccoli, sliced olives, zucchini or squash, or corn)

1½ cups shredded mozzarella cheese

1 cup shredded sharp Cheddar cheese

½ cup shredded Asiago cheese (optional)

½ cup shredded fresh Parmesan cheese

1 Adjust a rack in the oven to the lowest shelf. Place the baking stone on a cookie sheet and place in the oven on the low rack (a baking sheet will work, too, if you don't have a stone). Preheat the oven to 475 degrees. Let the stone heat in the oven for at least 30 minutes or up to 45 minutes.

2 Fifteen minutes before the stone is preheated, start making the pizza. Spray the center area of a piece of aluminum foil that is at least 18 inches long with nonstick cooking spray or dust with cornmeal. In the center of the foil, arrange the triangles of dough into a circle, with the small points all meeting in the center (they will overlap slightly).

3 In a small cup, combine the oil, garlic, basil, oregano, salt, and pepper. Drizzle the mixture over the dough.

4 In a mixing bowl, combine the vegetables, 1 cup of the mozzarella cheese, ½ cup of the Cheddar cheese, plus the Asiago cheese, if desired, and the Parmesan cheese. Arrange the mixture evenly over the dough, leaving a ½-inch border around the edge. Sprinkle the remaining ½ cup mozzarella cheese and remaining ½ cup Cheddar cheese on top of the pizza. Roll the edges of the dough toward the center to create a crust.

5 Remove the pizza stone from the oven and place near the pizza. Reduce the temperature to 400 degrees. Carefully transfer the pizza to the pizza stone by lifting it with the aluminum foil and centering it onto the stone.

6 Bake for 30 minutes, or until the vegetables are cooked and the crust is golden. Remove from the oven and, using the aluminum foil, carefully slide the pizza onto a large plate to serve.

Tip: *Be careful! The pizza stone will be very hot when you're transferring the pizza onto it. If you aren't certain that your foil will be strong enough to carry the weight of the pizza, use a double layer of foil.*

Per serving: *Calories 305 (From Fat 202); Fat 23g (Saturated 10g); Cholesterol 39mg; Sodium 641mg; Carbohydrate 12g (Dietary Fiber 0g); Protein 13g.*

Apple Turnovers

I like to make my turnovers with two different types of apples, one a sweeter baking apple and the other a tart apple. It adds a depth of flavor that I really enjoy. You can dice up any fruit to mix in with the apples, such as pears, peaches, or raspberries.

Preparation time: *20 minutes*

Baking time: *35 to 45 minutes*

Yield: *4 servings*

3 cups diced apples (about 4 medium apples)

½ cup plus 1 tablespoon sugar

½ cup apple juice

¼ teaspoon ground cinnamon, nutmeg, or cardamom

1 tablespoon cornstarch dissolved in 1 tablespoon water

1 package (17¼ ounces)frozen puff pastry (2 sheets), thawed

1 egg, beaten

1 Preheat the oven to 375 degrees. Combine the apples, ½ cup sugar, apple juice, and cinnamon in a heavy medium saucepan. Bring to a boil, stirring. Reduce heat to medium; simmer until apples are soft, about 6 minutes. Add the cornstarch mixture and stir until the mixture thickens and boils, about 1 minute. Cool.

2 Cut the pastry into four even squares (6 x 6 inches). Place ¼ cup apple mixture on top of the center of each pastry square. Brush the pastry edges with the beaten egg. Fold the pastry over the filling, forming triangles and pressing the edges gently with a fork to seal.

3 Transfer to a baking sheet. Repeat with the remaining pastry and apple mixture. Brush the tops of the turnovers with the beaten egg, if desired.

4 Bake for 35 to 45 minutes, or until golden brown. Remove and let cool slightly before serving, at least 15 minutes.

Per serving: *Calories 870 (From Fat 427); Fat 48g (Saturated 7g); Cholesterol 0mg; Sodium 311mg; Carbohydrate 104g (Dietary Fiber 4g); Protein 9g.*

Soft Pretzels

With the help of frozen bread dough, you can have these made in no time flat. They're great to serve at a party or have on hand for a snack. Serve them with dipping sauces, such as mustard, spaghetti sauce, or warmed cheese spread. You can also make smaller or larger pretzels by dividing the dough into more or fewer pieces. I've made them larger and then sliced them in half and used them as really tasty pretzel rolls. It's entirely up to you. Be sure to roll the pretzels into somewhat thin ropes because they will double in size when you bake them.

Preparation time: *15 minutes*

Baking time: *30 minutes*

Yield: *6 to 8 pretzels*

1 pound frozen bread dough, thawed according to manufacturer's instructions

¼ cup (½ stick) butter

1 to 2 tablespoons coarse salt, sesame seeds, or poppy seeds

1 Preheat the oven to 350 degrees. Divide the dough into 6 or 8 pieces (6 pieces will make larger and thicker pretzels). Melt the butter in the microwave in a glass pie plate or round, shallow dish, about 45 seconds.

2 Lightly dust your hands and work surface lightly with flour (do not use more than 1 teaspoon). Roll out each piece of dough into a 24- to 30-inch rope, about ⅓ inch thick. Twist the rope into a pretzel shape, pressing the two ends into the bottom of the pretzel.

3 Holding the bottom ends of the pretzel, dip it in the melted butter and place on a cookie sheet. Repeat with the remaining dough.

4 Sprinkle the top of each pretzel with the salt or seeds. Bake for 30 minutes, or until golden brown. Remove from the cookie sheet and cool for 15 minutes before eating.

Tip: *You can melt the butter over low heat and transfer the melted butter into a glass pie plate or round shallow dish. Alternatively, you can melt the butter in the oven while it's preheating.*

Per serving: *Calories 208 (From Fat 75); Fat 8g (Saturated 4g); Cholesterol 16mg; Sodium 737mg; Carbohydrate 29g (Dietary Fiber 2g); Protein 6g.*

Folded Peach and Berry Pie

This pie is perfect to make when you want a wow dessert with about two minutes of preparation. Using refrigerated pie dough and a few other ingredients, you have a lovely and delicious dessert. If you don't have access to fresh blackberries, use frozen or fresh blueberries or raspberries, or just make it plain peach. It will still be delicious. If you like a juicier pie, use only 2 tablespoons of tapioca. See the color section for a photo of this pie.

Preparation time: *5 minutes*

Baking time: *45 minutes*

Yield: *8 to 10 servings*

1 refrigerated 9-inch piecrust dough

16 ounces frozen sliced peaches

3 to 4 tablespoons light brown sugar

2 to 3 tablespoons tapioca

⅛ teaspoon ground cinnamon

⅛ teaspoon ground cardamom (optional)

1 cup fresh blackberries

1 Preheat the oven to 375 degrees. Unfold the piecrust into a 9-inch glass pie plate. Repair any crack in the piecrust by lightly pressing the split creases together.

2 In a mixing bowl, combine the peaches, brown sugar, tapioca, cinnamon, and cardamom, if desired. Make sure that the peach slices are separated and not frozen together in clumps. Let them thaw slightly, if necessary. Gently stir in the blackberries.

3 Transfer the peach mixture into the piecrust. Fold the edges of the piecrust over the filling. Press the edges of the crust together.

4 Bake for 45 minutes, until the crust is golden and the fruit is cooked and juicy.

Per serving: Calories 145 (From Fat 51); Fat 6g (Saturated 2g); Cholesterol 4mg; Sodium 80mg; Carbohydrate 23g (Dietary Fiber 2g); Protein 0g.

Chapter 16

Low-Fat Baking

*L*ow-fat and *fat-free* seem to be the buzzwords when it comes to talk about baking or cooking in general. One of the perks of baking things yourself is that you have control over what you put into your baked goods and, because of that, what you put into your body. Although everyone should be conscious of how they eat and what they eat, all the media attention on fat has made it a four-letter word. In this chapter, I take a closer look at fat, its role in baking, and ways to reduce it if you're watching what you eat.

Getting the Skinny on Fat

You actually *need* fat in your diet. Not only is fat a fuel source for many of our tissues, but it also is a concentrated source of energy, transports essential vitamins, and helps the body use carbohydrates and protein. A totally fat-free diet would be very unhealthy.

Fats also help make foods taste good. They hold flavor and act as a flavor carrier, which is why when recipes cut down on fats, they call for more seasoning, to compensate for this loss of flavor. Fats contribute to the *mouth feel,* the sensation lingering on your tongue and coating your taste buds. And after a meal, they contribute to your feeling full and satisfied, because fats digest more slowly. So, if they do all this good stuff, why do fats have such a bad reputation?

All calories are not created equal. Fat calories don't work the same as calories you get from proteins or carbohydrates. Fat calories provide the most concentrated energy source. Your body converts fat calories into body fat more easily than other calories, so your body uses them more efficiently, thereby needing less and storing the rest. The result? You gain weight more easily than if you had an excess of another type of calorie. Keep in mind that although fat is metabolized and stored most easily, the excess of any kind of calorie will be stored as fat. Because it takes fewer fat calories to get the same job done as would it take with carbohydrate or protein calories, you actually need fewer calories from fat. Or at least it would be smarter to get fewer calories from fat and make your body work a little harder and burn more calories instead of storing those calories.

Fat is a necessary part of baking for many reasons:

  ✔ It adds flavor to baked goods.

  ✔ It creates a flakiness and tenderness people have grown to like.

  ✔ It contributes moisture to baked products.

Because our society seems to be caught up in a huge frenzy, afraid to let anything with fat touch their lips, the first advice I give is to relax about it. *Remember:* Total deprivation is overkill, I think, and one rich dessert will not sacrifice your health forever. All things in moderation. If you're looking to cut down on fats for health reasons, you should keep in mind a few things when selecting what to bake. The rest of this chapter gives you plenty of tips for paying attention to your fat intake without sacrificing taste.

Being Smart about Fat

If you've decided to bake something either for yourself or for company, and you're trying to be fat-conscious, a few suggestions can help you cut down on the fats in a recipe:

  ✔ **Look for recipes that use a minimum of fat.** Angel food cake and meringue cookies are good choices. I include many lower-fat recipes in this chapter as well, so give them a shot.

  ✔ **Use fat substitutes.** Know which foods are rich in fat, and try to find adequate substitutions for them, without sacrificing flavor.

> ✔ **Reduce portion sizes.** Above all, don't feel guilty if you really want to make a rich cake. Just serve smaller slices and top the cake with slices of fresh fruit instead of ice cream or whipped cream.

Having a rich dessert every so often is fine. You don't need to feel guilty about it.

Don't substitute reduced-fat or low-fat butter, margarine, or spreads with less than 65 percent fat for butter in recipes. They won't perform the way regular margarine or butter will, causing your baked good to turn out gummy or spongy.

Fats do more than add tenderness and moisture to baked goods. When beaten with sugar, fats aerate the batter and contribute to the grain and texture of the final product. Thick fruit purees and applesauce can be successfully substituted for part of the fat in a recipe, so you may also want to start experimenting with your own favorite recipes, if you want to do a recipe redo. You can experiment with a how-low-can-you-go by substituting the puree for the butter. The texture won't be the same, though.

Lowering the Fat in Your Favorite Recipes

The fats used in baking are primarily butter, margarine, shortening, and oil, but they aren't the only sources of fat. Dairy products also have lots of fat in them, as do nuts. Choosing reduced-fat items in these categories or reducing the amount you use in a recipe will help lower the amount of fat. *Remember:* A reduction of fat in a recipe automatically means a reduction in calories all the way around. Don't go crazy, though — you still want your dessert to taste good.

Easy freezing for eggs

You can freeze any extra egg whites or yolks you have left over. Add a pinch of sugar to the egg yolks to prevent them from becoming sticky. Freeze both the yolks and whites in ice-cube trays, so you know it's one yolk or white per tray. Always defrost frozen eggs in the refrigerator. If you want to freeze whole eggs, beat the egg lightly, sprinkle in a few grains of salt or sugar, and freeze in the tray. If you don't use ice-cube trays, be sure you mark how many eggs you've frozen per container so you'll be able to defrost the right amount when you need them.

If you're trying to reduce the fat in your recipes, here are some tips that can help:

✔ **To cut down on the eggs in a recipe, you can substitute egg whites, which have no fat.** To substitute one whole egg, use two whites. For two whole eggs, use one whole egg plus one white, or three egg whites. Keep in mind that too many egg whites will have a drying effect, so try not to reduce the eggs by more than half.

✔ **Low-fat or nonfat plain yogurt makes a great substitution for the heavier sour cream.** You can also buy reduced-fat and nonfat sour cream, but be careful because they're not always the best choice for baking — they contain too much water. Check the label and make sure it says it's made from cultured skim milk.

✔ **Melt some premium frozen vanilla yogurt in a saucepan over very low heat.** Drizzle the melted yogurt over desserts, and it tastes just like cream.

✔ **Use frozen yogurts as a substitution for ice cream or whipped cream toppings.**

✔ **Choose skim milk in place of whole milk if it is called for in a recipe.** You can also substitute buttermilk, which is low in fat and gives the flavor a nice tang.

✔ **If you like the flavor of nuts in a recipe, cut the amount down to mere tablespoons.** If you finely chop them, they will stretch farther in a recipe. Toasted nuts also have a richer flavor, so you'll need less of them.

✔ **Use a nonstick cooking spray when greasing pans.** It has great releasing action, and you don't add calories to your pan like you do when you use butter.

Making Great-Tasting Low-Fat Recipes

Just because a recipe is low in fat doesn't mean it's low on flavor. The recipes in this chapter are sure to please.

Light Banana Bundt Cake

Moist, tender and full of flavor, these baby Bundt cakes are a favorite. I use my mini Bundt pans for this recipe. You can purchase these pans at Williams-Sonoma (it is one baking tray with six pans on it). You can also use muffin cups to make this same recipe. You will find Sunsweet Lighter Bake Butter and Oil replacement in the baking aisle of your grocery store.

Preparation time: *45 minutes*

Baking time: *20 to 30 minutes*

Yield: *12 to 14 servings*

¼ cup low-fat plain or vanilla yogurt

2 eggs

2 tablespoons Sunsweet Lighter Bake Butter and Oil replacement or light olive oil

3 tablespoons maple syrup

1 cup mashed ripe bananas (about 3)

1 tablespoon fresh lemon juice

1 cup whole-wheat pastry flour or cake flour

½ cup wheat germ

½ teaspoon baking powder

½ teaspoon baking soda

1 teaspoon grated orange zest

½ cup raisins (optional)

1 Preheat the oven to 350 degrees. Spray the mini Bundt pans with nonstick cooking spray.

2 In a mixing bowl, mix together with a spoon the yogurt, eggs, butter and oil replacement, maple syrup, bananas, and lemon juice. Add the flour, wheat germ, baking powder, baking soda, orange zest and blend just until the flour is incorporated. If desired, stir in the raisins.

3 Divide the batter evenly into the Bundt pans. Bake for 20 to 30 minutes, or until golden brown. Let cool for 10 minutes and then remove the mini-Bundts from the pan. Let cool before serving.

Tip: *These taste delicious with a basic glaze drizzled over the cakes. Try either of the glaze recipes in Chapter 9.*

Per serving: *Calories 191 (From Fat 30); Fat 3g (Saturated 1g); Cholesterol 71mg; Sodium 168mg; Carbohydrate 35g (Dietary Fiber 4g); Protein 8g.*

Creamy Chocolate Cheesecake

Usually cheesecakes pack on the pounds. Not this one. Blended with cottage cheese and low-fat cream cheese, this creamy, chocolaty treat is sure to please (and no one will even know it's low-fat!).

Preparation time: *20 minutes, plus 8 hours to overnight for setting*

Baking time: *1 hour*

Yield: *12 to 14 servings*

½ cup coarsely ground chocolate or graham crackers (about 6 whole squares)

1 cup sugar

1½ packages (12 ounces total) Neufchâtel cream cheese

1 cup fat-free cottage cheese

6 tablespoons unsweetened cocoa

2 teaspoons almond or vanilla extract

¼ teaspoon salt

1 egg

3 tablespoons mini chocolate chips

1 Preheat the oven to 325 degrees.

2 Press the cracker crumbs into the bottom of an 8-inch springform pan.

3 In a food processor, blender, or mixing bowl, combine the sugar, cream cheese, cottage cheese, cocoa, almond or vanilla extract, salt, and egg. Blend or mix until smooth. Tap the container or bowl on the counter a few times to allow any air bubbles to rise to the surface.

4 Pour the mixture into the pan. Sprinkle the top with the chocolate chips. Bake for 1 hour or until the center is just set (it won't be liquidy, but it might jiggle a little). Remove from the oven and let cool to room temperature. Cover and chill for 8 hours or overnight.

Per serving: *Calories 226 (From Fat 85); Fat 9g (Saturated 5g); Cholesterol 40mg; Sodium 276mg; Carbohydrate 29g (Dietary Fiber 1g); Protein 7g.*

Baked Apples

Baked apples are so homey, and these are no exception. Sweetened with brown sugar and kissed with lemon, all you need is a dollop of vanilla frozen yogurt, and you have a satisfying dessert.

Preparation time: *20 minutes*

Baking time: *40 minutes*

Yield: *4 servings*

4 Golden Delicious apples

⅓ cup light brown sugar, firmly packed

¼ cup dark rum

2 tablespoons finely chopped pecans or walnuts

2 tablespoons raisins, chopped

½ teaspoon ground ginger

2 tablespoons unsalted butter

Four 2-x-½-inch strips fresh lemon zest

One 1-inch-long cinnamon stick

4 whole cloves

1 Preheat the oven to 375 degrees. Grease a baking dish just large enough to hold the apples (a loaf pan usually works fine).

2 Cut off the top third of each apple and reserve. Peel the apples halfway down. Scoop out the cores using an apple corer, a paring knife (see Figure 16-1), a melon-ball cutter, or a round teaspoon measure to form a cavity (making sure not to puncture the bottoms). Stand the apples in a baking dish just large enough to hold them.

3 Heat the brown sugar, rum, pecans, raisins, ginger, butter, lemon zest, cinnamon stick, and cloves in a small saucepan over moderate heat, stirring, until the sugar is dissolved. Pour some of the syrup into the cavity of each apple and the remainder into the baking dish. Return the apple tops to the apples and cover the dish loosely with foil.

4 Bake until tender, about 40 minutes. Remove the cinnamon stick and pick out the cloves. Serve each apple with some of the sauce on top.

Per serving: Calories 289 (From Fat 83); Fat 9g (Saturated 4g); Cholesterol 16mg; Sodium 9mg; Carbohydrate 55g (Dietary Fiber 6g); Protein 1g.

How to Core an Apple

Figure 16-1: Coring an apple.

 Run a paring knife clockwise around the core (leaving ¼" at the bottom)...  ...and pop out the core!

Cinnamon-Almond Angel Food Cake

The cinnamon and almond of this recipe turn low-fat angel food cake into a special treat.

Specialty tool: *Tube pan with removable bottom; an electric mixer*

Preparation time: *15 minutes*

Baking time: *40 minutes*

Yield: *12 to 16 servings*

1 cup cake flour (not self-rising)	*1 teaspoon vanilla extract*
1¼ cups superfine sugar	*1 teaspoon almond extract*
1 tablespoon ground cinnamon	*1 teaspoon cream of tartar*
1½ cups egg whites (10 to 11 eggs)	*½ teaspoon salt*

1 Preheat the oven to 375 degrees. Mix together the flour, ¼ cup of the sugar, and the cinnamon.

2 Using an electric stand mixer, beat the whites on medium speed until frothy. Add the vanilla extract, almond extract, cream of tartar, and salt. Increase the speed to medium-high and beat just until soft peaks begin to form. (See Chapter 5 for more on whipping egg whites.) Gradually beat in the remaining 1 cup sugar, 2 tablespoons at a time, occasionally scraping down the sides of the bowl. Increase the speed to high and beat until stiff, glossy peaks form. Do not overbeat.

3 Sift one-third of the flour mixture over the whites. Beat on low speed just until blended. Sift and beat in the remaining flour in two more batches.

4 Gently pour the batter into an ungreased tube pan and smooth the top. Run a rubber spatula or long knife through the batter to eliminate any large air bubbles.

5 Bake the cake until golden and a tester comes out clean, about 40 minutes. Remove the cake from the oven and immediately invert the pan. (If the pan has legs or the tube part of the pan is higher than the sides of the pan, just rest it upside down. Otherwise, place the pan over the neck of a filled bottle.) Cool the cake completely, upside down.

6 Turn the pan right side up. Run a long, thin knife around the outer edge of the pan with a smooth (not sawing) motion. Do the same around the center tube. Remove the outer rim of the pan and run the knife under the bottom of the cake to release. Invert to release the cake from the tube, and invert again onto a serving plate.

Per serving: Calories 95 (From Fat 1); Fat 0g (Saturated 0g); Cholesterol 0mg; Sodium 107mg; Carbohydrate 21g (Dietary Fiber 0g); Protein 3g.

Apricot-Pecan Gems

Apricot and pecans give these cookies a wonderful flavor. Look for whole-wheat pastry flour in the bulk section of your whole foods store. If you can't find it, you can use all white flour. Because these cookies are lower in fat, it's important to line the baking sheets with parchment so they don't stick to the pan.

Preparation time: *10 minutes*

Baking time: *12 to 14 minutes*

Yield: *1½ dozen cookies*

3 tablespoons Sunsweet Lighter Bake Butter and Oil replacement, vegetable oil, or melted butter

¾ cup apricot preserves (no sugar added)

¼ cup egg substitute or 2 eggs

½ cup flour

½ cup whole-wheat pastry flour

1 teaspoon baking powder

½ teaspoon nutmeg

⅓ cup chopped pecans

½ cup chopped dried apricots

1 Preheat the oven to 350 degrees. Line baking sheets with parchment paper or waxed paper.

2 In a mixing bowl, combine the butter and oil replacement, apricot preserves, and egg substitute and beat until smooth. Stir in both flours, the baking powder, nutmeg, pecan and apricots.

3 Drop the cookie dough by rounded teaspoonfuls onto a cookie sheet. Bake for 12 to 14 minutes, until golden brown. Remove to a wire rack to cool.

Per serving: *Calories 79 (From Fat 16); Fat 2g (Saturated 0g); Cholesterol 0mg; Sodium 33mg; Carbohydrate 15g (Dietary Fiber 1g); Protein 2g.*

Part IV
Other Important Stuff

The 5th Wave   By Rich Tennant

"Oh for gosh sake – you've got to figure out what you're doing wrong when you make upside-down cake, or you're gonna kill yourself."

In this part . . .

After devoting your time and energy to creating a special baked treat, you'll want to ensure that it remains fresh as long as possible. This part gives you ideas for the best ways to store your homemade goods. This part is also chock-full of tips for special presentations and how to do some easy cake decorating when you want to make your cakes extra special.

Chapter 17

Storing Your Creations

*O*kay, so you've baked your cakes, cookies, pies, and breads, and now you're wondering what to do with them. You want them to stay fresh and tasting good, but maybe you're not sure how long something will keep or what the best method for storage is.

There are many ways to store something. The most important thing to keep in mind is that you don't want your baked things to sit in the open. Baked goods will dry out if they're left out; foods such as slices of bread or cakes can get dry and stale in just a few hours. If you know that your baked goods will stick around for a few days, you may want to keep them refrigerated or even frozen. This chapter offers some advice on storage and the best ways to keep your treats fresh.

Wrapping

No kitchen is complete without a supply of plastic wrap, aluminum foil, and waxed paper. If you go to the trouble of baking something special, you need to be able to store it properly. Foils and wraps can keep air away from your creations, which will dry them out and make them stale. Home-baked items don't have preservatives, so it's up to you to store everything properly so that it will last until tomorrow. However, like many tasty treats, it may not last that long. . . .

Plastic wrap

Plastic wrap seals bowls, wrap cakes, and covers containers. I like plastic wrap because you can see though it and know what you've stored. Plastic wrap has a number of other advantages, too:

- ✔ It is nonreactive, which means that it won't react with acidic or alkaline ingredients, making it good for storing just about anything.
- ✔ It is microwave safe.
- ✔ It creates airtight seals over bowls and other containers.

Find the brand of plastic wrap you like best. It should cling to itself, and you should be able to pull it tightly without ripping it.

Under no circumstances should plastic wrap be put in the oven or over a hot item that just came out of the oven. It will melt immediately and is not good for you to breathe or ingest.

Aluminum foil

Aluminum foil is a great tool in the kitchen because it won't cling to items like plastic wrap can. Unlike plastic wrap, aluminum foil can be used in the oven for baking. Foil is also better for wrapping and stabilizing loose or irregularly shaped items like cookies on a paper plate or unfrosted cakes because you can mold it to whatever shape you need it to be. Because aluminum foil molds to itself, you can create an airtight seal with it. And it works well in the freezer. You can write directly on the foil so that you know what you've wrapped. The one drawback to aluminum foil is that it can't be used in the microwave.

Waxed paper

In the old days before plastic wrap and foil, there was waxed paper. Cooks used it for everything from storing leftovers to keeping cakes fresh in the ice box. Waxed paper is underutilized these days for storage, in my opinion. The waxy paper offers a breathable seal for your baked goods, so they stay fresh but don't get soggy-moist. Waxed paper is very useful in the kitchen because you can use it to line baking sheets and pans and place it between layers for storage. It's also safe for the microwave and for wrapping items (as long as an airtight seal is not required).

Foil foils messy cleanup

If you're using a baking sheet to catch drips from a pie or overflowing cake pan, place a piece of aluminum foil on top of the baking sheet. All the burned-on mess will drip onto the foil, not the baking sheet, making cleanup a snap.

A sheet of waxed paper can act as a movable part of your kitchen counter or a bowl you don't need to wash. Spread out a sheet on your counter and sift ingredients onto it, or use it to hold breadcrumbs or other coating.

Plastic ware

I'm a big fan of plastic ware. I find it to be perfect for everything from packing lunches to holding leftovers to storing everything I've baked. Sealable plastic containers make great storage items because the airtight seals keep your baked items fresher longer. Clear plastic allows you to see what you've stored (which is a great memory aid), and they're generally spacious and can hold many items.

Know that sturdy plastic ware will more than likely outlive you, so don't skimp on quality when you purchase it. Look for sturdy containers with good lids that offer airtight closure. Be sure that the lids fit well and you don't have to struggle every time you want to seal it. If you have a microwave, you may want to choose microwave-safe plastic ware.

Now, you can buy inexpensive reusable plastic containers that make me want to bake and share with everyone. They come in a variety of shapes and sizes and are perfect for storing large and small items and giving, without worrying about getting them back.

Tins

Decorative tins can serve as both holder and wrapping if you like to give baked goods as gifts. They're also great items to recycle, so you can use them many times and for many different purposes. Keep a few things in mind, though, when you choose decorative tins:

✔ **Tins generally don't have airtight seals.** Baked items won't stay as fresh for as long in tins as they do when stored in plastic containers.

✔ **Tins don't have as much holding capacity as plastic containers.** So you may want to pack two dozen cookies in a decorative tin but find that you can fit only one dozen! If you have many cookies to store, tins aren't the best choice.

Tins are great if you want to give a sampling of cookies or brownies to a friend, but if you want to send a few dozen cookies as a care package, send them in a plastic container instead. That way, you can be sure they'll be fresh when they arrive.

Storing at Room Temperature

Chances are if you live with roommates or have a family, you won't have to worry too much about anything freshly baked hanging around too long. From the first sniff of anything baking, you'll have an audience in the kitchen, waiting for the treats to be cool enough to sink their teeth into. In those cases, as long as you want the items to be consumed right away, most freshly baked items are fine if you leave them on a plate for a while.

Cookies

Most cookies, cakes, and pies can sit on the counter for the better part of a day (about 12 hours) before they need to be stored. If they need to be stored in the refrigerator, the recipe will say so. Otherwise, most cookies can be stored in an airtight plastic container on the kitchen counter for up to three days.

Cookie jars are cute, but unfortunately, most of them don't have an airtight seal. If you have a high turnover for your cookies (meaning that they'll float out of the cookie jar within a few days), a cookie jar is fine to use. If you don't put them in an airtight container, you run the risk of the cookies turning stale faster. If you love the cookie jar but still want to keep your cookies fresh, store them in a sealable plastic bag in the jar.

Cakes

As long as your cake doesn't contain custard, raw egg, fresh whipped cream, or meringue topping — all of which require refrigeration — most cakes can be stored at room temperature for several days.

To store your cakes, you can purchase a *cake keeper,* which is a large plastic cake holder with an airtight lid that fits on top. I find cake keepers very useful, because I can fit a cake on a serving plate on the base of the cake keeper, snap on the lid and, even if the plate slides around, it doesn't damage the frosted sides of the cake at all. You can also use a *cake dome,* usually a metal or plastic cover with a lid that you place over the cake itself. The dome doesn't provide an airtight seal, but if the cake will sit for just a few days, that shouldn't matter.

If you don't have either a cake keeper or a cake dome, you can invert a large mixing bowl over the cake. Just make sure the bowl is large enough that it won't smash down the top of the cake or touch the sides. A bowl is slightly more difficult to lift, because it doesn't have a handle, but it does provide an adequate cover.

Another way to prevent the cut surface of a cake from becoming stale while it's being stored is to press a piece of waxed paper or aluminum foil against the cut surface.

If you will be traveling with your cake and its appearance is important to you, pack some extra frosting and your frosting spatula (and pastry bag, if necessary) with you. That way, if you reach your destination and find that your cake has suffered some nicks and bruises, you can fix it up in a jiffy and people will be none the wiser.

Pies

Whole fresh fruit pies can be kept on the kitchen counter, covered, for about a day. Store any leftovers, covered, in the refrigerator. I have a large sealable plastic container that I use to store pies. My 9-inch pie plate fits perfectly in the container, and the lid is high enough that it doesn't damage my crust. It's a great container to use in the refrigerator because I can store items on top of the container (and maximize fridge space) without my pie picking up other flavors or getting bumped around in the fridge.

Bread

Bread can be stored at room temperature, sealed in a plastic or paper bag, for several days. Homemade bread tends to lose its freshness faster at room temperature, so you may want to keep it in the refrigerator even if you plan to use it up within a day or so.

If you don't eat a lot of bread, freezing is an excellent way to keep bread fresh. Then you can defrost what you need and warm it briefly in a toaster oven. Just be sure to wrap the bread tightly in freezer plastic (which is different from regular plastic wrap), foil, or freezer-plastic bags.

Keeping Things Cool

Many baked goods, such as cookies and breads, can be stored at room temperature. However, some items must be kept in the refrigerator to ensure that they won't melt or spoil. If you aren't sure whether you should refrigerate items, refrigeration won't harm them, so go ahead and wrap them up and keep them in the fridge. Note the time of year, too. In the winter and fall, items can stay at room temperature longer than in the summertime, when even pies should be stored in the refrigerator to ensure that they don't mold or go bad.

If you're traveling with a cake or pie that needs to be refrigerated, keep it in the air-conditioned part of the car with you. Don't put it in the trunk. If you don't have air conditioning, keep it in a cooler (if it fits), or you can double-box the cake and surround it with ice packs (one box to hold the cake, and the other box to hold the ice packs around the boxed cake).

Baked goods that should be chilled

All cheesecakes must be stored in the refrigerator, as should cakes, cookies, and pies that contain custard, raw egg, fresh whipped cream, or meringue topping (although they will weep a little from the cold). Any cake *can* be stored in the refrigerator, unless otherwise specified in the instructions, to extend its freshness. If you keep a cake in the refrigerator, be sure that it's well covered either in a cake saver or with a cake dome or bowl placed over it (see the earlier section "Storing at Room Temperature").

If you place a cut cake uncovered and unwrapped in the refrigerator for more than a few hours, it will most likely pick up refrigerator flavors, the icing will harden, and the cake will dry up and become stale.

Cookies

You can store cookies in the refrigerator in an airtight plastic container for about two weeks. After the first week, they won't be as fresh as they once were, but you can always pop them in the oven for a few minutes or even zap them in the microwave for a few seconds if you want that fresh-from-the-oven feeling. If you don't want to be bothered, I find that a not-so-fresh cookie makes a perfect dunker in milk. It sops up lots of milk but doesn't fall apart. Mmm.

Pies

Pies can be stored in the refrigerator for several days as long as they're well wrapped (with plastic or foil) and not made with custard, cream, or meringue. You can store pies in a cake saver or just cover with plastic wrap or aluminum foil. After a day or two, the crust may become a bit soggy, but you can rewarm the pie in the oven if you like. If your house is quite hot in the summer, be sure to keep the pie in the refrigerator so that it doesn't mold quickly or get too runny.

Breads

Because homemade breads lack the preservatives that store-bought breads have to increase their shelf life, your breads will not keep for nearly as long. To extend the life of your bread, store it in the refrigerator. I have kept bread, wrapped in a plastic bag, for up to one week without a molding problem.

Bread, sliced or unsliced, also freezes well. You can always rewarm breads in the oven for 10 or 15 minutes to get the crust crispy and fresh again. Also, choose a recipe with some fat in it (butter, eggs, or oil). Fat acts as a preservative for breads and extends their life by several days.

Freezing

The freezer is a huge help to bakers because it enables you to prepare foods when you have the time. Then you can remove them from the freezer and defrost them when you need them.

Even though most items freeze well, keep in mind that if you have the time to bake your items fresh, that's always the better choice. Frozen goods experience an inescapable loss of moisture and tend to dry out faster after they're brought back to room temperature for baking. Never freeze custards or cream pies.

Always label and date items you put in the freezer. You may even want to keep a master list on the freezer door so you know what's inside. Frozen unbaked doughs have a relatively short freezer life, so you need to know what you have on hand so that you can use it up in time.

Cookies

Baked cookies are pretty easy to freeze. Just stack them in an airtight plastic container with waxed paper in between each layer and freeze. You also can store cookies in sealable plastic bags. Most every cookie freezes well, but you may find that filled cookies and some bar cookies with dried fruit are a bit softer after they're defrosted — but they're still just as good in flavor.

Cookie dough

Uncooked cookie dough will last about two months frozen. Before freezing, shape the cookie dough into long logs and wrap the logs in plastic wrap. After they're frozen, double-wrap the logs in aluminum foil or an airtight container. Be sure to label the dough. You can even slice the cookies before you freeze them to make preparing them later easier.

The best cookie doughs to freeze are those with a lot of fat in them. If you want to experiment with different doughs, start with chocolate chip, oatmeal, or peanut butter cookies. Roll the dough into 2-inches-round x 12-inches-long logs. Slice the logs (either still frozen or refrigerated) into 1-inch slices. Bake the slices on a cookie sheet in a 350- to 375-degree oven for 8 to 10 minutes (frozen dough may take a few minutes longer). It couldn't be any easier.

Instead of logs, you can scoop out the cookies, freeze them on a cookie sheet, and then transfer the frozen balls of dough into a freezer-plastic sealable bag. Then just drop them onto a cookie sheet and bake as directed in the preceding paragraph.

Bread dough

To freeze bread dough, prepare the dough as usual but add a teaspoon more yeast to the recipe. Allow the dough to rise once, punch down the dough, and then shape it into loaves. (You can freeze the loaves in the pans you will bake them in; then remove the frozen dough from the pan and wrap it in freezer plastic until you're ready to bake it.) Do not keep frozen bread dough for more than ten days in the freezer. Defrost the loaves at room temperature or in the refrigerator overnight, let rise a second time, and then bake as instructed.

Rolls can be frozen in the same manner, but don't keep them in the freezer for more than a week. Freeze the individual rolls on a baking tray for 2 hours and then wrap them in freezer plastic and store them in an airtight container. When defrosting rolls, allow them to rise in a warm area, covered, until doubled in bulk (anywhere from 1½ to 4 hours) and bake as instructed.

Cakes

Most cakes can be frozen for up to two months. For unfrosted cake layers, cool the layers completely before wrapping them: first in freezer-plastic wrap and then in aluminum foil. You also can wrap the layers well and then seal them in a large freezer-plastic bag. The purpose is to create an airtight package for your cake layers. Label each item (you can write directly on the plastic bag or foil or label a piece of masking tape and stick it onto the bag or foil).

You also can freeze frosted layer cakes. Place the frosted cake in the freezer, unwrapped (you can place toothpicks in the cake to keep the plastic wrap from touching the cake if you like, but doing so is not necessary). When the cake has frozen through (the frosting should be frozen solid), wrap the cake in plastic and then wrap it in aluminum foil.

Cake layers, unfrosted, can be frozen for up to two months. A frosted layer cake will keep frozen for up to four months. Spice cakes should not be frozen for more than one month, to ensure that the flavor stays true. To defrost the cake, place it at room temperature, unwrapped but covered with a cake dome or cake saver lid, until you're ready to serve it.

I don't recommend freezing cake batter. The leavening used to make cakes rise may react differently after being defrosted, and the flavor of the cake will change.

Pies

Assemble the pie in a pie plate you don't mind sacrificing to the freezer for a while. If this is a problem, you may want to purchase aluminum foil pie plates for freezing. The best pies to freeze are fresh fruit pies because the fruit filling and pie dough do not seem to sacrifice their quality in the freezer. You can't freeze pies made with pudding, custard, meringue, or other creamy fillings.

- ✔ **Uncooked pies:** To freeze an uncooked pie, prepare the pie as usual, except use 1½ times the amount of cornstarch, tapioca, or flour in the filling (for example, if the recipe calls for 1 tablespoon, increase it to 1½ tablespoons). Freeze the pie solid before wrapping it in plastic wrap and aluminum foil or an airtight container. Bake the unthawed pie for 15 minutes in a 425-degree oven, and then reduce the temperature to 375 degrees and continue baking for about 40 minutes more. If the pie has a top crust, be sure to poke air holes in that crust before baking.

- ✔ **Baked pies:** Before freezing a baked pie, make sure that it's completely cool. When you're ready to serve it, thaw the pie for several hours at room temperature if you want to serve it cold. To serve the pie warm, place the frozen pie in a preheated 375-degree oven for about 30 minutes. Again, do not freeze baked pudding, custard, or meringue pies.

✔ **Pie pastry:** Pie pastry made with shortening or butter freezes very well. You can freeze pie pastry in many different ways.

- You can just wrap the dough in an airtight container. Defrost the dough, roll it out, and use as instructed. Label whether it's dough for an 8- or 9-inch pie.

- You can roll out the dough and place it on a greased baking sheet to freeze. After the dough is frozen, just wrap and label. Defrost and use as normal.

- You can press the piecrust into a pie plate and freeze it like that. You may want to use a disposable foil pie plate unless you don't mind storing the pie plate in the freezer for a while. Freeze the crust on the pie plate until frozen solid, and then wrap tightly and seal in an airtight container or double-bag it in large sealable plastic bags. You can bake these shells without thawing them at 425 degrees for 10 to 15 minutes.

Avoiding freezer burn

Air left in containers dries out food during storage. That air can cause freezer burn and will draw additional moisture from the food, which forms those ice crystals that you find on the lids of many home-frozen items. Freezer burn also can happen if foods aren't wrapped tightly enough.

When wrapping food for freezing, choose wrappers that are moisture-proof to keep your foods from drying out and to prevent freezer odor from penetrating the foods. Heavy-duty aluminum foil is great for the freezer because you can mold it to shape the item being frozen. Large, sealable freezer-plastic bags also are a good choice for freezing irregularly shaped items. You can press out all the air to get a good seal. Double-wrapping or double-bagging items also is a good idea. Plastic wrap should be nonporous freezer plastic and can be used with heavy-duty aluminum foil for the best seal. Also, look for hard, plastic freezer containers to protect your baked goods from damage in the freezer.

Chapter 18

Making the Ordinary Extraordinary

In This Chapter

▶ Slicing a cake into neat, even portions

▶ Making simple decorations

▶ Sprucing up the flavor of creams

*W*hen you spend time baking, you want to be able to show off your finished products and enjoy all the oohs and ahhs when you put them on display. In this chapter, I give you some ideas for making everything you bake just a little more special.

Cutting Your Baked Goods Neatly and Evenly

Believe it or not, there is a correct way to cut cakes and pies. Well, it may not be "correct," but it does ensure that you get slices of equal sizes.

Most people cut out one slice and then work their way around, eyeballing each piece and ending up with irregularly sized slices. The problem reveals itself when you get to slice number eight and realize how tiny slices nine and ten will have to be. A simple technique for slicing cakes and pies makes it easy to know how many slices you'll get *before* you make the first cut. Plus, you've gone to all this trouble to bake from scratch; why just hack away at it? Neat slices add to the appeal of your creations.

Pies and layer cakes can be cut the same way. You want to use a long, thin, sharp knife to cut. You also may want to use a cake server (a fancy triangular spatula) to transfer the slices to plates.

Cutting cakes and pies into even slices

When you serve a layer cake, follow these steps to ensure even slices (Figure 18-1 shows you what to do.):

1. **Slice the cake completely in half.**

2. **Depending on the richness of the cake and/or the number of people you have to serve, cut each cake half in half again, and then cut each quarter in half or in thirds.**

   This method of even division ensures that you make even cuts instead of going around the cake and eyeballing each cut.

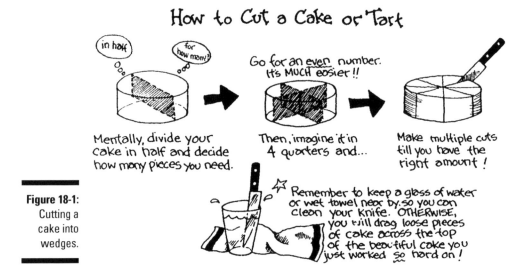

Figure 18-1: Cutting a cake into wedges.

If you want to measure out the wedges *before* you cut into the cake, do the following:

1. **Make a nick in the icing by gently letting the knife blade sink into the icing.**

2. **Mark the cake all the way around, using the method explained in the preceding steps to cut each section into halves, thirds, or quarters.**

   If you want to vary the sizes of the slices, divide one-quarter of the cake in thirds and the other in half.

3. **If you're satisfied with the sizes of the wedges, go ahead and cut all the way through the cake according to the nicks you made.**

   If you need more wedges, "erase" the cut marks by smearing the icing and then re-mark the cake until you have the number of slices you need.

The same goes for pies. You can make a nick in the crust or a small cut in the top, or, if the pie doesn't have a top crust, you can mark the filling.

Cutting cheesecakes cleanly

Cheesecake can get messy when you cut it. The moist cake tends to stick to the knife, increasing the thickness of the knife with each slice. You can conquer this problem in a few ways.

If you're planning to cut the cheesecake before you present it:

 ✔ Wet a nonserrated knife with hot water, shake off any excess water (but don't dry it), and then cut the cake. The heat and moisture from the knife enable you to get a clean slice each time. You will have to rewet the knife every second slice or so.

 ✔ Slice the cheesecake with clean dental floss. Get a piece of floss a few inches longer than the cake. Wrap the ends of the floss around your fingers and press the floss down and through the cake. Then release one side of the floss and pull it through the cake. Repeat this process until the whole cake is sliced. Doing so gives you neat, clean slices.

If you have to cut the cake at the table, you can always use two knives: one to slice and the other to scrape off the slicing knife between slices.

Cutting sheet cakes, bar cookies, and brownies

Sheet cakes, bar cookies, and brownies share the same cutting technique. It's easy, but you need to use a thin, sharp knife. You just have to cut the cake into equal-sized squares. If necessary, you can use the same technique you used on layer cakes to mark the icing before you slice to make sure that you'll get a high enough yield out of your cake or bars.

Cutting loaves and rolled cakes

Slice loaves and rolled cakes with a serrated knife. (A regular blade can compress the crumb of the cake and doesn't offer as nice a cut as a serrated knife does.) If you have an electric serrated knife, you can use that. It may be a little more horsepower than you need for cake or bread cutting, but it does the trick and enables you to cut thinner slices. Don't press straight down when you cut; use a gentle sawing motion. The thickness of each slice depends on the richness of the bread or cake.

Presenting with Flair

Decorated store-bought cakes tend to be ornamental and have that fussed-over appearance. That's all well and good for some people's taste, but I prefer the simple and basic. Not being a terribly artistic person myself, I think that less is definitely more. When I try to get too fancy, I usually have to explain my abstract art to the people looking at the cake: "Okay, this is the baby stroller, and this is Anne. . . ."

Food should look nice as well as taste good, so how you present your desserts really does make a difference. Although it doesn't have to be picture perfect, you can do some simple things to jazz up the presentation of your desserts.

Try piping a simple shell border or stars around the edge of the cake instead of going crazy with design. I recommend simple designs for beginner designers. See Chapter 8 for tips on decorating cakes. The following are suggestions for decorating cakes without having to apply to art school first:

- **Anniversary:** A big heart, two interlocking rings, the number of years celebrated

- **Birthday:** Balloons (if the name is short, you can put the letters of the person's name in the balloons), the person's age, a present with a bow

- **Good luck/bon voyage:** A horseshoe, champagne glasses toasting with colored confetti (sprinkles or colored icings), a four-leaf clover, a hot-air balloon

- **New baby:** A baby bottle, blocks with letters on them, a rattle

If you have a lot of people to serve, sheet cakes are a good solution. They're the easiest to frost, and their large, flat tops give you lots of decorating room.

If you don't have a platter or plate large enough to accommodate a sheet cake, you can make your own. Find a sturdy corrugated cardboard box and cut out a large enough piece of cardboard to accommodate your cake. (Use the cake pan to see how large your cake will be and leave at least a 2-inch border around the edge.) Wrap aluminum foil around the cardboard and — voilà! — you have a serving platter.

Remember, no one was born with the natural ability to decorate cakes and other baked goods, so go easy on yourself if you don't get it just right the first few times. Techniques take time to perfect.

Creating Quick, Spiffy Garnishes

Sometimes, frosting a cake just isn't enough — you want to dress it up a little more. Garnishing a cake lets you add your personal touch. The following sections give you some ideas for making simple, fun garnishes.

Garnishes for cakes

You don't have to limit cake garnishes to sugary flowers or fancy decorations. The following are a few suggestions for simple garnishes made of ingredients you probably have on hand:

✔ Press sliced almonds, chopped nuts, shaved chocolate, or crushed candy (peppermint works great) onto the sides of a frosted cake. To do so, frost the sides of the cake (but not the top), hold the cake with one hand, and press the garnish onto the side with the palm of your other hand. Or sprinkle the garnish onto a piece of waxed paper and roll the cake sides into the garnish (see Figure 18-2). Set the cake back on the serving plate and then finish frosting the top.

Figure 18-2:
Press the garnish onto the cake with the palm of your hand or roll the cake in the garnish to coat.

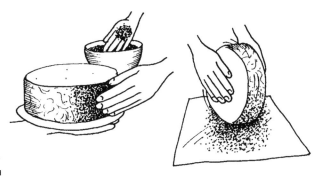

✔ Lightly dust the top of an iced yellow, carrot, spice, or chocolate cake with ground spice — cinnamon, nutmeg, or allspice. Don't shake the spice onto the cake directly from the jar; you might add too much. Instead, take a pinch of spice and sprinkle it on top.

✔ Melt some chocolate and dip a fork in it; then drizzle the chocolate over top of a frosted cake.

✔ Make balloons with whole cookies (vanilla wafers or chocolate cream-filled cookies) and use licorice for strings.

✔ Add a little color to your cakes with colored and chocolate sprinkles or beads.

✔ Give a cake a polka-dotted top by sprinkling candy-covered chocolates on top of the frosting.

✔ Forget the frosting and dust the top of the cake with confectioners' sugar or cocoa or a mixture of the two. You can cut out a message in a piece of paper, lay the paper on top of the cake, and then dust the top of the cake. When you remove the paper, your message will be written in sugar. You also can make a pretty pattern by using the same method — just use a paper doily instead of a paper cutout.

Also, check your local kitchen-supply store. There you'll find many garnishes, such as candy flowers, candy letters, and even edible glitter.

Fruit garnishes

Fresh fruit always makes a simple, elegant garnish. Cut up the fruit at the last minute to make sure that it stays fresh. You also can garnish with whole pieces of fruit dipped in chocolate — strawberries are just about everyone's favorite, or you can use raspberries, blackberries, or even sliced peaches. Prevent discoloration by tossing the peaches in lemon juice before you use them for garnish. You can either garnish each slice of cake with fruit or top whole cakes or tarts with fruit.

Whipped cream and flavored creams

A dollop of whipped cream on top of cakes and pies is always a welcome treat. Although a variety of premade whipped toppings are available, making your own is easy. Just follow these steps to make 2 cups of whipped cream:

1. **Place 1 pint of heavy (whipping) cream into a chilled bowl.**

   Do not substitute light cream or half-and-half; it will not whip up.

2. **With an electric or hand mixer or a wire whisk, beat the cream until it begins to thicken and stiffen.**

   If you can, chill these tools, too; your cream will thicken faster.

3. **Add 2 tablespoons of sugar or 4 tablespoons of confectioners' sugar, plus 1 teaspoon of vanilla, and beat a little bit longer until soft peaks form.**

   See Chapter 5 for tips on whipping.

4. **Taste and add more sugar if desired.**

Try substituting different flavored extracts for the vanilla. Some of my favorites are almond, lemon, and maple. Almond cream is great in coffee, on cherry pies, and in fruit cobblers. Lemon cream is great paired with lemon tarts or anything minty, and maple cream is delightful on pancakes, pies, and baked apples.

Flavorful combinations

Maybe you're feeling creative in the kitchen. Or maybe you're looking to jazz up a recipe. If you're looking for that little extra something, try the following flavoring combinations. You can flavor whipped cream or plain frosting with a few drops of extract or 1 teaspoon of spice. You may be pleasantly surprised by the flavor boost it gives your desserts. If you aren't feeling particularly adventurous, try flavoring the cream you serve with the coffee or select a corresponding flavor of ice cream or sorbet to match your dessert.

If Your Dominant Flavor Will Be . . .	You Can Accent with These Flavors
Blueberry	Lemon
Chocolate	Almond, apricot, cinnamon, mint, orange, raspberry
Pumpkin	Cinnamon, maple, rum
Strawberry	Almond, lemon
Vanilla	Anise, cherry, hazelnut, lemon, mango, maple, strawberry

Decorating plates

If you're serving a simple dessert that you don't want to bombard with creams or toppings, but you want to enhance its appearance, you can decorate the plates on which you serve it. Try a few of these tricks:

- ✔ Grease the edge of the dessert plate with shortening (just a thin coating). Sprinkle the edge with spices (cinnamon has a nice color) or cocoa and then tap off the excess. Place your dessert in the center of the plate and let your guests ogle.

- ✔ Get some squeeze bottles at a dime store and fill them with fruit sauce or chocolate sauce. Squeeze out a decoration (squiggles, lines, circles) onto each plate before serving. You can make your own fruit purees by peeling and slicing fresh fruits such as mango, peaches, nectarines, or raspberries and pureeing them in a food processor or blender. Press the fruit through a fine mesh strainer if it has lots of seeds (as raspberries do) and then transfer it to a squeeze bottle.

- ✔ A simple slice of colorful fresh fruit makes a nice garnish for plates.

Part V
The Part of Tens

The 5th Wave   By Rich Tennant

"I know it tastes a little odd. Let's just say you should store your bundt cake in a cool dry place, <u>other</u> than your husband's cigar humidor."

In this part . . .

If your cake turns out too dry, your cookies are baking unevenly, or your bread isn't rising, this part is the place to turn. I have an entire chapter devoted to solving common baking problems. This part also suggests resources for all your baking needs, whether you need an odd-shaped pan, good-quality chocolate, or crystallized flowers for cake decorations.

Chapter 19

Ten Troubleshooting Tips

In This Chapter

▶ Finding simple solutions for near-disasters in the kitchen

▶ Getting help with a dry cake, a reluctant cake, cookies baking unevenly, and much more

*O*kay, now you're baking. You've chosen a recipe and followed the instructions, but something doesn't seem quite right. Small frustrations while baking can quickly turn your whole baking experience sour, and they can also be time-consuming and costly. So equip yourself with the know-how to troubleshoot and problem-solve even if you feel like your recipe is on the decline. In this chapter, you'll discover that although some baking disasters are not salvageable in their present form, you *can* do some things to help disaster from consuming your baking experience.

Cake Too Dry

One way to tell whether your cake has finished cooking is to look at it: It will pull away from the side of the pan when it's finished. This space is usually just a fraction of an inch, but sometimes when a cake is overcooked, it will have pulled away a considerable amount, maybe a quarter of an inch or so.

There is a little trick we used to do in the bakery when cakes were overdone: We painted them with a simple sugar syrup that remoistens the cake. You can add flavorings to this syrup, if you like, to give your dry cake a bit of a boost. Frost as usual after the cake has had a chance to absorb the syrup.

Simple Syrup

This recipe makes enough for a 9-inch layer cake and can be stored in the refrigerator for several weeks.

1 cup water   *1 cup sugar*

1 Combine the water and sugar in a small saucepan. Place over medium heat and cook, stirring, until the sugar dissolves and the mixture comes to a boil, about 3 minutes.

2 Remove from the heat and cool the syrup to room temperature.

3 With a pastry brush, paint the syrup all over the top and bottom of the cake to moisten it, allowing the syrup to soak in. Frost as usual.

Vary It! *Add 2 or 3 tablespoons of liquor (rum, brandy, or bourbon) just before using. If you're using an extract, such as lemon or vanilla, add just 2 teaspoons.*

If your cake still seems hopelessly dry, don't throw it away. Cut the cake into small squares and split the squares open. Melt ½ cup to 1 cup of jam and pour a few tablespoons on top of each serving to moisten it. Then top with whipped cream or ice cream. Call it something fancy like Secret Strawberry Surprise, and no one will be the wiser!

Cake Stuck in Pan

The purpose of greasing and flouring baking pans is to alleviate the problem of having your cakes and muffins stick in them after they've finished baking. For the most part, cakes, if cooked all the way through, usually leave the pan without a fight. Teflon coatings also make life a bit easier for the cook by providing a nonstick surface, yet the surface will loose its properties after a while, so if you're ever in doubt, it's always better to grease the pan, just to be sure. Despite your well-laid plans, there will be times when the cake just refuses to leave the pan. When this happens, you can use a couple little tricks to make cakes turn out of pans easier.

First, run a butter knife or a long thin blade around the inside edge of the cake pan or muffin tin. This will loosen any cake that may be sticking to the sides. Place the cooling rack on top of the cake and flip the whole thing over. The cake should easily come out of the pan to finish cooling.

To remove an angel food cake from the pan, run a long, thin blade between the cake and the side of the pan to free it. Also run the knife gently between the cake and the inside tube. Place a plate onto the top of the cake and turn the cake upside down, onto the plate. Gently wiggle or shake the pan to loosen the cake.

Bundt cakes can be a bit trickier, especially if they're not well greased (all those nooks and crannies of the pan can make it a bit difficult for the cake to loosen). Here's a neat trick I learned to remove the Bundt cake from the pan:

1. **Fold a kitchen towel or bathroom towel and wet it with steaming hot water.**

   Leave it folded, in the sink.

2. **Remove the Bundt cake from the oven and place it on the hot, wet towel for about 30 seconds.**

3. **Turn out the Bundt cake from the pan.**

   It will come out cleanly and in one piece.

When you take a cake out of the oven, set it on a wire cooling rack for a few minutes. If you try to remove the cake from the pan too quickly, the bottom of the cake will have a tendency to stick to the bottom of the pan and split the layer in half.

Lopsided Cake

If the lopsidedness is caused by a sloping oven, this is a problem indeed — and a rather difficult problem to overcome. If your oven is free-standing, you can insert little squares of heavy-duty cardboard underneath it to give your oven an even platform. You can see if your oven is uneven by placing a glass baking dish halfway filled with water on your oven rack and checking to see if the waterline is straight. If your oven is severely lopsided, you can also place the cake pans on a baking sheet and prop something ovenproof (like a small stack of nickels) under the pan to offset the tilt. You'll have to experiment with this to get the level just right.

Repurposing your baking mess-ups

When I worked at the bakery, we had to level cakes all the time — mostly carrot and chocolate cakes. Instead of throwing out the domed tops, we saved them (after we finished snacking, that is). Later, we turned the domed tops into crumbs by putting them in the food processor and adding these moist, flavorful crumbs to our cheesecake crumb bottoms or sticky roll filling. This trick is a great way to use up the tops. Also, by leveling out the layers of the cake, we were able to sample what the cake tasted like without having to cut out a slice.

If your cake comes out of the oven lopsided, a sloping oven is rarely the problem. Your cake may come out of the oven with an irregular domed top (sometimes caused by overbeating the batter or too much batter in the center of the cake and not enough on the sides). This is okay, but if you're making a layer cake, it could cause your layers to shift and slide. To even out your layers, level your cake top by cutting it with a serrated knife as follows:

1. **Mark the area of the cake you want to cut off.**

   You can simply make a few marks on the cake to show what you want to cut away.

2. **Hold the knife parallel to the cake top and slowly, gently cut straight across to level off the cake.**

   Be sure you're making an even cut across the top of the cake and you aren't cutting down into the layer.

3. **Remove the cake dome.**

   You should have a flat, even cake top.

Flat Cookies

Baking a test cookie to see how the rest of your batch will turn out is important. If you discover a problem, it's better to find out by baking just one cookie instead of ruining a whole batch and wasting dough.

If your cookies are spreading all over the baking tray while they bake in the oven, you can try several tricks to get them back in shape. First, ask yourself if you're letting the baking sheet cool down between batches of cookies. The baking sheet should be cool enough for you to comfortably touch it before you put any dough on it. If you are letting the baking sheet cool, then try adding a tablespoon or two of flour to the cookie dough and bake another test cookie. You can add up to 6 tablespoons of extra flour, mix it well, and bake another test cookie.

If your cookies are still spreading out too much, cover the dough and place it in the refrigerator for at least 30 minutes (but no more than 2 hours). Then bake another test cookie and see what that does. Keep the dough chilled while your cookies bake. You can also lower the oven temperature by 25 degrees, and see if that keeps your cookies from spreading as much. Also, make sure that you have more than one cookie sheet so that you can have one cooling while the other one bakes.

Cookies Baking Unevenly

Sometimes, you bake a batch of cookies and find that the ones on the sides are done, but the ones in the middle aren't. Or the cookies toward the back of the oven are burned, but the cookies in the front of the oven are nicely done. What a pain! If your cookies are baking unevenly, three common reasons are

✔ Your oven racks are too close to the heating element.

✔ Your baking sheets aren't insulating the cookie dough sufficiently.

✔ Your oven may have hot spots.

Check your rack position

Nothing is more frustrating than removing your cookies from the oven to find they have scorched little bottoms and doughy, raw tops. The first thing to do is check to see whether your oven rack is in the right position. The rack should be in the center of the oven, and not near the bottom or the top of the oven. If the rack is positioned too close to the bottom of the oven, where it's hotter, the bottoms of the cookies will burn too quickly, without allowing the rest of the cookie to bake.

Evaluate your baking sheets

If the rack is in the right position, then your baking pans may be to blame. Darker baking sheets tend to absorb heat more than shiny metal ones do, which will result in cookie bottoms baking faster than cookie tops. Lower your oven temperature by 25 degrees and keep your eyes out for a sale on shiny metal baking sheets. They're a good investment and can save you frustration in the kitchen.

If you're already using the shiny metal sheets and you're still having problems with the cookies baking unevenly, then maybe the cookie sheets you're using are too thin, allowing too much heat to penetrate and baking the bottom of the cookie too quickly, before the top has finished baking. The easy way to fix this is to place one cookie sheet on top of another and create your own "insulated" cookie sheet. This trick should prevent the bottom of your cookies from burning.

If your cookies have burned a bit on the bottom, what I usually do is scrape off the burned part and put the cookies in the freezer. Then, when I need a cookie crumb crust, I just take my frozen cookies, process them into crumbs in the food processor, and — voilà! — I have a great cookie crumb crust. You can use just about any flavor of cookie (chocolate chip, gingerbread, peanut butter, oatmeal, sugar) for this great trick.

Compensate for hot spots

You may peer into the oven to discover that the cookies on the outside of the baking sheet are finished baking while the cookies toward the center of the sheet are not. Or you may find that half the sheet of cookies is browning, while the other half isn't. Unless you have a high-tech convection oven (you'd know if you did — they have a fan in the back that blows around the air so every spot of the oven is the same temperature), your oven has hot spots and cool spots. For the most part, these hot and cool spots don't interfere much with baking. But, from time to time, you may be reminded of your imperfect oven.

To combat hot spots and produce nice, evenly baked cookies, start by making sure that all your cookies are the same size. Making all your cookies the same size ensures even baking and means that they'll all require the same amount of time to bake. If you make some of the cookies big and some small, the smaller cookies will burn while the larger cookies will be gooey and raw.

Bake only one sheet of cookies at a time in the oven. Halfway through baking them (most likely at the 5-minute mark), give the cookie sheet a 180-degree turn in the oven so that the cookies in the back are up front and those on the right are on the left. That way, if your oven has hot spots, each side of the cookie tray will be evenly heated. This goes for sheet pans (brownies and single layer cakes), too.

And finally, don't overfill the cookie sheet. Leave about a 1-inch space between each cookie and about 1½ inches around the edge of the pan.

Burning Piecrust

Sometimes a recipe calls for a pie filling to go into a partially baked piecrust, or sometimes a filling takes longer to bake than the pie pastry does, and you find the crust of the pie is browning too quickly.

If this sounds familiar, there is no need for alarm. If you wrap up the edges of the pie in aluminum foil or, if it is a double-crust pie, cover the whole top with aluminum foil, this will slow down the browning of the pastry so the filling can finish baking without burning the pastry itself.

Lumpy Melted Chocolate

When you're melting chocolate, you need to be careful. Even the smallest drop of moisture (from a wet spoon or even the steam from the double boiler) can cause melted chocolate to become lumpy. Don't panic if this happens. Instead, stir in 1 tablespoon of shortening (not butter or margarine, because they contain water) for every 3 ounces of chocolate. Stir constantly until smooth.

When melting chocolate in a double boiler, be sure the water level in the bottom pan is about 1 inch away from the bottom of the top pan.

Chocolate burns easily if you melt it over too high a heat. If you suspect your chocolate is burned, taste it. If it tastes burned, throw it away and start again. That burned taste will be transferred to your baked good.

Bread Failing to Rise

Your bread may not be excited about rising for one of several reasons. First, yeast likes to be warm and cozy. If you've left the bowl in a cool, drafty place, you'll make the yeast sluggish, causing it to take a very long time to rise. If the outside temperature is cold on baking day, preheat your oven to the lowest setting (usually 200 degrees) for a few minutes (but no longer than 5 minutes) just to take the chill off of it. If you have a gas stove with a pilot light, that alone should be warm enough. Turn off the oven, place your bowl of dough in the warm oven, covered with a damp kitchen towel, and let it sit in the oven to rise with the door shut. If you still don't see a change in the dough within an hour, the yeast is probably dead.

Your yeast may be dead because of several reasons:

- ✔ **You used water warmer than 110 to 115 degrees.** Hot water kills yeast. You only want to use water that is slightly above body temperature, otherwise the heat from the water can kill the yeast.

- ✔ **You used yeast that is past its expiration date.** If you still have the packet of yeast you used, check the expiration date. If it has expired, you know why your bread isn't rising. The simple solution: Purchase new yeast.

✔ **You proofed rapid-rising yeast.** Rapid-rise yeast is a special strain of yeast that has been made to cut down the rising time of breads. If you've used this type of yeast and proofed it before mixing into the dough, that initial proofing could have used up all the yeast's energy, leaving it exhausted and unable to make your dough rise. Next time, skip the proofing step if you want to use rapid-rise yeast. (To find out more about proofing — what it is and how to do it — see the sidebar "Oh yeah? Proof it!" in Chapter 13.)

Risen Dough Left Unattended

Your dough has risen to perfection. Suddenly, your friend calls and tells you that her car has broken down and that she needs you to pick her up. What do you do? Punch down the dough, cover it with plastic wrap, and put it in the refrigerator. The dough can stay in the fridge overnight and will be ready for you in the morning. If your friend broke down a few minutes away and you'll be back home within an hour, you can punch down the dough, re-cover it with the towel, and let it rise again at room temperature. No harm done.

If the dough is in the loaf pans, has finished rising, and is mere moments from going in the oven to bake and you're faced with an emergency, you can brush the top of the loaves with butter and pop them into the refrigerator. This will slow down the rising. If the dough rises too much, you can still take them out of the loaf pans, knead the dough for a few minutes, and set them back into the loaf pans to rise again.

Muffins Like Hockey Pucks

Muffins toughen and become hard because the batter has been overworked. If this happens, you can't do much at this point to help, except learn from your mistake. Muffins really don't need much mixing — just a couple of turns with a wooden spoon and they're mixed. I suggest that you finish baking the muffins, even if you think you've overworked the batter. You can eat the muffins as they are. Or, depending on the flavor of the muffins you made, you can do several things with them:

✔ If they're a sweeter variety of muffin, cut them up and make a bread pudding with them. The additional moisture from the eggs, along with the act of baking them, will greatly improve their texture.

✔ If they're a savory variety, like corn muffins or bran muffins, cut them into chunks and make homemade croutons out of them. Sauté them in a little butter and add olive oil and seasonings (oregano, basil, onion, garlic) until they're lightly toasted and brown.

Chapter 20

Ten Great Baking Sources

No doubt the information in this book will motivate you to bake. The sources in this chapter offer not only great baking goods, but also the most essential ingredient of any recipe — inspiration!

Chef's Catalog

3215 Commercial Avenue, Northbrook, IL 60062; 800-338-3232; www.chefscatalog.com

If you're looking to purchase or upgrade your kitchen equipment, start with Chef's. Its prices are better than department store prices, and it's a good company to deal with. You can find your choice of stand mixers, quality food processors, and many great baking supplies — including my favorite bakery-style hot mitts (that are extra long to prevent oven burns).

Epicurious

www.epicurious.com

This is a fantastic Web site for cooks of every skill level. Questions are answered, trends are tracked, and volumes of *Gourmet* and *Bon Appétit* recipes are cataloged. You'll be exposed to much more than baking when you visit this site — and you may end up using it so often as a resource that you'll end up bookmarking it in your Web browser.

You have access to a wealth of information at Epicurious. For example, when you click on Learn, you discover etiquette guides, expert advice, a food dictionary, technique videos, and references. You can surf more than 13,000 recipes, plus you can shop, learn about foods and beverages, and do much more. It's a great tool for everyone who cooks!

King Arthur's Flour Bakers Catalog

P.O. Box 876, U.S. Route 5 South, Norwich, VT 05055; 800-827-6836; www.kingarthurflour.com

King Arthur's Flour Bakers Catalog is a great catalog for bakers at any level. You can find a large variety of quality flours, dried fruits, quality chocolate, and some baking equipment — all at a reasonable cost. Even if you're just curious about some specialty products, check out the King Arthur's Web site (from which you can place an order).

Kitchen Kapers

1250 Marlkress Road, Cherry Hill, NJ 08003; 800-455-5567; www.kitchenkapers.com

Kitchen Kapers is a regional retail store that offers well-priced baking equipment and ingredients, plus many other kitchen supplies. Although you can only go in person to stores located in the New Jersey, eastern Pennsylvania, and northern Delaware area, you can experience the great goods, prices, and customer service via the catalog and Web site (check out the nice sale items, too). If you live in the New Jersey/Philadelphia area, Kitchen Kapers also offers cooking classes at select retail stores.

Meadowsweets

173 Kramer Road, Middleburgh, NY 12122; 888-827-6477; www.candiedflowers.com

If you're looking for crystallized flowers, which are very special accessories for your cakes and cupcakes, call this company. The quality is second to none. Meadowsweets sells by mail order and has a great selection. Although you won't use this source often, you'll be glad you know about it when you need it.

NY Cake and Baking Distributors

56 West 22nd Street, New York, NY 10010; 800-94-CAKE-9

This store has just about every baking supply and ingredient known to man. That may be a *small* exaggeration, but it *is* an amazing place. It sells all the usual baking supplies, plus it has special decorating supplies and equipment, including edible gold and silver decorating dust and paste, a variety of quality chocolate supplies, a variety of coloring pastes and powders, videos, books, and more. If there were a candy store for bakers, this would be it.

Parrish Cake Decorating Supplies

225 West 146 Street, Gardena, CA 90248; 800-736-8443

For extraordinarily superb supplies, this is the place to go. You'll find bakery-quality cake-making and cake-decorating equipment (including custom-made cake pans), custom chocolate molds, beautiful cake accessories (for wedding or special event cakes), and much more. Shopping at this store is a bit of a splurge, but it's a great resource if you need to make something very special and need the supplies.

Sahadi

187–189 Atlantic Avenue, Brooklyn, NY 11201; 800-SAHADI-1

Near and dear to my heart, Sahadi is a great resource for well-priced baking ingredients. I used to live about five blocks from this store, and it was packed with shoppers at every hour. You can't beat the selection or prices of spices, seeds, flours, nuts, and other bulk items. Although Sahadi will ship anywhere in the United States, it's well worth a trip to the store if you live in the area.

Williams-Sonoma

P.O. Box 7456, San Francisco, CA 94120; 800-541-1262; www.williamssonoma.com

Chances are, you're acquainted with the Williams-Sonoma catalog — and you also can find its stores in shopping centers across the U.S. Williams-Sonoma offers an assortment of higher-end cooking and baking supplies (plus, the catalog offers you recipes to use with the equipment). It sells a host of seasonal baking supplies and ideas. Although you may find lower prices elsewhere, Williams-Sonoma does offer nationwide retail stores, so you can go in and shop around for what you need. Plus, it's a good source for specialty ingredients.

Wilton

2240 West 75th Street, Woodbridge, IL 60517; 800-772-7111; www.wilton.com

If you're looking for any baking supply (including specialty shaped pans), sign up for the Wilton catalogue. Or log on to its Web site for recipes, ideas, or decorating tips. Wilton has been in the baking business for many decades and is a name well trusted for quality products.

Appendix A

Glossary of Baking Terms

*F*or the most part, baking recipes is pretty straightforward. You're probably familiar with terms such as *beat, whip,* and *bake.* But from time to time, you come across words like *scald, flute,* or *macerate,* which set your head spinning and make you want to put down this book and head straight for the local bakery. Here is a list of commonly used baking terms to clear up any confusion in the kitchen.

bain-marie: See *water bath.*

bake: To cook in a hot, dry environment in a closed area (your oven!). Foods are baked uncovered for dry, crisp surfaces and covered for moistness and to prevent excess browning.

batter: An uncooked semiliquid mixture containing flour and other ingredients used to make a cake or bread. Generally a batter contains more liquid, and sometimes more fat and/or sugar, than a dough does.

beat: A mixing method in which ingredients are vigorously agitated to incorporate air and develop gluten, a protein that is found in wheat and other varieties of flour and that, when beaten, becomes more elastic and gives a cohesiveness to doughs. Beating requires the use of a spoon, beaters, or a mixer with a paddle attachment.

bind: To add an ingredient that holds other ingredients together. Most commonly, binding occurs when an ingredient is added to a hot liquid (flour, eggs, cream, cheese), causing it to thicken.

blanch: A technique in which food is plunged into boiling water for a short time (about 30 seconds) and then sometimes plunged into ice water to stop the cooking, followed by draining well. This technique preserves the color, taste, and texture of the food. Blanching is also used to remove the skins of harder-to-peel fruits, vegetables, and nuts.

blend: A mixing method in which two or more ingredients are combined just until they are evenly distributed; a spoon, rubber spatula, whisk, beaters, or mixer with a paddle attachment is generally used.

boil: To heat a liquid until bubbles rise to the surface and break, and steam is given off. Water boils at 212 degrees. A *rolling boil* means the bubbles are forming rapidly and cannot be stopped when stirred.

broil: To cook foods directly under a very hot heat source. Generally, this technique is used for quickly browning tops of dishes or cooking meats and fish with little or no added fat.

caramelize: To cook sugar over medium heat until it liquefies and turns a rich caramel brown.

chill: To place hot or room-temperature foods in the refrigerator or freezer. Gelatin and puddings change from liquids to solids when chilled. Creams also thicken upon chilling.

chop: To cut foods into coarse or fine pieces using a large chef's knife, food processor, or blender.

coat: To cover food evenly with flour, sugar, a crumb mixture, or a sauce.

come together: A term used in pastry-making. When small amounts of water are added to the crumbled mixture, it "comes together" and forms a rough dough.

cool: To allow hot foods to come to room temperature. Putting food on a wire rack allows air to circulate around it; stirring hot liquids cools them faster because it allows the steam to escape. You can also cool liquids in the refrigerator.

core: To remove the center of fruits, usually apples, pears, and pineapples.

cream: A mixing method in which a softened fat and sugar are vigorously combined to incorporate air; used for quick breads, cookies, and some cakes. Creaming can be done with a wooden spoon or electric mixer, and the fat becomes lighter when you're finished.

crush: To press into very fine bits.

curdle: The separation of milk or egg mixtures into solid or liquid components; caused by overcooking, high heat, or acidic ingredients (such as lemon juice or vinegar). If you add lemon juice to milk, the milk thickens and curdles. This is fine if you're making sour milk or buttermilk.

cut-in: A mixing method in which solid fat is incorporated into dry ingredients, using a pastry blender, two knives, or a fork, resulting in a coarse texture, as when making piecrust, biscuits, crumb toppings, and so on.

dash: Less than ⅛ teaspoon of an ingredient.

dough: A mixture of flour and other ingredients used in baking; it has a low moisture content and is often stiff enough to hold a shape.

drain: To remove excess liquid by placing the food in a colander or strainer that has been set over the sink, or over a bowl if you have to reserve the liquids you are draining.

drizzle: To pour a liquid (such as a sauce, frosting, or topping) in a thin stream over food. Usually, this is done quickly with a small amount of liquid.

dust: To sprinkle lightly with flour, confectioners' sugar, cocoa, and the like.

egg wash: A beaten egg (sometimes mixed with a little water or milk), brushed on top of pastry or dough before baking. It gives a sheen to bread, piecrusts, pastries, and so on after they're baked.

finely chop (mince): To cut into very small pieces. Done with a knife or in a food processor or blender.

flute: To pinch pastry edges with your fingers to make a decorative edge and extend the height of the crust edge, helping to hold in juicy pie fillings.

fold: A mixing method used to gently incorporate light, airy products into heavier ingredients (for example, mixing beaten egg whites into a cake batter). Usually a rubber spatula is used. First, you cut down vertically through the mixture, and then you slide the spatula across the bottom of the bowl and up the other side, turning the mixture over. You continue this down-across-up-over motion while rotating the bowl a quarter turn each time. Continue this motion just until the ingredients are incorporated. Do not use a stirring motion.

garnish: Any food used as an attractive decoration. Popular garnishes for baked goods include chocolate curls, whole strawberries, edible or sugar flowers, chopped nuts, and orange halves.

glaze: A shiny coating applied to food or a thin, sometimes flavored, coating poured or dripped onto a cake or pastry.

grate: To shred food (such as cheese) by rubbing it against a serrated metal plate known as a grater.

grease: To rub the inside of a baking pan with a thin, even coating of butter, margarine, or shortening (or to spray with a nonstick cooking spray) to prevent foods from sticking to the pan while baking. Generally used for cakes. Use shortening, not butter, if baking sheets need to be greased for cookies.

grind: To pulverize or reduce food to very small particles by using a mechanical grinder, mortar and pestle, or food processor.

hull: To remove the caps from strawberries. This can be done with a small knife, an inexpensive tool called a strawberry huller (short, fat tweezers), or a straw. With the knife or huller, just pinch off the green cap. To use the straw, insert the straw in the narrow end of the strawberry and push it through to the top of the strawberry. The green cap should pop right off.

knead: To work dough to develop the gluten present in the flours. During kneading, the gluten strands stretch and expand throughout the dough, enabling the dough to hold in the gas bubbles released by the leavener (usually yeast). You can knead by hand by repeating a series of steps: pressing into the dough with the heel of your hand, folding the dough in half, and giving a turn. You can also use a large mixer with a dough hook or a food processor equipped with a plastic blade. Well-kneaded dough becomes smooth and elastic.

macerate: To soak foods in a liquid (often juice or liqueur) to soften them, absorb the flavor of the soaking liquid, and release its flavor. Both liquids and solids are used for the dish, as in a dessert fruit topping.

melt: A process where certain foods, especially those high in fat, gradually soften and then liquefy when heated.

mix: To combine ingredients by hand or with an electric appliance so they are evenly dispersed.

nonreactive: Used when talking about cooking equipment. Nonreactive equipment is made of a metal that will not react with acidic foods. Examples of nonreactive materials are stainless steel, Teflon, and glass. Reactive metals are aluminum and copper. When foods and metal equipment do react, generally the foods turn an undesirable brown color. Tomato sauces, red wine sauces, and lemon juice are examples of foods that will react with metals.

pare: To peel. A paring knife is a small, short knife.

pipe: To force a softened mixture (frosting or whipped cream) through a pastry bag in order to decorate a cake.

pit: To remove the hard seeds from the center of fruits.

preheat: To allow the oven to reach its proper baking temperature before food is placed in it. An oven takes between 10 and 20 minutes to properly preheat.

proof: A test given to yeast to determine whether it is alive. The yeast is dissolved in warm water (wrist temperature, not above 115 degrees) with a pinch of sugar and then set aside for about 5 minutes. If the mixture becomes foamy, it is alive.

pulse: Short on-and-off bursts of a food processor. Pulsing is generally used to chop or mince foods.

punch down: To firmly push your fist into risen dough with your fist to deflate it so it will become more tender and even-grained.

puree: To process food to achieve a smooth pulp. Usually done by using a food processor or blender or by pushing softened foods through a fine mesh strainer or food mill.

reduce: To cook a liquid until its quantity decreases due to evaporation. Typically this is done to intensify flavors and thicken the liquid.

rest: To allow dough to stand for a certain period of time before shaping it into a shape such as a roll or braid. The dough will relax and be easier to work with after a rest.

scald: To heat a liquid, usually milk, uncovered, to just below the boiling point.

score: To cut very shallow slits across food before cooking. Scoring can be decorative, as when making French bread. Scoring also can be functional: It helps loosen skin in preparation for peeling foods such as peaches or tomatoes, and it helps marinated foods absorb flavors.

seed: To remove the seeds from a fruit or vegetable.

set: To chill a custard or gelatin, transforming it from a liquid to a solid.

shave: To cut in very thin layers with a vegetable peeler (usually done with chocolate).

shell: To remove the hard outer casing of nuts.

shred: To cut into thin but irregular pieces. Often done with a grater or food processor with a shredding disk.

sift: To shake a dry ingredient (such as flour or sugar) through a sieve or sifter to remove lumps and incorporate air. Sifting also is used to combine dry ingredients.

simmer: To maintain the temperature of a liquid just below the boiling point. Small bubbles continually but gently break the surface of the cooking mixture.

slice: To cut an item into relatively broad, thin pieces.

soften: To allow food, usually butter, cream cheese, or margarine, to stand at room temperature until it is no longer hard. Perishable foods should not stay at room temperature any longer than 30 minutes.

sprinkle: To scatter something, usually a garnish, lightly over the surface of food.

steep: To soak foods in a hot liquid in order to extract flavor or to soften the texture, such as when you make tea.

stir: A mixing method in which ingredients are gently combined until blended.

strain: To pour foods through a sieve, mesh strainer, or cheesecloth to separate or remove the liquid or smaller particles from larger particles.

toast: To brown food in an oven or broiler. Nuts and spices are toasted by cooking them in a dry skillet over very low heat for several minutes, stirring often, until they brown slightly and become aromatic.

unmold: To remove food — usually a cake, custard, or gelatin — from its container and place it on a serving plate.

water bath: Also called a *bain-marie*, a large baking dish filled with hot water in which food in individual cups is gently baked. Usually used for custards and baked puddings.

whip: A mixing method in which foods are vigorously beaten in order to incorporate air. A handheld whisk or an electric mixer with a whisk attachment is used.

whisk: A wire whip used to beat foods to incorporate air into them.

work in: A mixing method in which an ingredient is incorporated into other ingredients, resulting in a uniform mixture. For example, butter is worked into flour to create a delicate pastry.

yield: The total amount of a product made from a specific recipe or the number of servings a recipe will produce.

zest: The outer skin of citrus fruits that contains the fragrant oils. You want to avoid the white underneath (the pith), which tastes bitter.

Appendix B

Metric Conversion Guide

*N**ote:* The recipes in this cookbook were not developed or tested using metric measures. There may be some variation in quality when converting to metric units.

Common Abbreviations

Abbreviation(s)	What It Stands For
C, c	cup
g	gram
kg	kilogram
L, l	liter
lb	pound
mL, ml	milliliter
oz	ounce
pt	pint
t, tsp	teaspoon
T, TB, Tbl, Tbsp	tablespoon

Volume

U.S Units	Canadian Metric	Australian Metric
¼ teaspoon	1 mL	1 ml
½ teaspoon	2 mL	2 ml
1 teaspoon	5 mL	5 ml
1 tablespoon	15 mL	20 ml
¼ cup	50 mL	60 ml
⅓ cup	75 mL	80 ml
½ cup	125 mL	125 ml
⅔ cup	150 mL	170 ml
¾ cup	175 mL	190 ml
1 cup	250 mL	250 ml
1 quart	1 liter	1 liter
1½ quarts	1.5 liters	1.5 liters
2 quarts	2 liters	2 liters
2½ quarts	2.5 liters	2.5 liters
3 quarts	3 liters	3 liters
4 quarts	4 liters	4 liters

Weight

U.S. Units	Canadian Metric	Australian Metric
1 ounce	30 grams	30 grams
2 ounces	55 grams	60 grams
3 ounces	85 grams	90 grams
4 ounces (¼ pound)	115 grams	125 grams
8 ounces (½ pound)	225 grams	225 grams
16 ounces (1 pound)	455 grams	500 grams
1 pound	455 grams	½ kilogram

Measurements

Inches	Centimeters
½	1.5
1	2.5
2	5.0
3	7.5
4	10.0
5	12.5
6	15.0
7	17.5
8	20.5
9	23.0
10	25.5
11	28.0
12	30.5
13	33.0

Temperature (Degrees)

Fahrenheit	Celsius
32	0
212	100
250	120
275	140
300	150
325	160
350	180
375	190
400	200
425	220
450	230
475	240
500	260

Index

• *M* •

• R •

• S •